The **BIG BOOK** of

HAÏR METAL

The Illustrated Oral History of
HEAVY METAL'S DEBAUCHED DECADE

MARTIN POPOFF

Voyageur
Press

Quarto is the authority on a wide range of topics.

Quarto educates, entertains and enriches the lives of our readers—enthusiasts and lovers of hands-on living.

www.quartoknows.com

First published in 2014 by Voyageur Press, an imprint of Quarto Publishing Group USA Inc., 400 First Avenue North, Suite 400, Minneapolis, MN 55401 USA.
Telephone: (612) 344-8100 Fax: (612) 344-8692

quartoknows.com
Visit our blogs at quartoknows.com

Voyageur Press titles are also available at discounts in bulk quantity for industrial or sales-promotional use. For details contact the Special Sales Manager at Quarto Publishing Group USA Inc., 400 First Avenue North, Suite 400, Minneapolis, MN 55401 USA.

10 9 8 7 6 5 4 3

ISBN: 978-0-7603-4546-7

Digital edition published in 2014
eISBN: 978-1-6278-8375-7

Library of Congress Cataloging-in-Publication Data

Popoff, Martin, 1963- author.
  The big book of hair metal : the illustrated oral history of heavy metal's debauched decade / Martin Popoff.
    pages cm
  ISBN 978-0-7603-4546-7 (hardback)
  1. Heavy metal (Music)--History and criticism. 2. Rock musicians--Interviews. I. Title.
  ML3534.P66 2014
  781.66--dc23
                    2014001234

Acquiring Editor: Dennis Pernu
Project Manager: Madeleine Vasaly
Art Director: Cindy Samargia Laun
Cover Designer: Brad Norr
Design and Layout: Karl Laun

Printed in China

contents

introduction

Well, cats, here it is, and I'm pretty proud of it. Had a blast writing this book. Why? Well, it's chock full of interesting talking points 'n' concepts, but more so because hair metal makes me happy. Now obviously, the time's gotta be right (can't play this stuff all the time), but man, it's a mood lifter for any occasion, ain't it?

Much of the cool summarizing stuff I wanna say, you'll see, I say it in my year-opening remarks throughout the book, ergo, I don't feel the need to speak much of my piece here. Any of youse who've argued with me about metal of all skunk stripes—ha ha—you'll see that I get some of these batty points across in my state of the glam nation address at the start of each yearly chapter.

A few things I do want to say, however, number one being, I'm really digging this synthesis of timeline and oral history, because subtle bits of new knowledge come out of the very abutment of date to date (sounds like backstage at Mötley). As well, it allows us to explore all manner of trivia and not have it eat up space or that accursed precious word count.

Main thing I'm proud of here, besides some of the philosophical points made, is the fact that all of the quotes 'n' dialogue are from my own interviews, a list of speakers of which is shoved in the rear (sounds like backstage . . . oh, never mind). I love it—it's like the memories of talking to all these guys just flashing before my eyes as I rechecked all these old chats for points that matter, obviously leaving out so much more that could have been said. But then again, do you really want five pages on Kick Axe's debut (actually, I know a couple dozen buyers of this book who do).

Did I mention running out of room? Well, yes, I did. Fact is, I coulda made this twice as long, especially when it came to the long and complicated prehistory of hair metal. For that reason, I've left out a lot of the minor bands, didn't talk much about tour dates or compilations or live albums, all of this to allow for the salient points about hair metal to breathe, often with multiple perspectives.

Wait, a couple points of methodology, just so I can fool you a little longer that I'm not an idiot. When I didn't know an exact date, say in 1989, for instance, '89 is put at the beginning of the year, June '89 is put at the beginning of the month, and "Spring" or "Early" is put somewhere vaguely logical. As for labeling speakers, if the dude is in the band talked about in that entry, then it's just his name; if it's someone from a band not talked about in the entry, then I mention the band the guy's from.

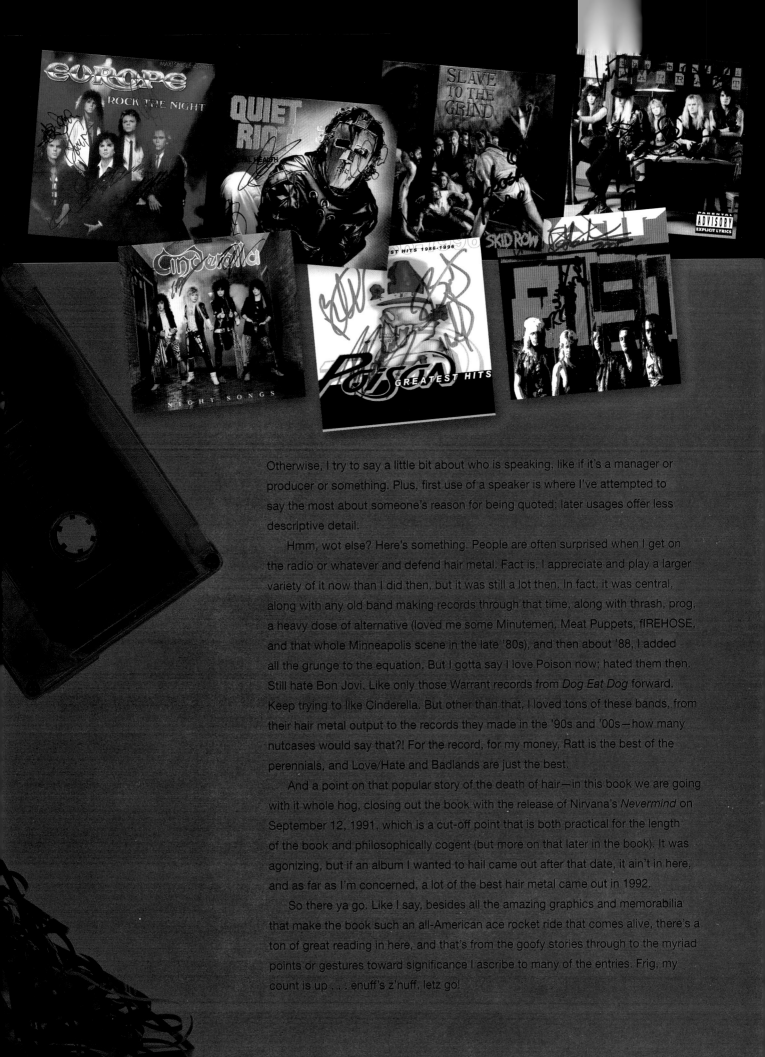

Otherwise, I try to say a little bit about who is speaking, like if it's a manager or producer or something. Plus, first use of a speaker is where I've attempted to say the most about someone's reason for being quoted; later usages offer less descriptive detail.

Hmm, wot else? Here's something. People are often surprised when I get on the radio or whatever and defend hair metal. Fact is, I appreciate and play a larger variety of it now than I did then, but it was still a lot then. In fact, it was central, along with any old band making records through that time, along with thrash, prog, a heavy dose of alternative (loved me some Minutemen, Meat Puppets, fIREHOSE, and that whole Minneapolis scene in the late '80s), and then about '88, I added all the grunge to the equation. But I gotta say I love Poison now; hated them then. Still hate Bon Jovi. Like only those Warrant records from *Dog Eat Dog* forward. Keep trying to like Cinderella. But other than that, I loved tons of these bands, from their hair metal output to the records they made in the '90s and '00s—how many nutcases would say that?! For the record, for my money, Ratt is the best of the perennials, and Love/Hate and Badlands are just the best.

And a point on that popular story of the death of hair—in this book we are going with it whole hog, closing out the book with the release of Nirvana's *Nevermind* on September 12, 1991, which is a cut-off point that is both practical for the length of the book and philosophically cogent (but more on that later in the book). It was agonizing, but if an album I wanted to hail came out after that date, it ain't in here, and as far as I'm concerned, a lot of the best hair metal came out in 1992.

So there ya go. Like I say, besides all the amazing graphics and memorabilia that make the book such an all-American ace rocket ride that comes alive, there's a ton of great reading in here, and that's from the goofy stories through to the myriad points or gestures toward significance I ascribe to many of the entries. Frig, my count is up . . . . enuff's z'nuff, letz go!

1950 – 1959

ROCK 'N' ROLL IS BORN, as is showmanship, nice hair, and, in Little Richard's case, a bit of disconcerting makeup. Plus there's lascivious lyrics that would make Mötley blush. Bottom line, while it might be a stretch to say black metal or doom metal or power metal is born in the '50s, it really ain't that far from "Tutti Frutti" to Faster Pussycat.

1950   **1951**   **1952**   **1953**   **1954**

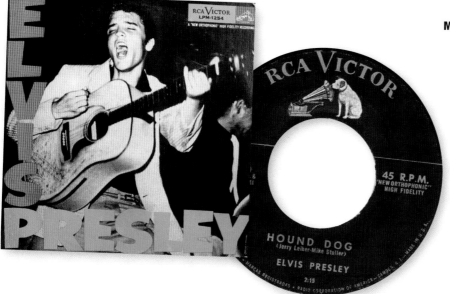

1950s: Aqua Net is invented. This hairspray will enjoy a huge boom in the hair metal era. It is considered the hardest helmet-creating product, surpassing the power of any gel or mousse.

March 3 or 5, 1951: "Rocket 88" is first recorded, credited to Jackie Brenston and his Delta Cats. The band didn't exist and was put together by Ike Turner. Jackie Brenston sung the vocal. It is credited as the first rock 'n' roll song but doesn't actually include the phrase "rock 'n' roll," leaving Billy Ward's claim to the phrase as valid.

1952: The first Gibson Les Paul is released. It will become a favorite guitar of '80s rockers.

November 1955: Little Richard's "Tutti Frutti" is released. Elvis will include the song on his January 31, 1956, self-titled debut album. Little Richard becomes arguably the first glam rocker, with his fancy hair, his slightly androgynous look, frilly sleeves, and conspicuous makeup.

July 13, 1956: Elvis Presley's version of "Hound Dog" is released (as a B-side). The song features an early wailing vocal, which will become another glam element (like his shiny suits). Elvis is also, in effect, the first rock star—a dangerous threat to social order, perhaps even intending to shock.

March 31, 1958: Chuck Berry's "Johnny B. Goode" is released, possibly the most popular early example of a good-time rock 'n' roll party song.

| **1955** | **1956** | **1957** | **1958** | **1959** |

1960–1969

THERE'S NOT A LOT OF CONNECTION

between the '60s and hair metal, other than in the late '60s with the half-birth of heavy metal itself. Not included in the entries to follow is the rise of psychedelic rock, which puts an emphasis on explosive color and expensive clothes. Most significant in the decade is the birth of Led Zeppelin, with their proto–hair metal golden god frontman Robert Plant and guitar hero Jimmy Page. Guitar will, of course, be of utmost importance in hair metal, with many of the bands sporting their very own heroic, virtuosic figure, and Page is the first and best prototype (although in a general rock sense, Eric Clapton, Jeff Beck, and Jimi Hendrix must also be cited). Finally, Led Zeppelin also draws up the blueprint for hair metal success from a musical standpoint, mixing fast, hard rock, the blues, and balladry, all of which would later be cards successfully played by any number of gold and platinum hair metal acts.

1960   **1961**   **1962**   **1963**   **1964**

January 11, 1964: The Whiskey a Go Go opens at 8901 Sunset Strip, West Hollywood.

August 4, 1964: The Kinks release "You Really Got Me," in which Dave Davies simultaneously popularizes blocked power chords and a fuzz tone. The track is a pioneering hard rock classic later famously covered by Van Halen.

October 23, 1964: The Kinks issue "All Day and All of the Night," a second proto–riff rocker (on the heels of August's "You Really Got Me").

DAVE DAVIES (GUITARIST, THE KINKS):

When I was young I used to listen to records and just listen to the guitar work. I used to listen to James Burton, Scotty Moore, I loved John Lee Hooker, Howlin' Wolf. Even before that, I was a big fan of the Ventures' rhythm guitar playing. And if you listen to it, it's kind of like bar chords; they don't really play the whole chord—and I used to copy that. So it was a combination of different influences and coupled with my frustrations at not being able to get the sound out of an amplifier. Because the amplifiers in those days were very clean-cut sounding and I wasn't very happy with that, so coupled with a variety of influences, and my own sort of aggression about how I wanted a guitar to sound . . . and I got an amplifier and I just cut the speaker with a razor blade and I came out with this raunchy sound and that was the sound I liked, which was used on "You Really Got Me." A lot of bands like the Beatles and the Hollies were more poppy-sounding, which was brilliant. The Yardbirds were quite heavy, a much heavier band, but that was rhythmically heavy.

1965   **1966**   **1967**   **1968**   **1969**

JIM MCCARTY (DRUMMER, THE YARDBIRDS, ON THE BAND'S CONTRIBUTION TO HARD ROCK):
I suppose definitely more the *Little Games* element. But yeah, "Think About It," "Tinker Tailor," "Dazed and Confused," obviously. It all came from heavy blues riffs. "I Wish You Would," for instance, quite a heavy blues riff. "Smokestack Lightning," which Jimmy [Page] actually sort of simplified. He used to do many of these blues riffs very cleverly in his own way, simplifying some of them and making some of them more complex. But I think it was all about the riffs.

May 12, 1967: The Jimi Hendrix Experience's debut, *Are You Experienced?*, is released in the U.K. It contains heavy tracks "Foxy Lady," "Manic Depression," and "Fire," among others. Hendrix is said to be one of the first to experiment with the new fuzz pedals and is lauded as a pioneering hard rocker. Like contemporaries Cream, Pink Floyd, and Deep Purple (Mk. I), he's also quite extravagant in his dress, although this could possibly be considered more psychedelic than proto-glam.

January 1968: Sweet form as the Sweetshop. They will go on to become the most "heavy metal" of early glam bands, scoring many of the major hits that will inspire and, indeed, be covered by '80s hair metal rockers.

January 1968: Blue Cheer's *Vincebus Eruptum* is released. The record is, in fact, one of the heaviest rocking albums of the '60s but is soon overshadowed by records by MC5 and the Stooges.

1960　　　　**1961**　　　　**1962**　　　　**1963**　　　　**1964**

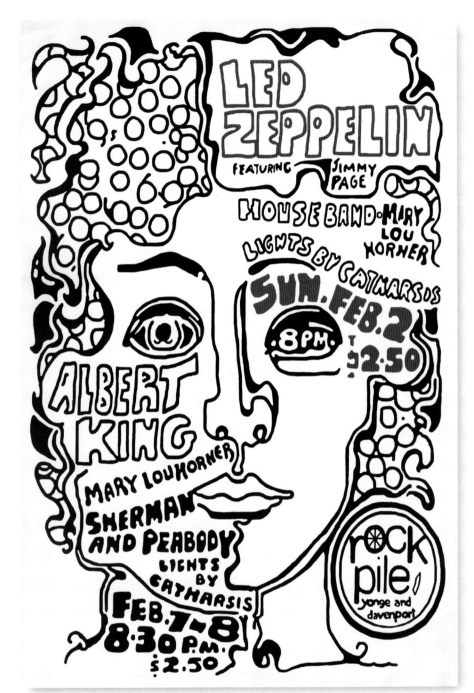

January 12, 1969: Led Zeppelin's self-titled debut is released. Led Zeppelin will become the most cited influence among '80s hair metal bands, more so musically than visually, although Robert Plant is considered the prototype for the typical hair metal front man.

August 1969: Alice Cooper issue their debut album, *Pretties for You*. The band is already well-known around L.A. for their androgynous look, long hair, and audacious shock-rocking theatrics. Alice will be cited as a major hair metal influence and even reinvent himself as a successful hair metal icon.

October 22, 1969: Led Zeppelin *II* is released, containing seminal metal track "Whole Lotta Love," plus other influential hard rock tracks "Heartbreaker," "Living Loving Maid (She's Just a Woman)," "Moby Dick," and "Ramble On."

1965   **1966**   **1967**   **1968**   **1969**

1970 – 1979

IF WE WERE TO PICK *the one key influence on hair metal, it would be Van Halen. Aerosmith, essentially a shaggier, bluesier precursor to Diamond Dave and his hotshot guitarist, would be our second pick. Also in the proto zone would be Ted Nugent, Kiss, and the likes of Montrose, Boston, and Starz. Pushing further into the obscure, we would find Legs Diamond, Riot, Moxy, April Wine, and Teaze. And then there's the conundrum of U.K. glam (the real "glam" if you ask some critics). Most thinkers on this stuff, however, prefer to call hair metal "hair metal" and leave it at that. U.K. glam, as it existed from sort of '72 to '75, is as much or more a look than one musical style, and frankly, that look bears little resemblance to hair metal fashion other than androgyny. Still, bands like Slade, Sweet, and Mott the Hoople lend musical inspiration to future hair farmers, as do rare American act, the New York Dolls. But with nuthin' going on in L.A. for this stuff in the late '70s, Van Halen shoot like a rocket into rock consciousness, essentially establishing the template for future hair bands, with their shredder of a guitar hero and their irrepressible party animal of a front man.*

1970 **1971** **1972** **1973** **1974**

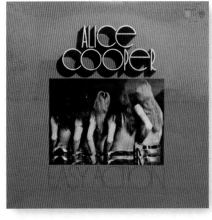

March 1970: Alice Cooper's second album, *Easy Action*, is released, featuring some of the first glam visuals ever, if not the music to match.

October 5, 1970: Led Zeppelin *III* is released. Its use of light and shade later will be utilized on hair metal records, significantly on power ballads.

JOHN PAUL JONES (BASSIST, LED ZEPPELIN):

We were into Joni Mitchell a lot and listened to a lot of Fairport Convention as well. There was a lot of music around that was softer. Remember Ian Matthews' Southern Comfort? And there was an American group, Poco. We kind of listened to a lot of that and we thought we had done a couple of heavy albums. It's funny, though, a lot of heavy Zeppelin songs were written on the acoustic guitar. And there was a lot of acoustic stuff on the first album, which people forget. You know, after the second album, they always go, "Oh, the third album's acoustic. What are you doing?" And we were like, "What about 'Babe I'm Gonna Leave You'?" I mean, there are acoustic numbers, but they had heavier parts. And I had started playing mandolin by then, as well, so like "Going to California" and "That's the Way," those were all my mandolin parts. It just seemed a nice thing to do. And by then we realized that, again, there were no rules. We didn't have to do it this way or that way. We just made our own judgment and said, "Well, this is nice, this is good, let's use it."

1975   **1976**   **1977**   **1978**   **1979**

November 28, 1970: Slade issue *Play It Loud*. Slade will become pretty much the archetypal glam band, plus a fairly heavy one to boot. Their "Cum on Feel the Noize" and "Mama Weer All Crazee Now" would famously be covered by Quiet Riot. "Gudbuy T'Jane" would be covered by L.A. Guns.

February 21, 1971: Alice Cooper's third album, *Love It to Death,* is issued, with *Killer* to follow in November. More of a shock rocker, Alice and his band nonetheless very much presented themselves as a glam band in the early days, wearing shiny suits, makeup, and very long hair.

November 8, 1971: Led Zeppelin's fourth album (self-titled but popularly known as *IV*) is released. It is arguably the premiere complete LP with respect to influencing later hair metal bands—"Stairway to Heaven" is a prototype power ballad; "Black Dog," consummate cock rock.

JOHN PAUL JONES:

"Black Dog" I wrote on the train [laughs]. I didn't have an instrument. I write them in my head. Literally, I didn't even have manuscript paper. I have a system my father taught me, where you just use numbers and pluses and minuses and you can write a melody down on anything. As long as you've got a pen and a piece of paper, you can write music. And I remember coming back, I think it was from Page's house, after rehearsal. Yes, I remember, I was listening to one of the cuts off of *Electric Mud*, Muddy Waters, and there was a riff that they did that kept going around and around. You thought it was going to stop and it didn't. And I thought it would be great to write a riff that just kind of went around and around [laughs]. . . . So I got it down quick so I wouldn't forget it. I didn't actually do the arrangement, if you know what I mean. The vocal arrangement kind of dictated how that went. It didn't seem that Robert wanted to sing actually over the riff, so it kind of made sense that he sang a bit, then we played the riff, then he sang a bit more. Then Page did the other half [sings it], and then Robert did his stuff over that. Most of the stuff we did worked that way. Somebody would bring in an idea and the whole band would work on the idea and then we would add bits to it. And eventually it would become something through sort of an organic process. Out of all the different elements would come the final song.

1970   **1971**   **1972**   **1973**   **1974**

November 1971: Sweet release their first album, *Funny How Sweet Co-Co Can Be*, which includes bubblegum songs like "Co-Co," "Chop Chop," "Funny Funny," and "Tom Tom Turnaround." Hard rock vocals meet guitars and lots of melody.

1972: Van Halen form in Pasadena, California, as Mammoth, with Eddie and Alex, and Mark Stone on bass.

1972: Gary Glitter, looked upon as überglam but a bit of a parody and an older guy in a young man's game, has his biggest hit with "Rock and Roll" (or "The Hey Song").

1972: Silverhead, fronted by Michael Des Barres, issue their self-titled debut (*16 and Savaged* would follow in 1973). The band's sound is thuggish blues rock, but the look is typical UK glam.

April 16, 1972: The Rainbow Bar and Grill at 9015 Sunset Strip, West Hollywood, officially opens for business. Guest performer for the party is Elton John.

June 6, 1972: David Bowie issues *Ziggy Stardust and the Spiders from Mars*, probably the definitive glam album (the word glam, here and in most of these '70s entries, defined as a mostly UK music and fashion craze as it existed from about 1972 to 1975).

June 16, 1972: Roxy Music's self-titled first album releases. Proggy and foppish, the band is usually listed among the first half-dozen bands at the forefront of the UK glam movement.

July 21, 1972: T. Rex issue their third album, *The Slider*. Marc Bolan had the ultimate glam look, and the band's music, although not heavy, was very glam. Hits included "Jeepster," "Get It On," "Metal Guru," and "Telegram Sam."

JOHN PAUL JONES:

I remember "Stairway to Heaven" was done kind of around the fire, a big fireplace, sitting around drinking cider. Page had a few things worked out on the guitar. He had these different sections, and he was just playing them through and I remember picking up. . . . I had brought all my recorders and my bits and pieces and I picked up the bass recorder and started playing that rundown with the guitar. Then Robert started jotting a few lyrics down. Again, it was a very organic process, as most of our music was. Somebody would start something and somebody would follow, and it would turn into something else and you would sit down and work out what sections you've got and you'd put them together. It was all very easy, very relaxed.

JOE ELLIOTT (VOCALIST, DEF LEPPARD):

As kids, when you're first starting to sprout your own kind of wings and roots and stuff, twelve, thirteen years old, the music that was in the British marketplace, or psyche, the pop world of '72 to '74, were bands like Sweet, Slade, Mott the Hoople, Roxy Music, T. Rex. These are the kinds of bands that, before you can play an instrument, just before Christmas, you were tugging on your parents' sleeve saying, "I want a guitar for Christmas, please," so you can be Marc Bolan.

1975   **1976**   **1977**   **1978**   **1979**

September 8, 1972: Mott the Hoople release their fifth album, *All the Young Dudes*, with the David Bowie–penned title track as its biggest hit.

1973: David Essex issues his debut, *Rock On*, a cornerstone UK glam record.

January 13, 1973: Aerosmith release their self-titled debut. Although Led Zeppelin is more often cited by hair metal bands of the '80s as a chief influence, Aerosmith, also cited proudly and regularly as an Influence, is closer to hair metal both visually and musically.

July 1973: Sweet issue their self-titled album which includes pure UK glam rock hits like "Little Willy," "Wig-Wam Bam," "Block Buster," and "Hell Raiser." Sweet represents the best example of UK glam in collusion with hard rock.

July 20, 1973: Mott the Hoople's sixth album *Mott*, includes "Honaloochie Boogie" and "All the Way from Memphis," both archetypal UK glam songs.

August 1973: New York Dolls' self-titled debut is released. The band represents a major glam look married to a hard rock sound. Indeed, the band's hot mess image is much more a direct predecessor to hair metal than is UK glam. Androgyny and decadence collide, and what's more, the band is American.

SYL SYLVAIN (GUITARIST, NEW YORK DOLLS, ON LEAD SINGER DAVID JOHANSEN AND GUITARIST JOHNNY THUNDERS):

[David] was bad with alcohol. He was one of those mean drinkers and I hate that. He became known for that. And Johnny, his addiction with heroin. At the beginning there, he was so clean and beautiful and everything was great. And that helped destroy the band. It's true, you try heroin once and you become a junkie instantly for some people. And it's so hard, that they never get out of it. It changed him so much. He became like a Frankenstein and he couldn't help it. But at first he was the most beautiful fucking kid on the block and it was really sad to see that. It was so hard to see someone so beautiful turn so ugly. That shit had him by the balls. I'm not saying that alcohol and Johansen's big ego telling us all the time that we can be replaced, you know that didn't help.

1970   **1971**   **1972**   **1973**   **1974**

October 1973: Suzi Quatro issues her self-titled debut, and also in the same year, her second album, *Quatro*.

October 17, 1973: California-based Montrose release their classic self-titled debut of white-hot American hard rock, featuring proto–hair metal vocalist Sammy Hagar. Produced by Ted Templeman and issued on Warner Bros., the album is considered a precursor to the first Van Halen album. Both records are major early works of American stars-and-stripes party metal.

RONNIE MONTROSE (GUITARIST):

I had just come out of Edgar Winter's group and *They Only Come Out at Night* had gone platinum and I felt so fortunate to be playing that I couldn't believe I was being paid to play. I was like twenty-four years old then and that was a big thrill for me. And Ted walks in and goes, "Do you know that this record is selling five hundred to a thousand copies a day in some places?" We weren't taken very seriously around the Warner Bros. tent at that time because they weren't really convinced that our brand of music was going anywhere. But we would be in a town touring and I would go into the convenience store and as I was walking in I'd hear guys at the other side of the counter going, "Holy shit, man, we're going to see Montrose tonight." And I thought, well, I guess they're talking about me. *Montrose* took about ten years to go platinum. It sold slowly and it continues to sell to this day. It's a pleasant one of those things where it wasn't a boom smash success. A lot of fans took us seriously but the record company really didn't.

RONNIE MONTROSE (ON THE SELF-TITLED MONTROSE ALBUM BEING A CONFLUENCE OF FORTUNATE CIRCUMSTANCES):

One of the interesting comments about that record was made to me by my friend and old bandmate in Gamma, Mitchell Froom. He said to me, "Ronnie, the reason I think that record did great was that it was four young guys who were new at it." And it wasn't a question of how technically good you were, because I was really just playing a basic rudimentary style, guitar riffs and lead solos et cetera. It was rudimentary. But he made the comment and it was right. He said, "The point is that all four of you were playing up to one hundred percent plus of your ability at that time. So you were going all out. What you did is what you could do." It was an interesting comment. That first Montrose album was heralded much more in England. I met Cozy Powell when I was over there once and he said [in English accent], "I gotta tell you, Ronnie, that record, it's everyone's favorite over here."

1975   **1976**   **1977**   **1978**   **1979**

1974: Mammoth change their name to Van Halen.

March 1, 1974: Aerosmith release their second album, *Get Your Wings*, which finds the band ascending to more of an arena rock sound.

March 24, 1974: Monterey Pop impresario Lou Adler mounts a production of the wildly successful London musical *The Rocky Horror Show* at the Roxy in L.A. The show runs for nine months and is cited as a major influence in terms of bringing glam fashion to the West Coast.

JACK DOUGLAS (PRODUCER, AEROSMITH):

We loved Montrose because, first of all, you had a great singer and he was a fantastic guitar player. You had a great band, and he was really a progressive jazz player who was like our Jeff Beck. But by the time I got to him [for 1976's *Jump on It*] he had a different singer and was with a different band. I think maybe we had lost our way by the time we did that record. It didn't do all that well. But I had great respect for Ronnie and what they were doing. I thought it was different. But I loved everything Ted Templeman did. It was classic West Coast, but by then they were doing a lot of their stuff on Trident boards over at Cherokee, and that stuff sounded cool. I think Ronnie wanted to get heavier and join the crowd and thought that with my participation we would get him to the Aerosmith stage. But he never really was an arena show. And you know, you've got to keep the same lead singer, really, to keep things going.

NIC ADLER (SON OF LOU AND CURRENT OWNER OF THE ROXY):

Yeah, I think it was definitely a seed that grew into something bigger. I don't know if you could've seen it when it was going on, because a lot of people walked into the Roxy and went, "What is this?!" But you quickly started to see the makeup, the tights, the outfits, the hair. It definitely grew out of, I think, *Rocky Horror*. I think it really took popular music, rock 'n' roll music, and mixed it with this "You can be anybody you want, you can dress like you want" kind of thing. And obviously we saw what followed that. And the way it happened, actually, my mom had seen it in London and had asked my dad, and said, "I just saw something you need to see. You need to bring this to L.A." And he actually flew out on a couple days' notice, and that's how he actually found the *Rocky Horror Show*.

KIM FOWLEY (MANAGER, THE RUNAWAYS):

Rocky Horror was cosmetically Bowie and Iggy and Lou Reed, but musically it was Broadway via London's West End. Whenever you have . . . if you have gonorrhea and you fuck Janie and then Janie fucks Tommy, Tommy will get gonorrhea too, but it won't be as severe a strain. It will be a slightly different strain of gonorrhea. So a New Zealand guy wrote the music. Richard O'Brien, he wrote the music for *Rocky Horror*. He was the guy who played the bald actor in the original production of the movie. He goes from New Zealand, which is by the South Pole, all the way to the mother country, England. He does it in England. By the time they did the movie, Lou Adler and everybody in America, Meatloaf and all those guys, it had gone through three generations of virus change. From New Zealand to the West End to New York to L.A. So it was four downward steps. The metal and rock community did not embrace it musically. They embraced it as auxiliary parallel universe entertainment because Gene Simmons

1970   **1971**   **1972**   **1973**   **1974**

brought it up, but only the visuals. They took possibly the visuals of the New York Dolls, which they added to what they had done in New Zealand, and so that audience tolerated it as visual entertainment, not as audiovisual entertainment. And there's a delineation and a differential that you must take into account.

DEREK SHULMAN (A&R MAN):

Original glam? David Bowie would have to be there, if you're talking about imaging. What these bands in the glam era effectively tried to do is play rock music that appealed to a female audience. And, you know, Bowie and/or Sweet, Mott, Slade, the late-'60s, early '70s bands, who were quite rock oriented, they wanted to appeal to a female demographic also. And that's how they had a cross-demographic appeal. I mean, in certain respects, there are bands like Kiss. Where do they fit? Aerosmith. Kiss . . . they all fit into that quasi-glam, because glam has so many kinds of definitions. The real, real glam is, how can I put this, has a quasi-androgynous feel. They had the makeup, which was the androgyny part, but they played rock music. The New York Dolls, if you like, although the New York thing was much more punk-oriented and didn't really appeal to the female demographic.

SYL SYLVAIN (GUITARIST, NEW YORK DOLLS):

Maybe it wasn't the most perfect thing but we were just starting to invent stuff. You really don't know there's going to be an explosion, you know what I mean? You don't know what's going to happen around the corner; it's a blind turn. David and Johnny, don't forget, by then they were sleeping with each other's girlfriends and wives and stuff like that, which is really . . . forget it, when stuff like that happens and they're all on drugs and alcohol, it's going up and then down again. The second album, don't forget, it wasn't quite like the first time going up there. The Dolls . . . were playing three-thousand-seaters. We brought the "glitter rock tour" to Toronto, which was Aerosmith as the opening band, Kiss in the middle as a special guest, and then the New York Dolls—that was in 1973 at Massey Hall. But I think if we would have gotten Todd Rundgren [to produce] the second album and then included those new songs on there, I think we really would have gotten to that point that they described later on as punk or new wave. That's what we were working on. We were the first ones to really bring that out from the bands that we were inspired by, which were the girl groups from the '60s, the Shangri-Las of course, the Ronettes. Don't forget, we used to do "Give Her a Great Big Kiss." Oh, check this out! When I was in Europe, they have a Chiclets commercial and they used that song in the commercial [laughs]. After they told us we fucking sucked and we couldn't even damn sing.

April 1974: Sweet issue *Sweet Fanny Adams* in the UK only. LP includes melodic glam rock songs like "AC-DC," but also pure metal monsters like "Set Me Free," "No You Don't," "Sweet F.A.," and "In to the Night," some of which will become high-profile covers in the future.

May 1974: New York Dolls release their second and last album, the appropriately titled *Too Much Too Soon*, before imploding. America wasn't ready.

1975   **1976**   **1977**   **1978**   **1979**

November 1974: Sweet issue *Desolation Boulevard*, which includes "The Six Teens" and "Fox on the Run." The hit US version of the album would include "Ballroom Blitz."

April 8, 1975: Aerosmith release their third album, *Toys in the Attic*, which includes "Walk this Way." The song employs a proto-rap vocal, which will, of course, show up years later in a collaboration with rappers Run-D.M.C.

May 1975: Blackie Lawless (né Steven Edward Duren) replaces Johnny Thunders for two New York Dolls gigs in Florida. Blackie was from Staten Island, New York, and purportedly was in a street gang with Ace Frehley when they were kids. Going under the name Blackie Goozeman, Lawless will move to L.A. with the Dolls' Arthur Kane, where they form Killer Kane, also known as the Killer Kane Band.

September 10, 1975: Kiss issue their fourth album, *Alive!*. The explosive double live album comes just in the nick of time, with the band and their record label, Casablanca, rapidly running out of money. The album lights a fire under many a budding rocker who sees his future mapped out in smoke, leather, and fire.

1976: Blackie Lawless forms Sister in L.A. Blackie's act includes black leather, eating worms, and lighting his boots on fire, which Sister bandmate Nikki Sixx would later adopt in Mötley Crüe. In fact, Sister guitarist Lizzie Grey claims much of Crüe's look was stolen from Sister. Sister was said to have utilized an inverted pentagram as well. W.A.S.P. guitarist Randy Piper proves to be a longstanding member.

JACK DOUGLAS:

[Aerosmith] got a lot from the New York Dolls but mainly they listened to old blues records, they listened to James Brown, they listened to Led Zeppelin and all of the English stuff was very important to them. I mean, you know, classical music . . . we listened to quite a bit because we liked to steal as much as we could from Prokofiev [laughs]. Those were the people we were stealing from, and from R&B and blues-based guys. From the Dolls, it was the ability to just let it go, let fly. And you know that they were managed by the same people and they were very close. They were all friends, so you would find the guys from Aerosmith at Dolls shows quite often watching the show because . . . in fact, the guys in Aerosmith weren't the greatest players in the world either, but they wanted to be better. But they wanted to see what was possible, if you weren't a good player at all—how could you still do a show? And the other big influence, of course, was the Stones. There was some physical resemblance and there were a lot of parallels between Joe and Steven.

LIZZIE GREY (GUITARIST, SISTER, LONDON):

Blackie Lawless wanted to be Alice Cooper, pretty much. What he was doing was shock rock. At the time with Sister, he was doing things like eating earthworms onstage, nightcrawlers, and throwing meat at the audience in his later W.A.S.P. band. Alice Cooper had a huge appeal to people like Blackie and myself. I was a huge Alice Cooper fan, although as a guitarist, not as someone doing the theatrics, but as someone who is creating the music for those sorts of theatrics. Kiss was an influence as well. Blackie and Gene Simmons had kind of a rift going between them because of a girl named Star Stowe, who had known both of them or something [laughs]. Star's really well-known because she did a really great *Playboy* spread, where she was holding a Rickenbacker guitar over her crotch, and I think that was one of the first times it was really done to that degree. So she kind of gets kudos for that.

BILL AUCOIN (MANAGER, KISS):

[*Destroyer* producer] Bob Ezrin was a genius and an eccentric, exactly the best of both worlds for me. It wasn't necessarily for the group in the sense that Ace and Peter just didn't get along with Bob at all. It was oil and water. On the other hand, Gene and Paul did and Bob was strong enough to pull it all through. We could all get ideas to Bob and he could get them done. But it turned out to be a great album, and after all was said and done, I think they knew it and the response was good, and of course "Beth" came out of that album. No one wanted it on the album. I had to kind of demand that it went on. For obvious reasons, you know, it wasn't a Kiss song, but why don't we do this anyway? And I think part of the reason I got it on there was that Peter and Ace felt so bad about this whole album and not getting along with Bob that when I knew that "Beth" was absolutely a hit song, I just said to Gene and Paul, "Look, for Peter's sake and for the album's sake, we have to put this on. At least it's a rock 'n' roll song in terms of what happens in the lyric to an artist, and we have to go with it." So that's how that got on the album. After it was said and done they certainly enjoyed the rewards of that album.

STEPHEN PEARCY (VOCALIST, RATT, ON AEROSMITH'S *ROCKS*):

I had a song called "Out of the Cellar" that I wrote in 1976; that's where that title came from. Ratt . . . "Rats in the Cellar" . . . there you go. I would be very forward to say, "Thank you, Aerosmith." I was a rat in the cellar [laughs].

KEVIN DUBROW
(VOCALIST, QUIET RIOT, ON BAND'S DEBUT ALBUM):

Well [laughs], it's not really very good, really. It's a case of having one of the world's greatest guitar players, and not being able to tell on that record. It was produced by a guy who didn't get it. We knew what we wanted to do, but he couldn't get it for us, and he didn't know how to get it. Because that was our first time in the studio, pretty much. And believe it or not, the guy produced Deep Purple in the early days. It's not very representative. It's still a band growing up.

March 1976: Sweet issue *Give Us a Wink*, which, despite including glam hit "Action," is more of a straight heavy metal album establishing a temporal link between the waning days of glam and a continued slow burn of metal's early years.

March 15, 1976: Kiss issue their seminal *Destroyer* album. *Destroyer* cut "Beth," although not a power ballad, introduced the idea of putting completely uncharacteristic soft rock songs on heavy metal albums, a gambit that will prove a lucrative trope for hair metal bands.

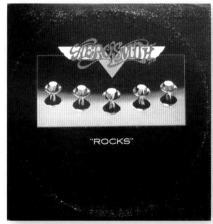

May 3, 1976: Aerosmith's fourth album, *Rocks*, is issued. It will be cited by Nikki Sixx as the greatest record of all time, and likely many hair metal rockers would rank it among their top albums ever.

March 2, 1977: Quiet Riot release their self-titled debut album, which is more like glam pop than hard rock glam. Featuring guitarist Randy Rhoads, it's issued in Japan only, on Sony.

1975   **1976**   **1977**   **1978**   **1979**

KELLY GARNI (BASSIST, QUIET RIOT, ON SUNSET STRIP IN THE LATE 1970S):

It was kind of a mishmash, really, at first. Nobody was really going in one single direction; there were lots of different kinds of bands around. The Sunset Strip had a lot of bands that maybe were leftovers from the '60s, really. Probably the best thing, I think, that was ever on the Sunset Strip was Rodney Bingenheimer's club—that place was just amazing. It wasn't that big of a place, but the things that went on inside were just incredible. It was right when the whole glam scene hit. And that was a part of the '70s, to be sure, in Hollywood. Everybody was walking around in sparkly this and sparkly that, and eight-inch-high heels, and a lot of people were sexually ambiguous-looking. The Brits were well ahead of us as far as rock 'n' roll at that time, I felt. You had Sweet, Slade, which we covered. David Bowie, Suzi Quatro, T. Rex. Iggy Pop was around. And they were all very diverse. And right around '74, '75, that kind of died out. And that's when kind of the more mainstream rock 'n' roll started to hit the Strip. And that was pretty much at the point where I got into playing the Strip a lot. Me and Randy Rhoads had a band called Smoky, and we did play the clubs quite a bit, and usually we would be second billed to Shaun Cassidy. That's how diverse it once was [laughs]. But from then we went on to Quiet Riot, and then basically we lived at the Starwood for quite a few years after that. We did do other clubs like the Troubadour and shows that were big venues that were like two-thousand-seaters and stuff. We played with Black Oak Arkansas and Journey, and these were all bands that were at their zenith right about then and really starting to make an impact. But then you started hearing things like Scorpions and Judas Priest. So it was an evolving thing. Original glam lasted like four years, and then after that it was a big evolution that was happening on the Strip. We came in at just the right time to be able to do what we were doing, and of course we had Van Halen down the street at Gazzarri's, and they were doing what they were doing, and then the Starwood was really the place to be. I mean, the Starwood was just an awesome club.

LIZZIE GREY:

Quiet Riot was sort of hard rock, Slade-influenced, the British hard rock that influenced all of us so much—Slade, Sweet, Mott the Hoople, Mark Bolan, T. Rex., Quiet Riot were a bit older than us, and guys like Nikki Sixx and I . . . we used to go watch Quiet Riot, and Randy Rhoads was so awesome to watch. He was so fluid and had such a great feel for that kind of music. And needless to say Kevin DuBrow's voice was pretty much a dead ringer for [Slade's] Noddy Holder. Quiet Riot was really popular, and Sister was very unpopular [laughs]. There wasn't that much draw for that kind of thing in the late '70s. Because you had Rodney Bingenheimer doing disco on the Sunset Strip, and you

1970 **1971** **1972** **1973** **1974**

had Fowley doing the Runaways, and there was this sort of foppish, poppish leftover from the late '70s. Arthur Kane was a good friend of mine before he passed away, and he used to talk about how the whole New York Dolls thing and the whole glitter rock thing only lasted for a couple years from like '74 to '76. Then it got kind of eclipsed by the whole disco thing. So it was really fun, back in '76, '77, when I would see Blackie kind of moping around Hollywood, because there wasn't much appeal for the shock rock thing, other than Alice Cooper who was doing it his first time around [laughs]. But we would be hanging around the Starwood. That place was just phenomenal because you had all these influences, like disco going on in one room, and then you had the foppish metal rock, whatever you want to call it, Quiet Riot. We call it glitter more than glam. Our distinction is that glitter rock was everything going on in the '70s and glam rock was kind of like the second coming of glitter rock, and that was bands like Poison and London and all that.

KELLY GARNI:

Van Halen were somewhat rivals of ours, mainly due to, of course, the two guitar legends that were basically opposed against each other, within the scene. And we didn't really feel a whole lot of competition from them, so to speak. We kind of controlled the Starwood. We were basically the house band there for years and years and years, and one of the highest-paid bands there. And Van Halen, they pretty much stay down at Gazzarri's, where they had more of a college, preppy, upper-scale kind of clientele that hung out at Gazzarri's at that time. Whereas at the Starwood, it was all ages, and you could be a twelve-year-old kid and walk up to the bar and get a beer and they would give it to you—it was more of a street rock 'n' roll place. In fact, we never ever once played Gazzarri's—ever. Most bands didn't. It was pretty much like Van Halen was there every night playing, and it was like a job for them, and they played basically cover tunes. They mixed their other stuff in with that too, but they were playing cover tunes that were popular at that time, and they were like one of the first really good successful cover bands, I guess.

KIM FOWLEY:

Van Halen were at Gazzarri's next door to the Rainbow and the Roxy, where all the out-crowd kids who weren't cool enough to go to the Whiskey hung out. They went out playing dreaded cover songs, and their own originals, and were stuck down there. One day Eddie and David came to me and said, "Can we open for the Runaways?" I went and saw them and said, "Yeah, you guys are really good." And they opened for us New Year's Eve 1977 at the Whiskey. To this day holds the record for the most admissions. They had a giant fanbase. They came into the gig in their alter ego, Atomic Punks. Or that was the

May 1977: Ted Nugent issues his third solo album, *Cat Scratch Fever*. Ted's gold and platinum success in the mid- and late '70s, as well as his lustful party rock anthems and guitar hero pyrotechnics, inspire many adolescent and teenage boys to form bands.

September and October 1977: Van Halen record their self-titled debut album.

1975   **1976**   **1977**   **1978**   **1979**

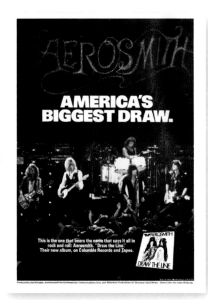

December 1, 1977: Aerosmith issue *Draw the Line*, arguably the last Aerosmith album important to the story of American party metal until '87's *Permanent Vacation*.

January 1978: New Jersey band Starz issue their third album, *Attention Shoppers!*, essentially forsaking their hard rock sound in a case of bad timing. The album, however, signifies the industry vibe at the time that hard rock was dead. And, granted, in America, for four or five years anyway, it was. The band's first two albums, *Starz* and *Violation*, were indeed proto–hair metal semi-classics, and their fourth and last, *Coliseum Rock*, was a return to a hard rock sound. Starz, like Angel, were ahead of their time, and as a result, in the wrong place at the wrong time.

next time we played as the Runaways. They showed up as the Sex Pistols and the Damned, with lipstick and black eyeliner and dyed their hair and everything. I said, "What are you doing?" They said, "We're debating whether we should dump metal and be a punk band." I said, "No, you're great at being metal; you're almost laughable being Atomic Punks. Do it for fun; don't do it for real." So I'm the one that kept them on the straight and narrow. They said, "Would you like to produce us?" I said, "Let me see what the guy at Mercury says." I was producing at Mercury and I brought him to see Van Halen. I said, "What do you think?" He said, "Led Zeppelin imitators with a lead singer trying to be Jim Dandy from Black Oak Arkansas—fuck off."

RICHIE RANNO (GUITARIST, STARZ):

Attention Shoppers! was a big problem, actually, and we don't look back on it fondly, although there are people who like it. I'm always surprised. Our manager said, "You know, these two albums, they aren't good enough." And I was like, "What are you talking about!?" And he said, "Yeah, these aren't good enough. You need more pop songs. You have to write a whole album of pop songs, and you have to get away from this hard rock thing." And I was like, "You know, we're already building a great following as a hard rock group. If we do a light album, everybody's going to hate our guts. They're going to feel that we sold out." And everybody in the group said, "You know, look, this is too much pressure. Let's just go in and not write songs based on anything except just writing some songs." So we went ahead with it and did it that way and it kind of came out. I mean, there were some hard rock songs on there and there were definitely some that weren't, and they didn't become hits. And I said to the manager, "Now we've done what you asked, they aren't hits, we're through." And basically we were through.

1978: Blackie Lawless' Sister now includes Nikki Sixx on bass and influential underground glam metaller Lizzie Grey on guitar. Guitarist Chris Holmes will join later. The same year, Lizzie and Nikki form London, the most promising proto–hair metal band that never made it. London was based in Hollywood and wound up being a feeder group, with members leaving to move on to much more famous acts. The band's first drummer was Dane Rage, a.k.a. Dane Scarborough, who became an inventor and founder of the toy company Uberstix in 2005. An early Sister vocalist was Michael White, a Robert Plant lookalike and soundalike who went on to form The White and also make solo albums.

February 10, 1978: Van Halen issue their self-titled debut. The solo guitar piece "Eruption" establishes Eddie Van Halen as the first "shredder," or at least the first since Jimi Hendrix. Party metal songs collide with more extreme metal, along with celebrated cover songs, most notably the Kinks' "You Really Got Me." Van Halen, the band, almost singlehandedly jump-start American hard rock, something that was becoming a rarity, although the shockwave wouldn't be felt for a good five years with the birth of hair metal, not coincidentally in the band's hometown of Los Angeles.

Van Halen

If you haven't heard them yet, it's not their fault.

Van Halen has been making a lot of noise since their album was released 4 months ago. California's hardest-rocking band has placed 3 scorching singles on the radio, earned reviews comparing them to Zeppelin and Aerosmith, and destroyed audiences from coast to coast.

Turn on a radio or talk to a friend. Then you'll know why everyone's excited about Van Halen. VAN HALEN Featuring the singles 'You Really Got Me,' 'Runnin' With The Devil,' and 'Jamie's Crying.'

Produced by Ted Templeman On Warner Bros. records and tapes.

1975   1976   1977   1978   1979

LIZZIE GREY:

Creem magazine was like the center of the universe. And so we were just mimicking the makeup and the glitter-ness of the '70s glitter bands who were big acts. London was the first band to really go over the top. One of the big things we did, on Halloween '78, to kind of break ourselves out to the L.A. scene was that we all went in drag to the Starwood. It really created this buzz. We were like the new New York Dolls of L.A., and I mean the band was hot. And the thing that we had that I thought made London so unique was the songs, which were centered around these really strong, melodic, Mott the Hoople–esque hooks. And so the music was pop with raunchy guitars, which became . . . I mean Poison took that whole concept and ran to the mountain with that ten years later. I would even have CC DeVille come up to me at the Rainbow on any given drunken night and just put his arms around me and say, "Lizzie Grey, man, you are the godfather of the music that I love" [laughs]. He was always a very, very nice guy.

KELLY GARNI:

Bands like Slade had an influence as far as what people looked like; you started seeing bands coming out of England that kind of had a little bit more of a visual thing going on. This was way after Alice Cooper, actually, and really nobody went there until Kiss finally did, and they certainly influenced a lot of stuff. And that's where bands like Sister, who came to be known as W.A.S.P., got their image. Plus Judas Priest and Scorpions, even in their early genesis, they were doing that hardcore look with the studs and the leather, and bands like Sister wanted to have that harder-edged image that was basically invented by people like Scorpions and Judas Priest.

MIKE TRAMP (VOCALIST, WHITE LION):

I was in Spain, where I was living prior to America, and saw Van Halen for the first time on TV. I had the record, but I'd never seen what it was. And that day, what I saw them doing, and on that second album when they came around, I saw something that I hadn't seen before. Obviously, I was not exposed to American television every day, but when I saw what Roth was doing at that moment I went "Okay," and from that fucking instant moment, the next night when I went out on stage, even though I was just a pup, I became David Lee Roth. I mean, in my own version. From that day on, and that never changed. . . . But the thing was, I wasn't David Lee Roth. I was just somebody putting on a pair of tight pants and rushing to grow my hair even longer and trying to jump and do the little things—"Okay, you've got to move around."

1970   **1971**   **1972**   **1973**   **1974**

RUDY SARZO (BASSIST, QUIET RIOT, WHITESNAKE, DIO):

You know, once they signed Van Halen, they slammed the door on metal. I was here, so I could tell you, and I struggled with it, and I suffered and I starved because of it. But what doesn't kill you makes you stronger [laughs]. It happened that I survived just along with everybody else, and they survived the same thing. There was a huge movement going on in England and in Europe, especially Germany, with Scorpions and so on. Meanwhile, back in L.A., no one knew about it, no one really cared. Unless you were a band that was new wave or punk that showcased locally at the Starwood or the Whiskey or the Roxy, the record company didn't care up here. I know, because I went through that with Quiet Riot and Randy Rhoads, which is the major reason he decided to leave L.A. and join Ozzy and move over to England. So yeah, they slammed the door on metal, hard rock, as soon as Van Halen got signed. We were caught with the bands that were trying to get a record deal. Everybody was competing for that one record deal from an independent that might happen. And you had bands like Mötley Crüe that, at one time, they were a band called London. You had Dokken and Ratt, which was also known as Mickey Ratt. You had Great White . . . and Quiet Riot [laughs].

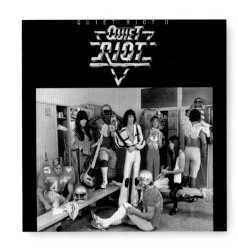

April 24, 1978: *Quiet Riot II* is issued, again in Japan only. The band is led by Kevin DuBrow but also features Randy Rhoads, the only "shredder" on the scene comparable to Eddie Van Halen. But so far it seems that Quiet Riot has missed California's bubbling-under hard rock revolution started by Van Halen.

KEVIN DUBROW (ON *QUIET RIOT II*):

The second album, we were over-produced, just drowned in echo. Another one where you couldn't really tell that we had one of the greatest guitar players in the world. Really lame singing [laughs]. And everything is played too slow. Our influences at the time were Sweet and Queen, not so much Cheap Trick. I think we were together before they came out with their first album. We started in 1975. I mean, I saw them that first tour and they were good. But it was more about the English bands. I learned more about music from Randy than any other person. He taught me how to play guitar. He was awesome. I'd never met a musician quite like him. He had a passion and a fire about his playing and his musicianship that I've never seen in anybody else. And that's why some people who can play his solos don't seem to have that same approach, because Randy had something special. One of the nicest people I ever worked with. He was pretty funny, he was a pretty wild guy. That's one thing people really don't know about him. After a cocktail, he was pretty out there. He was a lot of fun to go out and party with. I always used to say that Randy used to get me into trouble. I just don't remember, but we used to go to parties and Randy would do some mischievous things and I would get blamed for it.

1975   **1976**   **1977**   **1978**   **1979**

CARLOS CAVAZO (GUITARIST, QUIET RIOT, ON THE BIRTH OF HAIR METAL):

There was still a lot of punk and new wave at that point, but there were a lot of metal bands starting to emerge. I remember Dokken being around then, Great White, the BulletBoys. They weren't formed yet, but all those members were around playing the Hollywood scene. And obviously Quiet Riot was. Ratt was starting to come on the scene in the late '70s, early '80s. I'd come into the L.A. scene in late 1978, like October, with my band, Snow, through '81, when the band broke up. I had known Kevin from his band, DuBrow, which was also Quiet Riot with Randy Rhoads in the band. After Snow had broken up in '81, I got a call from these guys saying they needed a guitar player, so I knew them, and I wrote songs with them for about a half year and got the deal about three-quarters of a year later. Snow . . . moved up to L.A. from Orange County. Me and my brother had bands all throughout our childhood, since we started playing at nine or ten years old. Snow started out as a cover band, then we eventually started writing songs. We were influenced by bands like Led Zeppelin, The Who, the Beatles; we liked UFO and did ZZ Top covers.

KELLY GARNI:

I always say that we, along with Van Halen, dug the trenches along the Sunset Strip that led the other bands and eased the way to get where they wanted to be. Compared to what we had to go through, for bands like Ratt and Dokken and Mötley Crüe, they kind of made their own life hard on themselves [laughs] by the crap they used to get into. But you know, for a lot of bands, it was really quite easy for them. Bands that you never hear about anymore, like Black 'N Blue. But bands like that, all they have to do is walk through those trenches that we dug with our fingernails. And those trenches lead right to the clubs and right to the record companies and everybody got a nice free ride. It's very true. There were so many one-hit wonders around at the time, and everybody was getting signed left and right. All you had to do was look like a rocker and walk up the Sunset Strip and some guy would pull over in a Mercedes and offer you a record contract.

DEREK SHULMAN (A&R MAN):

The glam bands drew from the whole Sunset Strip scene. That was an entity unto itself—that whole L.A./Sunset Strip, stickering, flyering, the posters.

CARLOS CAVAZO (ON POSTERING, A HAIR METAL PROMOTION STAPLE):

There was a lot of that, yes. I used to do that with my band Snow. We used to take a lot of posters and pin them up. But there were people who'd tear people's posters down and hang theirs up in front of theirs, a lot of that going on, sure.

1970   **1971**   **1972**   **1973**   **1974**

DUFF MCKAGAN (BASSIST, GUNS N' ROSES):

"Night Train" we wrote on acoustic guitars in Izzy's apartment, one night before we went out flyering for a gig. So we were all drunk, on Night Train, and walking around the streets postering, and singing the chorus to "Night Train."

MARK KENDALL (GUITARIST, GREAT WHITE):

We were just kids with dreams. What we did was, when we got a band together, we tried to play more than all the other bands were playing. That was our big thing. Who's the best band in town and how often do they play? Oh, three nights; we're going to play six nights. So we tried to play more than everyone, because we knew that it would take a hell of a lot of luck to ever get a record deal. So we thought that if we put ourselves in a position to get lucky, at least we'll have a better chance of somebody being in the crowd, whether it be a record guy or a manager. So we just kept playing Hollywood until we were blue in the face. And sure enough, that's what happened. It was so ironic. I mean, you know what, we always kept our dreams alive, but we used to pretend like we were doing interviews with each other on cassette players. That's how crazy it was. The main competition was pretty much Van Halen, the hardest working band. It was very hard to keep up with them because they played almost every single night. But just on the local level, there were bands that were playing just on the weekends only. So we would play all during the week, whether it would be somebody's backyard or in a club. Even for free; we played for free a lot. That was our motto. We'll play for free. Put people in front of a stage somewhere and we will play.

BILL AUCOIN (MANAGER, NEW ENGLAND):

["Don't Ever Wanna Lose Ya"] sold hundreds of thousands. They were caught up in a couple of things. Number one, they were a band that was talented but I didn't know until years after that they didn't get along—even in the beginning. One of the things on me, which I did not expect, was that they said, "Look, you can't ever tell Bill that we don't get along that well" [laughs]. And it was also a new label on MCA that Ron Alexenberg was starting and there was eventually problems between Ron and MCA, and everything happened all at once. But sometimes things are not meant to be. And they ended up selling hundreds of thousands of units. They probably would have broken if they had stayed together. And Paul Stanley produced their first record. Paul said that he wanted to produce and I said, "Look, why don't you do this one?" Paul was pretty good. The great thing about Paul is that he cares so much.

November 1978: Jack Russell and Mark Kendall form Dante Fox, precursor to Great White.

1979: Boston-area band New England issue their self-titled debut, featuring the hit single "Don't Ever Wanna Lose Ya." New England are promising representatives of a genre known as pomp rock, a direct precursor to, and influence on, hair metal. Others within the realm include 707, the Babys, Trillion, Touch, Roadmaster, the Hounds, and, to some extent, Piper, Billy Squier, Night Ranger, Journey, and Angel.

1975   **1976**   **1977**   **1978**   **1979**

March 23, 1979: Van Halen issue *Van Halen II*, featuring "Dance the Night Away" as a first single and another novelty cover in "You're No Good." Hair metal bands would follow Van Halen's example and score many of their hits with cover songs.

May 25, 1979: Angel issue *Sinful*, their fifth and last studio album. The Casablanca-signed act were considered the white to Kiss's black and musically were by this point pomp rock, which was a form of pop metal, which was a form of proto–hair metal. Like Starz, they were before their time.

DEREK SHULMAN:

The L.A. glam/pop thing—bubblegum, effectively—was very, very thought-out by these bands who came from California, and that's a whole different entity to itself, the Mötley, Poison, Ratt thing. And that was also unfortunately accelerated by MTV. MTV had a very big influence in defining what that was. But remember, Van Halen did the groundwork. That's a whole different thing. . . . They were going as a band for a long time before they really broke through in a gigantic way. That's a whole different thing. Van Halen had a track record. Whereas a band like Quiet Riot, even though they were going, came through much later with kind of an MTV poppy Slade cover. So Van Halen were out front, and they weren't glam, actually, when they started. They were basically a rock band, like an Aerosmith, effectively. They had done their work, and they toured their asses off. And the fact that they had some big rock records . . . again, MTV was a huge catalyst in jumpstarting a lot of these bands' careers.

KELLY GARNI:

Record companies were signing bands left and right. I'd say Quiet Riot, Van Halen, and Mötley Crüe were the bands who really broke the ground for bands like Ratt and Dokken, all those bands. Autograph certainly made it through that. Even Mark Slaughter. There were just eight million bands. Gosh, I can't even remember half the names of them. But they were actually selling records and filling up venues. And it was real popular. And I would give Van Halen the main credit for that, sure. They had some good money behind them, plus Gene Simmons, and that gave them a lot of street cred, and their songs were hits. You know, "Running with the Devil," I remember hearing that for the first time on the radio and going, "Holy crap! That's rock." And then you had Night Ranger coming along, all these bands. And then finally the Scorpions and Judas Priest [became] really popular over here. And then it wasn't so much an L.A. scene—it turned into an international scene, as far as heavy metal goes, which is the best thing that has happened to it. And that's why it's endured, because it's become a really international thing.

1970   **1971**   **1972**   **1973**   **1974**

LIZZIE GREY (ON ANGEL'S LAST LP):

Unfortunately, Angel had their moment with that label. Their music was not '70s glitter or glam, but more like '70s mainstream rock. I thought the music sounded a little antiquated and their costuming was kind of foofy. You gotta remember, in glitter and glam, you've got guys putting on makeup who are kind of scary-looking. And the idea is that the makeup is a shock effect. I mean, Dee Snider took that to the mountain. Guys in makeup, but they really look like they could kick your asses if they wanted to [laughs]. Now, when you get into bands like Poison, these are guys who are pretty with makeup on, but these are guys that don't look like they could kick your ass. These are pretty guys who put on makeup and look like women.

CARLOS CAVAZO (ON THE GRIND OF BEING A GLAM BAND):

We would live off girls and also do temporary jobs. There are these companies called Manpower and Volt, and they would sign you up and say, "We've got you this, we've got that." You could go work there for two or three days, make your rent and then quit. Temporary work service. We would live off of women. Girls would come over and we'd be laying on the couch holding our stomachs. They would say, "What's wrong with you guys?" "We're hungry." "Oh, we'll go buy you groceries." "No, you can't do that!" So they would buy us groceries, pay our bills.

CARLOS CAVAZO (ON GEORGE LYNCH):

I remember seeing him before I was even playing the scene, in the mid-'70s. Saw him play in Orange County with the Boyz, and I knew he was going somewhere. But Eddie already had the right band and the right songs at the time. To this day, I think Eddie Van Halen still has more of the guitar hero in him than any guitar player [laughs]. He pretty much beat everybody. There are a lot of good guitar players out there, but still, when you think of guitar hero, you've got to think about Eddie Van Halen and Jimi Hendrix. I think Eddie Van Halen was just at the right place at the right time, had amazing talent, and had the right songs, and just exploded, went crazy. George wasn't exactly behind him—they came out of the same time—but Eddie just had success before him.

1979: Blackie Lawless starts a new band, Circus Circus. Randy Piper is on board for this, too. Blackie is at the center of a scene finding its legs. Others toiling away include Quiet Riot, George Lynch, and members of Ratt.

1979: A six-track Dokken EP called *Back in the Streets* is issued. According to Don Dokken, it should be considered a bootleg.

1979: In a strange twist of glam pedigree, vocalist Nigel Benjamin of Mott (the Ian Hunter–less version of Mott the Hoople) joins Hollywood's London.

1979: George Lynch auditions for Ozzy Osbourne's band, losing out to Randy Rhoads. He would try again in 1982, losing to Brad Gillis. Great White guitarist Mark Kendall says that Lynch was doing two-handed tapping before Eddie Van Halen was.

1979: In Mechanicsburg, Pennsylvania, future Poison stars Bret Michaels and Rikki Rockett form a band called Spectres.

1975　　**1976**　　**1977**　　**1978**　　**1979**

IN 1980, *the New Wave of British Heavy Metal (NWOBHM) is starting to mean something, with tons of fast, flash metal acts getting into the game, the most potentially hair metal of which is Def Leppard. Meanwhile, L.A. is starting to heat up, with bands frantically trying to get gigs, flyering, trading members, living off the avails of their low-level groupies, trying to make sense of a town that is still somewhere between post-punk, skinny-tie new wave, and the last vestiges of "glitter rock," a term that essentially means glam but somehow applies more so to the handful of American bands making fools of themselves. Bottom line: Significantly, all the big US hard rock bands (save for Blue Öyster Cult?!) have run out of gas around this time, and the UK behemoths aren't faring any better. Just as there needs to be a NWOBHM, it looks like a young wave of American rockers are about to take over for the likes of yer wilting Kiss, Aerosmith, and Deadly Tedly.*

1980   **1981**   **1982**   **1983**   **1984**

PHIL COLLEN (GUITARIST, GIRL AND DEF LEPPARD):

The first album was kind of like a concept. We were trying to be glam. We really liked all that stuff. But in England, they really didn't get it at all. It was actually quite funny, looking back on it. It used to really piss people off.

JOE ELLIOTT (VOCALIST, DEF LEPPARD):

The first album was a lot of fun to make and a lot of torture to listen to. We were at Ringo Starr's house, which used to belong to John Lennon. This is the place where he shot the "Imagine" video, in Ascot. We were eighteen, nineteen-year-old kids let loose in a candy store, really. It was Christmas time almost. We had three weeks to make the record. We got all the backing tracks done in one day and spent twenty-one days ruining it by doing too many overdubs [laughs], and not enough time on the vocals. So we had a great time doing it, but it was a good lesson in like . . . that's what records sounds like if you enjoy it too much. Whereas later on in our careers, we've made records that were absolute torture to make, but you could listen to them ten years after the fact and think, "That was well worth it." But the first album—shite. I immediately didn't like it. We had just been signed to the record label three months earlier. I mean, the first album had great intentions. It did show what we were trying to do with the vocal harmonies. But unfortunately it was only me and [bassist Rick Savage] who could sing in the band. So I had to handle nearly every vocal part on it, and I just didn't have the character of Freddie Mercury when he does that. And the other thing was, it was like, "My God, we're making a record," and I'm jumping up and down and getting drunk and running around John Lennon's bedroom. It's like, "You've got to sing," and I'm like, "Fuck off, I'm playing some video." We were just playing. We were just totally playing. We hadn't woken up to the fact that this was really hard work, get on with it. We didn't have a producer that was prepared to grab us by the hair and throw us in and say, "Look, stop fucking around." He'd join in with us, nice guy and everything. But yeah, you compare it to *Van Halen* and tell me it's competent [laughs]. Or the first Montrose album.

LIZZIE GREY (GUITARIST, LONDON):

Van Halen had so much of a Hollywood thing. They were kind of like a Valley band, definitely. When we first saw David Lee Roth, I saw them at Gazzarri's, and when we saw him on stage, I just said, "He's dressed up like . . . that's Jim Dandy." And I've got to give him credit. They nailed all the right points. They've got a singer doing the Jim Dandy thing and a guitar player who replaces the void left by Jimi Hendrix, and America just loves guitar heroes. But when they exploded

1980: Female metal band Vixen forms in St. Paul, Minnesota.

1980: Mickey Ratt moves from San Diego to L.A.

1980: Jon Bon Jovi is onto his third band, The Rest, after playing with Atlantic City Expressway and John Bongiovi and the Wild Ones.

January 1980: The UK's Girl unwittingly contributes to the invention of hair metal with their pouty, androgynous first album, *Sheer Greed*. The band features Phil Collen, later of Def Leppard, and Phil Lewis, later of L.A. Guns.

March 14, 1980: Def Leppard's debut album, *On Through the Night*, considered the most Americanized, professional, and accomplished of all NWOBHM albums, a pointer toward the next metal trend. It would be certified platinum on May 9, 1989. The band somewhat disowns it, considering *High 'n' Dry* their first "good" album. *On Through the Night* was produced by Tom Allom, known for commercializing Judas Priest.

1985   **1986**   **1987**   **1988**   **1989**

1980   **1981**   **1982**   **1983**   **1984**

the way they did, they almost helped create the '80s thing where L.A. bands became this marketable resource for the record labels. The guys that were running the labels, I think they were as clueless as they are now [laughs]. But the whole mentality at that time, there was a lot of influence by the drug of choice being coke. These guys would get drunk and do blow, and it was just madness. It was a decade of madness in Los Angeles. No question about it. People that love that will never let go of it. They will just never let go. When everybody came here, it was almost like the '49ers looking for gold in the 1800s, the gold rush. The labels pushed so hard with so much money back in the '80s, that they made these people into icons that are just not going to go away.

JOE ELLIOTT (ON APPEASING NWOBHM FANS):

We didn't want anything to do with that. So we were absolutely the enemy. We spent every given opportunity in the press telling everybody how crap they all were. I mean, even recently, you only do it . . . not that you have anything personal against anybody, apart from maybe Saxon. But like, we've known Maiden for over twenty-one years and they're decent guys. You can sit at the bar with these guys or go for a curry with them and have a really good time, because they're all nice guys. Known them since they were this big. But we don't have anything in common with them musically. In fact, we've got a lot more in common with Oasis than we have with Iron Maiden. And that blows people's minds. And I say, think about it! We don't do the obligatory guitar solos because we're a rock band. I mean, we've worn leathers, but we've worn leathers the same way Lou Reed has worn leathers. It's not because of the "We swear allegiance to rock" bullshit. You take a look at Lou Reed on the front of *Metal Machine Music*, and you could argue that he could have been the lead singer for Judas Priest. You shouldn't be tainted by it, but unfortunately you are. You've got to be very careful if you wear a leather jacket nowadays. George Michael can wear one and nobody thinks he's in a heavy metal band. We wear one, and all of a sudden we're metal. And we've been trying so long to just get out of any movement and be our own thing. We don't want to be part of any movement.

DAVID BATES (A&R MAN WHO SIGNED DEF LEPPARD TO POLYGRAM IN THE UK):

They were clearly into Led Zeppelin, Judas Priest, bands like that I think, a couple of rock bands. But deeply, they were into Sweet, which was a glam pop rock band, and I think they liked Bolan and Bowie. So yeah, they had the rock thing which they liked, but equally, they were just as big on Sweet as they were on anything else.

March 26, 1980: Van Halen's third album, *Women and Children First*, is released.

March 28, 1980: Vancouver's Loverboy help pioneer the hair metal sound and look with a string of party rock anthems on their self-titled double platinum debut. Hits include "Turn Me Loose," "The Kid Is Hot Tonite," and "Working for the Weekend."

August 22–24, 1980: Def Leppard play the Reading Festival in England. Already there is a slight backlash brewing to the band's Americanized sound.

1985   1986   1987   1988   1989

1980

BIG NEWS IN '81 INCLUDES the success of Def
Leppard with High 'n' Dry and the LP's slightly mechanized sound,
the continued success of hooky keyboard rockers Loverboy, a debut
record from the shocking and nasty Mötley Crüe, and, most pertinently,
the debut of MTV. Also, one shouldn't underestimate the continued
impression of a still-growing NWOBHM on latent metalheads in L.A.,
San Francisco, and New York. Metal is hot in the UK, and sure as heck,
it is about to spread, although sweetened, to the record company
hotbed of Los Angeles. I say sweetened, but the fact of the matter is
the NWOBHM begat thrash as well as meat-and-potatoes US "power
metal" that countless bands up and down California are crafting. Many
of these acts wind up on Brian Slagel's Metal Blade Records, and quite
a few of them shift their sound toward hair metal.

LIZZIE GREY (ON LONDON):

I think any of us would've done anything to be a rock star. Nikki was driven like I was driven. We were like Heckyl and Jeckyl. We lived it. Every day was spent trying to conceive a new, better way to market the project. And I hate to use that word "marketing" because we were lousy businessmen. We were lovers of rock 'n' roll and the whole stigma of the glitter glam rock star. And as much as Mötley Crüe tried to sell themselves as a heavy, heavy metal band, I just see them as a really strong pop rock band more than anything.

JOE ELLIOTT (ON *HIGH 'N' DRY*):

We wanted Mutt to do the first album, but he wasn't available. And we weren't ready for him, truth be known, either. Peter Mensch, who was managing us at the time, had a relationship with Mutt through AC/DC. He had just done *Highway to Hell*, and they were about to do *Back in Black*, and Mutt had come and seen us opening for AC/DC. We had a gig in England, and he saw something. He saw a lot of bad things, but he could see something, otherwise he wouldn't have worked with us. And he said to Pete, "I think I can polish this lot up." So we brought Mutt on board for the second record, and the difference versus the debut is just ridiculous. And sonically, there's a big comparison between *Highway to Hell* and *High 'n' Dry* because of the studio, the producer, the equipment available. That's like, you can listen to Gerry and the Pacemakers and it doesn't sound that different to the early Beatles stuff either. It's a time thing as well. But of course, the way he got the two guitars to play against each other, or with each other, depending on what suited each part, was very much a Mutt Lange thing. If you listen to those Mutt albums, and compare them to the Vanda and Young AC/DC, you'll hear—maybe only a tiny bit—but you'll hear a difference. What he did is he stripped our riffs down. He'd tell [guitarists] Pete [Willis] or Steve [Clark] to take certain notes out and make it easier, rather than musical. You know, Steve never had a problem with that because he wasn't a musician [laughs], in the musician sense. Pete desperately wanted to be. Pete wanted to be in there with Robin Trower, people who are great musicians, but what we would deem like, boring. You know, same thing as the reason why punk came along. So Pete had a problem with it, but not Steve, who just wanted to be Jimmy Page. Page's stuff was pretty simple. So [Lange] was more about taking stuff out. He taught us that less was more. That was the big difference between those two records.

1981: Dante Fox change their name to Great White after an onstage quip singer Jack Russell made about guitarist Mark Kendall's hair. The band is managed by Alan Niven, famous for his early steerage of Mötley Crüe's career.

1981: Blackie Lawless joins Lizzie Grey in the band London, right around the time Nikki Sixx leaves to form Mötley Crüe.

January 12, 1981: Canadians April Wine score a US hit with their Capitol/EMI album, *The Nature of the Beast*, which goes platinum on the strength of "All Over Town" and "Just Between You and Me." The band's heavier album from 1979, *Harder . . . Faster* achieves gold status. April Wine joins the likes of Loverboy and Sammy Hagar as toilers in the wilderness of a melodic hard rock sound that, updated, becomes California-centric hair metal.

April 29, 1981: Van Halen's fourth album, *Fair Warning*, is released.

1985 **1986** **1987** **1988** **1989**

July 11, 1981: Def Leppard issue their second album, *High 'n' Dry*. It's now viewed, in retrospect, as a well-regarded proto–hair metal album—essentially good heavy party metal. It is produced by Mutt Lange, but, like his previous hit production credit, AC/DC's *Back in Black*, really lacks any of Lange's later excesses, as exemplified best by Def Leppard's *Hysteria* and *Adrenalize*. "Bringin' on the Heartbreak" is a candidate for first power ballad ever.

August 1, 1981: MTV launches. The first 25 videos belie the fact that heavy metal of any sort did not yet have much presence in America. However, REO Speedwagon was represented twice with proto–power ballads "Take It on the Run" and "Keep on Loving You." April Wine served a similar role with "Just Between You and Me."

October 7, 1981: Loverboy's second album, the one with the red leather pants, *Get Lucky*, is issued, eventually going 4x platinum on the strength of "When It's Over" and proto–hair anthem, "Working for the Weekend." Not often talked about in glam or hair metal circles, Loverboy is actually one of the earliest contributors to the form, creating melodic hard rock hits and power ballads, writing with Jim Vallance, and recording with Bruce Fairbairn.

Def Leppard's "High 'n' Dry." Hot as Summer.

Don't miss Def Leppard on tour.

Produced by Robert John "Mutt" Lange

RICK ALLEN (DRUMMER, DEF LEPPARD):

Mutt had just finished working on *Highway to Hell* [*sic*], so I think he was obviously in that mode. He had a certain idea, a certain sound, and I think *Highway to Hell* probably had a lot to do with that. That was a great record. Who wouldn't want to sound like that?

JEFF KEITH (VOCALIST, TESLA):

I love *High 'n' Dry*, the rawness. But you're right—they went commercial after that. I mean with Tesla, we had that. You've got to think a little bit commercial, but at the same time that was our niche or whatever you want to call it. Let's not sit there and try to get too commercial on everybody. Let's try to blow things out of the water. Try to stay true to the music, and we always hung with it and we were successful with it.

MIKE RENO (VOCALIST, LOVERBOY):

High-energy rock with positive lyrics, good times. We'll let U2 think about world starvation and poverty. We're not going to do that. We offer a kind of entertainment for two hours. That's what we do. And you know what, I love U2, don't get me wrong, but we chose not to do that.

1980   **1981**   **1982**   **1983**   **1984**

NIKKI SIXX (BASSIST, MÖTLEY CRÜE):

Our thing was a direct rebellion against what was going on in Los Angeles. The thing is, when this band got together, everybody in the band looked the way they looked. It wasn't like after we came out, it was "Let's look like this." It was just four guys that had the same passion and we looked like that. It became something that people talked about more than the music. And we were like, "I've always looked like this, what's the problem? What's the big deal?"

VINCE NEIL (VOCALIST, MÖTLEY CRÜE):

When we got together, I was a fan of Sweet and Nikki was a fan of the New York Dolls. We were all in these different bands, but we all stood out in each band that we were in because we all looked a little bit crazy. And then when we all got together, everybody thought, wow, how ingenious. But it wasn't, it was just us.

NIKKI SIXX:

Hard drugs? Not like that. Although even when we were doing our first session, during "Live Wire," Vince was shooting cocaine.

VINCE NEIL:

Because I had a rich girlfriend who was a drug dealer [laughs].

NIKKI SIXX:

Lovey! She's dead, you know? She got stabbed sixty times in a drug deal. Dead.

TOM ZUTAUT (A&R MAN):

Mötley Crüe started the glam metal thing, and they looked more like the New York Dolls when I found them. Or Slade or Sweet or any of those glam bands from the '70s. But as far as glam metal goes, I mean, nobody really thought of Sweet or Slade as metal, but when Mötley Crüe and Quiet Riot came out, and they were kind of dressing like girls and putting on makeup like the glam bands from the '70s, I think that's when glam metal sort of spawned. Quiet Riot's big hit was a Slade song.

LIZZIE GREY:

Mick Mars I know very little about. I think he was from the west side, like the beach town Huntington Beach area. He played in some Top 40 band called White Horse or something. I knew very little about him, and he actually had no presence that I ever experienced in the Hollywood rock scene. I think it was more like someone who answered an ad or something.

MÖTLEY CRÜE

STICK TO YOUR GUNS
TOAST OF THE TOWN

November 10, 1981: Mötley Crüe's debut album, *Too Fast for Love* is released on Leathür Records. Glam? The band is a mix of bad-boy rock, punk, Hanoi Rocks decadence, and, yes, something coming called hair metal. The record will see much wider re-release on Elektra the following year.

1985　　**1986**　　**1987**　　**1988**　　**1989**

EVEN BEFORE THERE IS *a hair metal proper, acts like Scorpions, Rainbow, and Judas Priest are accused of Americanizing their sound—that is, adding hooks, lessening the note-density of their riffs, chucking in more party songs and the occasional power ballad—basically dumbing it down. All the while, Van Halen continues to supercharge their way upward. The back cover of their* Diver Down *album essentially establishes what the dreams of all future hair metallers looked like. The fact that the album is short and pocked with cover songs and jokey bits . . . well, it is excused in the spirit of lazy L.A. Summary: 1982 isn't so much about hair metal being born as it is about the old guard getting a second wind (add to the list above: Kiss, Ozzy, and Sabbath) to keep up with the explosion of young UK bands firing and inspiring a new headbanging class on both sides of the pond.*

THE NEW HEAVY METAL REVUE

$1.00

NUMBER FIVE — JANUARY 1982

DEF LEPPARD

PLUS! GIRLSCHOOL, SAMSON, CIRITH UNGOL, AC/DC, DEMON FLIGHT, BITCH, MOTLEY CRUE & more!

LONDON

THURS. JAN. 19 — 9 p.m.

Chuck Landis'
COUNTRY CLUB
18415 Sherman Way
Reseda, California 91335
(213) 881-9800

PRODUCED IN ASSOCIATION WITH LUCY FORBES & RON NAGBY

PHIL LEWIS (VOCALIST, GIRL AND L.A. GUNS):

We weren't musicians, we really weren't. We hadn't been trained in anything. It was really like three-chord rock. We were surprised as anyone that we got a deal, and before we know it, we're on tour and our music is being taken seriously to the point of actually being analyzed. That was weird. Musically growing and growing in public is difficult, sometimes painful, and that's what we did. The first album was just kind of rough ideas, and then the second album we'd been on tour a couple of times and we had an idea of what was going to work live. Because when we wrote the first Girl album we'd never done a tour or anything. It was good production—they definitely captured something, the effervescence I think we had. The second album, we had been out on tour with some very heavy bands and we knew the riffs and the grooves that worked and we just sort of actualized them. But we just weren't that good. And it was weird to find us lumped in with the NWOBHM. We were listening to bands like Japan and David Bowie more than the metal. And Jet Records, they were tuned into the metal scene, and that's where they pushed it. But it was a little difficult because we weren't really that heavy.

1982: W.A.S.P. form.

1982: The UK band Girl issue their second and last album, *Wasted Youth*, a grittier affair than the smooth and glammy *Sheer Greed*.

1985   **1986**   **1987**   **1988**   **1989**

42

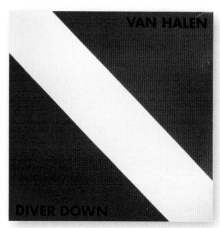

1982: Jon Bon Jovi is doing odd jobs at The Power Station recording studio in New York at the behest of his cousin, Tony Bongiovi. He already has the song "Runaway," which is about to become a regional proto–hair metal hit.

April 10, 1982: Scorpions release *Blackout*. The band started "Americanizing" their sound when guitarist Uli Jon Roth left and was replaced by Matthias Jabs prior to *Lovedrive* (1979) and *Animal Magnetism* (1980). Arguably, *Blackout* is the most transitional of the three, however, steering toward a glam sound with proto–power ballads "No One Like You" and "When the Smoke is Going Down." The album went gold immediately and platinum within two years.

April 14, 1982: Van Halen issue *Diver Down*, featuring a number of fun-time covers and a short duration (31:24). Immediate grousing about a lack of work ethic will be echoed regularly in regard to hair bands of Van Halen's fun-in-the-sun ilk.

JAY JAY FRENCH (GUITARIST, TWISTED SISTER):

Twisted Sister started out as a glam/Bowie band, and then me taking the lead vocals, we became a Mott the Hoople/Lou Reed–type band. When Dee Snider joined, he was very much influenced by Alice Cooper and Black Sabbath. So we became a glam band again, but not a pretty glam band like the original version. We became a more theatrical band. Not gross—that's probably not the best way to put it—but theatrical. The original band was a real attempt at female impersonation, but when Dee came in, it was a very theatrical glam look.

DEE SNIDER (VOCALIST, TWISTED SISTER, ON RECORDING *UNDER THE BLADE* AT JIMMY PAGE'S STUDIO):

There was nothing in the house that gave away that it was Page's. It was built by Gus Dudgeon, who was the producer of Elton John. He had spent sixteen million building his dream studio on a river with a guest house that had literally waterfalls breaking in front of the window. I remember sleeping on the bed and it was floor to ceiling windows and a brook flowed out from underneath my bed. It was the

1980   **1981**   **1982**   **1983**   **1984**

greatest recording environment. Windows in the control room, in the recording facilities, looking at an open meadow. I remember seeing snow falling and horses running across an open field. It was the most pleasant environment to record in. And what had happened is that the bottom had dropped out of the recording industry in the late '70s, and Gus went bankrupt. And Page literally apparently landed a helicopter and bought the place for three million. So he used to come in in the middle of the night when everybody was sleeping. You'd never really see evidence of him except for some stuff being moved around. And, you know, we were more creeped out by his legacy than anything that was technically happening. I remember we watched *Evil Dead*, and Jay Jay was sleeping in the main house—we were all in the band house—and he was kind of freaked out going back in there. But it was very nicely decorated, very old English and proper. But the coolest thing was I remember [bassist Mark] Mendoza coming to me one day, going, "Dee, come here," and he said, "Look at this." And he opened this closet and in there are all the master tapes for all the Zeppelin albums, just sitting there. You'd think they'd be in a vault someplace. But here they were, just in a closet—"Heartbreaker" outtakes, "Stairway to Heaven," "Whole Lotta Love," every friggin' track they ever did just sitting there. We just walked in and walked out.

JAY JAY FRENCH:

It was an exciting experience to finally get the chance to make a record after struggling for ten years. You know, it was primitive, but it was fine. Pete Way from UFO produced it, and you know, he did not do much producing. He was drinking a lot at the time, so Mark Mendoza ended up producing a lot of it. But it was a fun experience. We recorded it on a mobile truck in a barn in southern England, and the amplifiers are separated by hay bales. I remember that. I remember the farmer said that his chickens laid thirty percent more eggs when Mendoza did his basic tracks.

DEE SNIDER:

Pete Way was a functioning heroin addict. I don't think he's doing too much heroin now—he's off the road. He's a doll, a sweetheart, a lover of rock. He wasn't much of a producer, but at that time we were in an indie deal, and we were looking for anybody who could give us a bit of notoriety, and UFO were English legends. [Former Motörhead guitarist] Fast Eddie Clarke ended up coming down and jamming and doing a guitar duel with Jay Jay on "Tear it Loose." And Fast Eddie and Pete Way were forming Fastway at the time. So it brought a sort of attention, and hey, Pete put in the good word for us with Lemmy. So things happened for a reason. But Pete was an awesome guy. And some people feel that *Under the Blade* had a certain rawness. It was recorded literally in a barn with a mobile unit.

August 1982: Key NWOBHM band Tygers of Pan Tang go radically melodic and poppy on their third album, *The Cage*, placing themselves ahead of their time and confusing the home-country punters.

September 3–5, 1982: The first of two US Festivals, featuring twenty bands— none of them metal. (For an interesting contrast, see days two and three of the second—and last—US Festival in May 1983.)

September 18, 1982: Twisted Sister issue their debut album, *Under the Blade*. The music is a rudimentary and pure form of heavy metal, but direct and party-rocking. Visually, the band are pioneering a garish femininity last seen with Alice Cooper and somewhat practiced by Mötley Crüe.

1983

THE YEAR OF HAIR METAL'S *birthing proper. Great White issue their weighty EP, Quiet Riot issue* Metal Health *and then go on to play the enormous US Festival along with Mötley Crüe and the newly Americanized Scorpions and Judas Priest (the US Festival is framed as the final victory for heavy metal over other more anemic musics). Def Leppard issue* Pyromania, *and the production of the thing, along with the iconic videos for all of its smash hit songs . . . well, the term pop metal starts being thrown around and we're off to the races. New Yorkers Twisted Sister issue an "Americanized" album after the very British heft of their* Under the Blade *debut. New Yorkers Kiss issue an "Americanized" album after the very British heft of* Creatures of the Night. *As the year blossoms for serious hairstylists and haberdashers everywhere, Ratt produce their explosive and impressive debut EP, which quickly garners major-label attention, which, along with the smash success of Quiet Riot and the continued surge in Mötley Crüe's fortunes, shift the pendulum to L.A. The year ends with Quiet Riot taking* Metal Health *to No. 1 on the Billboard charts, the first heavy metal album to do so.*

1980   **1981**   **1982**   **1983**   **1984**

JACK RUSSELL (VOCALIST, GREAT WHITE):

We had every label wanting us, and we went with EMI America and they just ended up dropping the ball. We were on a huge Judas Priest tour, which was a sold-out tour. They just wanted us because everybody else wanted us, not because they really thought they could do something with the band. I mean, we were playing ten-thousand-seat arenas with Judas Priest. I would walk across the street to the record store and the record store had never even heard of the band. But whatever happens is meant to happen. We ended up with Capitol later on and did really well with them for years. I mean, this band has been with five major labels, almost a *Guinness Book of World Records* thing. I have no complaints about my career. It's been up and down and up and down but it's definitely been an adventure, excepting of course the tragedy. But other than that, everything else is bearable.

JAIME ST. JAMES (VOCALIST, BLACK 'N BLUE):

Most people think of us as a California band. Everybody in Black 'N Blue was born in Portland, Oregon, and we grew up in Portland and we formed the band in about 1981, but [guitarist] Tommy [Thayer] and I had been playing in bands since the late '70s. Basically we moved to California after about the first year of being in a band, and I had been going back and forth between Portland and L.A. for a while. And I just knew it was a better scene for us, for what we were trying to do. We didn't fit in up here. We were just a little too heavy playing our own music, and that was what was going on in Portland. We broke out of Los Angeles so we kind of have two homes.

DEREK SHULMAN (ON CINDERELLA'S TOM KEIFER):

Tom's influences really were blues-based, just like Aerosmith originally. We're talking late '60s, early '70s, mid-'70s they were a blues-based rock band. They hadn't become a pop-based band until the mid- to late '80s, where they flagged and they were almost defunct. So like *Toys in the Attic*, Aerosmith, their whole base was the same as the Stones. They were raised on blues music. So yeah, I guess Tom had to be influenced to a certain degree by Aerosmith, but not really by Aerosmith as a band, but their appeal as a blues-based rock band, based on what they did originally.

1983: Bret Michaels, Rikki Rockett, Bobby Dall, and guitarist Matt Smith play the Pennsylvania club circuit as Paris.

1983: Great White issue their independent and well-regarded *Out of the Night* EP, which sells eight thousand copies in three months, helping the band get a deal with EMI. Comparisons to Ratt's career arc are inevitable, that band also moving from independent EP to major label.

1983: Portland, Oregon's Black 'N Blue, like so many other hair metal hopefuls, migrate to L.A. The band had already garnered some recognition, with Metal Blade Records founder Brian Slagel adding the band to the first of his *Metal Massacre* compilations on the strength of their demo.

1983: Cinderella form in Philadelphia.

1985   **1986**   **1987**   **1988**   **1989**

1983: Pantera issue their first album, *Metal Magic*, which is fast, hard, and glam, with a fashion sense to match. Song titles include "Ride My Rocket," "Latest Lover," "Nothin' on (But the Radio)," and "Sad Lover."

January 20, 1983: Def Leppard's breakthrough record, *Pyromania*, ushers in the advent of "pop metal." Producer Mutt Lange painstakingly produces it to perfection, bringing the world synthetic drum sounds and inhuman gang vocals. The album goes 10x platinum and continues to sell briskly to this day. Hits include "Photograph," "Rock of Ages," and "Foolin'."

PHIL COLLEN (GUITARIST, GIRL AND DEF LEPPARD):

I knew the guys in [Def Leppard] anyway, because they had seen Girl play. And I had obviously seen them. And I'm from London, and when I was up in Sheffield, I just kind of hung out with them. So really, when I joined, I was really just helping out. Joe was like, "Shit, we lost Pete [Willis], he's gone and we've got all these solos and we want to split it fifty-fifty because we're a two-guitar band. Do you want to come down and do that?" So I ended up playing about five solos on *Pyromania*: "Photograph," "Foolin," "Rock of Ages," "Stagefright," "Rock! Rock! (Till You Drop)" and then I did some rhythm, and then I started singing, and it was like before I knew it, we were on tour. And I never got asked to join the band—it was just like, "Right, you're in." When I joined, I definitely could see that the difference between the first and the second album was pretty huge. And the difference between the second and third album was even bigger. And I also think the difference between *Pyromania* and *Hysteria* was massive. I think with each album, it got more open-minded. I think with a lot of rock bands, they are very close-minded. All this stuff we were talking about, the leather thing, "Oh no, you can't use that influence," all the clichés. When I joined the band I could sing a bit as well, which was different [laughs], because I know there were big vocals going on, but it all kicked in. The band really was influenced by Queen, and I think we wanted to be that, but not *just* that. We wanted Zeppelin, we wanted Stevie Wonder, the Police, the Fixx, a lot of the punk stuff, three-minute songs. And when I joined, all the songs were written already for *Pyromania*, so I just had to play solos on top, basically, and do a bit of singing. Just my impression of it was. I had never heard anything quite like it, because it was an absolute hybrid, a rock hybrid. We were still a rock band. When I heard a lot of American bands—and I'm not slamming these by any means—but Styx, REO Speedwagon, they were very sweet vocals, very high. We weren't. We owed our thing to punk and that's where we come from, you know, "Won't Get Fooled Again," "Holidays in the Sun," "God Save the Queen." That's where we were singing from, only we could do it in tune. It was a totally different attitude. But by doing that, it allowed us to still think we were cool. And we really didn't want to be in that bracket with all those other things.

RICK ALLEN (DRUMMER, DEF LEPPARD):

The original idea was a carryover from *High 'n' Dry*. And I think that was really Joe's obsession with Marilyn Monroe, and I guess his frustration of not ever being old enough to really know her or be around when she was at her peak. . . . I guess that's pretty natural for a red-blooded Englishman [laughs].

1980   **1981**   **1982**   **1983**   **1984**

Triumph's Rik Emmett

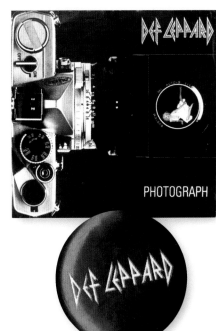

PHOTOGRAPH

DEREK SHULMAN:

Def Leppard, before *Pyromania*, were pretty popular but not big. . . . MTV was looking and scouring around for any videos they could find. And "Photograph" was one that blew the roof off the album.

BOBBY BLOTZER (DRUMMER, RATT, ON "ROUND AND ROUND"):

I just remember, when we were writing that tune, we were rehearsing in Redondo Beach at this place called Music Works. It was a guitar store that had a rehearsal room in the back. I was stoked because I was getting the guys to drive up from Hollywood, whereas I was always driving to Hollywood to rehearse, and this was in Redondo Beach, which was my hometown, so that was cool. As dumb as that might sound [laughs], that's my biggest memory of that, not having to drive to Hollywood. Then, of course, the song taking off, and rapidly. I mean, we did our first show April 9th of '84 in Colorado Springs, and by May we were playing huge gigs, and by June and July, the thing was a smash. And I don't know how the thing went that quick. Normally it takes a lot longer than that. Felt good, though, that's all I can say. And thank God for that song, and thanks to my partners for writing it.

January 28, 1983: Canada's Triumph, toiling away since 1976, find success in the US with a proto–hair metal sound, as evidenced on *Never Surrender*, issued on this day. The album goes gold, as does its follow-up, *Thunder Seven* (*Just a Game* from 1979 and *Allied Forces* from 1981 sell platinum). Comparisons with April Wine's career arc are inevitable.

February 1983: Def Leppard issue "Photograph" as the first single from *Pyromania*, and the band is on their way to having one of the biggest selling records of all time.

Spring 1983: Ratt work on their career-breaking hair metal anthem "Round and Round."

1985   **1986**   **1987**   **1988**   **1989**

SEPTEMBER 17, 1983
CONVENTION CENTER ARENA
SPECIAL SOUVENIR CONCERT PATCH

March 11, 1983: Quiet Riot's *Metal Health* is issued on Pasha/Columbia. Its only hits are "Metal Health (Bang Your Head)" and a cover of Slade's "Cum on Feel the Noize," but the album goes 6x platinum. The title track, issued as a single on the same day, will peak at No. 31.

March 11, 1983: Helix issue their third album and major-label debut, *No Rest for the Wicked*, on Capitol, scoring a minor hit with "Heavy Metal Love."

March 23, 1983: ZZ Top issue *Eliminator*. Not a glam band making a glam album, but it proves a very successful party rock/metal-ish record, nonetheless, fueled by MTV and helping to build a buzz about heavy metal in general. And like glam, the album was highly produced and its videos both sexist and visual.

CARLOS CAVAZO (GUITARIST, QUIET RIOT, ON TRANSITIONAL METAL ANTHEM "METAL HEALTH (BANG YOUR HEAD)"):

The original version was called "No More Booze," and the chorus was exactly the same [sings it], except the verse was different. The verse on the Snow version had a lot more chords going on and Kevin and I simplified it and made it darker. So basically the intro and chorus were the same, and then just the verse is different. And that title, Randy Rhoads had phoned Kevin from Europe, and he said, "There are these kids out here headbanging." And he goes, "What?!" "Yeah, they're banging their heads." And Kevin was like . . . he liked the term, so he used it as a title, and actually, I thought it was a stupid title. I went, "I don't know if I like that. Kinda weird." Goes to show what I know [laughs].

KEVIN DUBROW (VOCALIST, QUIET RIOT):

I found my direction. I found a trademark sound in my throat, pretty much. And that was the best song I had written over a period of like five years. See that's the problem with any band's first album. They compile these songs that's taken them years to put together, and unfortunately when you go to do the second one, you don't have five years to write it. That's why *Metal Health* was so good. It was just the cream of the crop songwriting-wise. I really like the *Metal Health* album. I think it's produced really well. I think the performances pretty much stand up. I really like everything about it, to be honest with you. There's one thing I don't care for on *Metal Health*. I never liked the vocal on "Thunderbird." I mean I demoed that song four times, and that is the fifth version of it. And I think I sang it better in all the first four demos.

CARLOS CAVAZO (ON HEAVYING UP THE BAND'S SOUND):

When me and Kevin got together, we said we wanted to play tougher music—we didn't want to play too pop. Because Quiet Riot was more pop. That's just the way that band was. I don't know why they were that way, it's just that at that time, at the moment, that's what they were doing. I never realized how good a guitar player Randy really was until he joined Ozzy, because he was able to open up with Ozzy. Ozzy's format was darker. But with the pop sound, I don't think he was able to explode the way he did. But bands like Black Sabbath, Iron Maiden, Judas Priest, mainly British bands, we liked what they were doing—heavy metal. We were reading *Kerrang!* magazine. A lot of those British bands were popular over here. Actually, Quiet Riot did shows with Accept and probably even Saxon. We did a lot of shows with those kinds of bands.

JAKSON SPIRES (DRUMMER, BLACKFOOT):

We came back from a European tour in 1982 and we just went right back out again, after taking just a few days off and doing headline

1980   **1981**   **1982**   **1983**   **1984**

stuff. Ted Nugent was out with his new band at the time with Carmine Appice, and when we came back, [vocalist] Rickey [Medlocke] and our manager, Al Nalli, were adamant about changing the band, which I didn't want to do. I love keyboards, but I've always had this thing about keyboard players that they were just flaky. I actually like the album, but Rickey and Al were in this number-crunching thing. Nobody believes me when I tell them this to this day, but we cut that album on a twelve-track Sun board in 1983, with all the multitracking and digital shit coming in. And still, some of the songs on the album were last-minute things that they threw on because the other stuff was too progressive or too heavy and all this shit. They always had an excuse for something, you know? I like most of the songs, but I think they overproduced the stuff to the point where it lost some of the drive.

RICK ALLEN (ON "ROCK OF AGES"):

We spent quite a bit of time getting the whole sort of cowbell intro going. It's funny, because Mutt had this whole country thing going, where, instead of saying "1-2-3-4," he would sort of make lighthearted fun of various groups around the world. And one of the counts was "Gutten-Gleben-Glatin-Globin" [sic], you know? And that was pretty interesting. Various people have written in saying, "Oh, it means running through the forest softly," all these different translations. Knowing Mutt and his background, he speaks Dutch really fluently, I think a lot of it came from his background. It was really just a bit of fun, as was "rock of ages" just being a play on the biblical Rock of Ages, as it were.

DAVID BATES (A&R MAN WHO SIGNED DEF LEPPARD, ON HAIR METAL'S LACK OF POPULARITY IN THE UK):

I think the UK and the US completely split, some years ago. If you take the start of MTV, at that point, we were coming up with Duran Duran, Tears for Fears, Culture Club, and you guys were still coming up with Journey and Ratt or whatever. So that's where we schismed, I think, there. Suddenly MTV had all these videos, and it's well-known that we had lots of videos and MTV took all those things, and that did quite well. And at that point, what American rock stations were into was not what was being played on radio in the UK. And I think even to this day we're miles apart. Britain has always looked for something new, something fresh, something different, something contemporary, something inventive, and North America has always gone very "steady as she goes." It's always been rock-influenced. And I think when you got to the point where the hair bands were going, you know, we were just into a million different things, and it didn't register. It didn't make any sense. Bon Jovi was truly the odd one out. When it came to *Top of the Pops* or Radio One, there weren't that many rock bands being played at that point. Bon Jovi was one, but you're absolutely right—Nikki Sixx and all those bands, no, it just didn't kick in.

May 1983: Yet another southern rock band tries their hand at hair metal. Blackfoot issue *Siogo*, featuring the keyboard textures of Uriah Heep's Ken Hensley.

May 1983: "Rock of Ages" becomes the second smash hit from Def Leppard's *Pyromania*.

May 1983: Ex-Runaway Lita Ford issues *Out for Blood* on Mercury. Her leather-and-studs image is indicative of the transition from traditional heavy metal to hair metal.

1985   **1986**   **1987**   **1988**   **1989**

May 28–30, June 4, 1983: The second and last US Festival is held. While the first one the previous year had no hard rock, in 1983 there were four days: a New Wave Day, a Heavy Metal Day, a Rock Day, and a Country Day. The Heavy Metal Day was the clear winner, with attendance at 375,000. Vince Neil famously said, "It was the day new wave died and rock 'n' roll took over." Heavy Metal Day featured Quiet Riot, Mötley Crüe, Ozzy Osbourne, Judas Priest, Triumph, Scorpions, and Van Halen.

Triumph's Mike Levine

MIKE LEVINE
(BASSIST/KEYBOARDIST, TRIUMPH, ON THE US FESTIVAL):

Best of my recollection [laughs], Quiet Riot opened the show, Mötley Crüe, Ozzy, Priest, Triumph, Scorpions, and Van Halen. It was a three-day event, but our day, the rock day, was called Heavy Metal Sunday and that drew the half-million people, and the other two days drew maybe 200,000 each. The day of, everybody just kind of kept to themselves. The night before, when I checked into the hotel, which was I guess a motel more than anything else—it was the closest place to where it was, where the park was—I had checked in to my room, but outside they had set up a real nice patio and stuff and some helipads. And there was Mike Anthony yelling to me, "Hey Levine, get over here, get over here. "So we started drinking and then Eddie came by and then Roth came by and a couple guys from Scorpions came by and pretty soon it was a party, and next thing I knew, it was two in the morning. But playing, that was probably the toughest entrance to a stage that I'd ever done. I was flabbergasted by the size of the audience—you couldn't see the end of the people. It was kind of like this endless horizon thing, like when you're looking at the ocean, waiting for the sun to set. Until the sun actually sets, you don't know where the horizon is. There was nothing at that venue that you could just focus on—it was just people as far as the eyes could see. And, man, everybody got paid a lot of dough for doing that show, because they are all headliners. Basically Steve Wozniak took out his checkbook and he had his wish list and he paid what he had to pay to get everybody there. It was by far our best payday.

JAY JAY FRENCH (ON TWISTED SISTER'S SECOND LP):

That's the way we were developing. The first album was really kind of clubby and driven by anger. The second one was more refined and driven by a mentality of doing hits. "I Am (I'm Me)" was written in the studio on the fly. It was a genius move, a great song. And "Shoot 'Em Down" is my favorite song, although it's on the first record. But we had a similar feel on the second record. That one went gold eventually in America, and worldwide I guess it reached platinum.

1980   **1981**   **1982**   **1983**   **1984**

DEE SNIDER:

Under the Blade was mostly stuff from the clubs. Very little of that material was specifically written for *Under the Blade*. So it was the culmination of a lot of years and it was very diverse. *You Can't Stop Rock 'n' Roll* was written while *Under the Blade* was being recorded. I was writing that album then because there was a lot of downtime. And by the way, *Under the Blade* was supposed to be called *You Can't Stop Rock 'n' Roll*. We were recording that song and it was decided by the record company at the last minute that album titles with "rock 'n' roll" in the title weren't happening. So we didn't put the track on *Under the Blade* because we had been playing that song for a long time. But we did wind up using it on the next album. But all of the next album was written specifically for *You Can't Stop Rock 'n' Roll*. So I was becoming more focused as a writer. The AC/DC influence was raging, and there was Judas Priest. So instead of songs being culled from the last four or five years, you were getting songs that were being written the year before. And then when I recorded *You Can't Stop Rock 'n' Roll*, I was writing *Stay Hungry*. So when people say that *Stay Hungry* was our attempt to be commercial, they don't know that it was written when we hadn't had any success at all. We still hadn't broken . . . we had just gotten signed by the skin of our teeth to Atlantic Records and we were toughing it out financially on every level.

STEPHEN PEARCY (VOCALIST, RATT):

Back then you had Great White, W.A.S.P., Black 'N Blue, Mötley Crüe, Quiet Riot. At one time in 1982, you could see every one of those bands in one weekend. Just walk down the street to the Troubadour and you could see W.A.S.P. Walk down to the Whiskey, then to Gazarri's. But we considered ourselves players. When we first started, this was heavy metal—'82, '83—and me and [guitarist] Robbin [Crosby] made a conscious effort to say, "Hey, we've got to, you know, let's be the nice guys. Mötley's the Jack Daniels, let's be the champagne." So it kind of worked like that. We kept ourselves a little bit out of the loop. We didn't let anybody know what we did or what was done. It was just one of those things. It was all about the songs, because we were one of the last bands to get signed in L.A., even though Ratt was right under Mötley, selling out the clubs, to where you can't play anymore. You had to wait a month to play the Palladium, then you moved up two months later. The only downfall to becoming popular in L.A., and maybe still to this day, if you're a local band, is that you can only play certain clubs close to the next club that you booked. So, you know, okay, we've got to wait a couple of months or a month because we're playing the Palladium. Oh shit, we're doing really good now—now we've gotta wait because we're going to coheadline Santa Monica Civic. We just did the same as Mötley, you just take steps. But everybody else was gone off and running, Quiet Riot, this and that.

June 27, 1983: Twisted Sister issue their second album and first for a major label (Atlantic), *You Can't Stop Rock 'n' Roll*. The record is seen as one of the foundations of hair metal, even though the band is from New York and the sound of the record is a simple, thumping metal along the lines of Kiss and AC/DC. The single "I Am (I'm Me)" is an anthemic precursor to the smash hits to come.

August 23, 1983: Ratt issue their self-titled EP.

August 24, 1983: Rainbow issue *Bent Out of Shape*, the last of their three records featuring American vocalist Joe Lynn Turner. Beginning as more of a gothic, old-school heavy metal band, Rainbow had morphed into a proto–hair metal band, breaking up just as this type of hard rock was about to break big.

August 27, 1983: Quiet Riot issue the single "Cum On Feel the Noize," a hit for Slade at the height of the UK's own glam explosion a decade earlier.

September 18, 1983: Dokken's debut album, *Breaking the Chains*, sees its US issue after having been released by France's Carrere Records as *Breakin' the Chains* back in 1981—making it a groundbreaking hair metal record before its time.

Quiet Riot's Kevin DuBrow and Carlos Cavazo

But I think it was the songs and the fact that we put out our own EP for three thousand dollars in two days, and it worked and you had that vibe and character.

TOM ZUTAUT:

My first signing was [Quiet] Riot. They were very early, and they had the song "Swords and Tequila." They were so close to breaking and making it on radio, and they paved the way for Dokken and Mötley Crüe. So Dokken and Mötley Crüe would be the next two, and then after that, Metallica and Tesla and Guns N' Roses, and I'm probably forgetting some. You know, I signed a bunch of bands. There were a bunch of bands like Ratt that I would've signed, but Nikki Sixx, you know, Robbin was his roommate and he didn't want me to sign his roommate, so that was kind of the end of that. I passed on Poison, because I wasn't sure if they were going to be a one-hit wonder or not. I was wrong about that.

JOE LYNN TURNER
(VOCAIST, RAINBOW, ON *BENT OUT OF SHAPE*):

I think it was a little more refined. I don't know if that is good or bad, refinement for a rock band. I think it's an extremely fine album because the material on it and the recording and the sound, everything is just probably one of our better efforts, although *Straight Between the Eyes*, in my opinion, has a magic that just cannot be duplicated. It was just that point in time, with "Stone Cold" and all those kinds of songs. But then again *Bent Out of Shape* with "Street of Dreams," we had something going on there. And I really believe that we were headed toward becoming a melodic, heavy Foreigner or heavy Journey. And I think with one more record we really would have broken through into the commercial market. Because we still had legions of fans that we were heavy enough and obscure enough to keep them. But at the same time we were picking up . . . you know, here in America we were in the Top 10 and things like that, we were on MTV, and it was just working. We were on the verge of something greater but unfortunately it broke up right at that time [laughs]. Ritchie [Blackmore] is a song guy, believe it or not, whereas people think he is a riff master. But at the same time he was all for the song. And traveling through America, you had Loverboy and all these hit bands. I just think Ritchie's ear was just remarkable and he picked up, in his own way of course—I don't think he ever sacrificed or compromised himself—but in his own way, he likes very hook-oriented, melodic rock. Bluesiness from a singer's point of view, but at the same time he likes the song. So there was no forcing Ritchie into any sort of square-peg-round-hole thing. He was all for it.

1980   **1981**   **1982**   **1983**   **1984**

DON DOKKEN (VOCALIST, DOKKEN):

I think what made us popular, in my opinion, is when we came back from Germany, we got passed by almost every American label and they all said the same thing. They said that your music is too heavy and your lyrics are too pop. And that the people who like your commercial melodies will think you're too heavy and the people who like your heavy side will think your lyrics are too commercial. So the people who like your heavy stuff will find you too light and vice versa, so you will lose both sides of the fence. And trying to get both sides, your chances are a billion to one. And I said, "Yeah, but it's the one I'm looking for. I mean, what if we got both sides of the fence?" If we're going to write these heavy songs, with George's heavy riffing, like this chunky stuff like "Breaking the Chains," that was a really heavy guitar riff for the time. And "Paris Is Burning," with the double bass, that's a heavy metal song. If you look back now, like we played that song live, it still sounds like a metal song and it was done in 1981, eighteen years ago. . . . That thing was flyin'. So it was really heavy and then I did this huge chorus going [singing really delicate] "Paris is burning" and they said, "Well, why don't you do some really heavy vocals? It's so melodic, yet it's so heavy." They said, "Why don't you do one or the other?" And I said, "Well I want to do both." And nobody was really doing that at the time. Either you had Journey doing melodic vocals and melodic music or you had Accept or Metal Church doing screaming vocals and screaming guitars. I remember David Wayne saying that I was an influence, and I was thinking, well that's a compliment. But my voice was not metal. It's not that I don't want to do it, it's that I can't. I don't have a ballsy voice. If I did, I'd use it. I wish I could sing that kind of gnarly aggressive vocal. I can do it for about ten minutes and then I'm hoarse. I can't force that growl. I have a wimpy voice, I guess [laughs].

VINCE NEIL (ON THE *SHOUT AT THE DEVIL*'S SATANIC VISUALS):

I think that was more of the press taking something and running with it, you know? If you forget about the music for a minute, image-wise, by the time *Too Fast for Love* came out [on Elektra in 1982], we had already evolved into doing this other thing, getting more macabre and theatrical. I mean, if you look at the way we looked on *Too Fast for Love* and then the way we look in the foldout to *Shout at the Devil*, the only difference is we had more money [laughs].

NIKKI SIXX:

"Shout at the Devil" was just a song, a political song at that. It had nothing to do with Satan. It was about Ronald Reagan, and that got twisted. Like Vince said, we were just getting theatrical. It's cool, it was fine with me, it was our *Goats Head Soup*. If you look at the photo session in the first album, the very next [Elektra] version of the record

Gene Simmons

Kiss' Vinnie Vincent

September 20, 1983: Kiss remove the makeup and go hair metal with considerable success, issuing *Lick It Up*. The band's non-makeup era would find them MTV staples throughout the '80s. The album is their first platinum certification in the last three tries.

1985   1986   1987   1988   1989

54

September 26, 1983: Mötley Crüe issue *Shout at the Devil*, the band firming up their reputation as the dark side of L.A. glam.

that came out [in 1982], there was a picture of us with the pentagram in that macabre setting. So that was before *Shout at the Devil* came out. So we were already there.

VINCE NEIL:

The first album, you have to remember, was basically a demo tape. We recorded that record in like three days and we ended up pressing it independently and sold like twenty thousand copies. That's what really got us our record deal. We weren't even signed when we did that. But when Elektra signed us, they re-released it. So *Shout at the Devil* was basically really our first album that we actually went in and recorded from scratch with Tom Werman and that's why it sounds so different, because it was really produced, rather than us just kind of throwing down the songs.

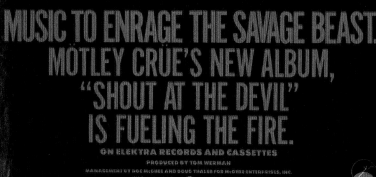

1980 **1981** **1982** **1983** **1984**

NIKKI SIXX:

Too Fast for Love, we had just kind of thrown it down and did it, and no one was interested. And all of a sudden, it started selling and there was a buzz, and Elektra signed us, and they said, "We want you to use [producer] Roy Thomas Baker." And we were like, "My God, Roy Thomas Baker—Queen, the Cars—this is going to be great." He was a complete disappointment. He just like laid around, hungover all the time. He would come in and say, "Oh, a little bit less reverb, darlings." Who the fuck's this wanker, man? This is the guy who did the Queen records. He had, you know, lost his edge. He was fuckin' just a guy who was going through the motions. So Tom Werman, being a guy who'd done some of our favorite bands, one being Cheap Trick, was brought in to talk about doing *Shout at the Devil*, and at first I was like, "Look, I don't really want anybody in there to do it. We can do it ourselves." And Elektra brought us in, and we met with [Werman]. He was kind of this square-looking Jewish cat, and I was like, "What does this guy know?" But he did do Cheap Trick, some of the greatest albums—Molly Hatchet, Ted Nugent—and we were like, "Man, maybe this is what we need," so we went with it. And Tom, in a lot of ways, was the perfect producer because he let us be us, enough to let us make *Shout at the Devil*. He sort of stayed out of the way. He organized the edges, brought them somewhat together. In other words, we never really could have gotten from brain to take to mastering. There were a lot of steps, and he was the guy who did all that. He said, "Look, these guys know what they're doing, just let them do what they're doing. Let me sprinkle a little magic here and there."

VINCE NEIL (ON THE IMPORTANCE OF VIDEOS):

We always enjoyed making them. They were a lot of fun. You can see as time progressed, from our first video to one of our last videos, just the technology advanced so much. There really was some thought to what we did. And I think it was great for fans to be able to turn on the TV and actually be able to see your favorite bands, rather than just listen to them and look at the album cover.

CARLOS CAVAZO (ON TOURING WITH LOVERBOY):

They were good, and they were accepted really well. They had a lot of fans. They were putting butts in seats in stadiums. They were really huge. They still get airplay here. I still hear their songs once in a while on the radio. Good band—they're good guys too. I'm sure everybody was talking about them at one point or another, as big as they were. Then they, like all bands from that era, had a backlash [laughs]. They weren't immune to it, nor were we.

November 8, 1983: Loverboy release their third album, the Bruce Fairbairn–produced *Keep It Up*. It will go double platinum, fueled by single "Hot Girls in Love."

November 26, 1983: Quiet Riot's *Metal Health* hits No. 1 on Billboard, where it stays for just one week—replaced by Lionel Ritchie's *Can't Slow Down*.

1985   **1986**   **1987**   **1988**   **1989**

1984

TONS OF RECORDS, all adopting elements of what is happening in L.A., are issued by bands all over the United States and beyond. Perhaps the most important of these is an album from that lovable transition band, Van Halen. Their 1984 LP, as much through its world-beating videos as its volatile raw music, defines the party atmosphere of L.A. rock like nothing before. Bands begin flocking to L.A. encouraged by other bands' successes, such as Ratt's Out of the Cellar, the Scorpions' Love at First Sting, W.A.S.P.'s notorious first mauling, and, to a lesser but still buzzy extent, Great White's self-titled debut and Dokken's second album, Tooth and Nail, the latter reemphasizing the concept of the hair metal guitar hero. Kiss enhance their hair metal look and sound with Animalize and sell lots of records in the process, fueled by MTV, as is the case with prettier and younger bands beginning to overtake them. The year ends on a morbid note, with the death of Hanoi Rocks drummer Razzle in a car accident, as well as a second car wreck in which Def Leppard drummer Rick Allen loses an arm.

1980   1981   1982   1983

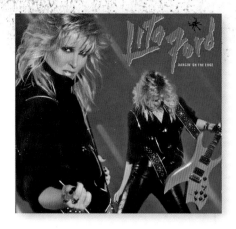

1984: The very glammy D'Molls form in Chicago.

July 1984: Lita Ford issues *Dancin' on the Edge*, featuring a hair metal title and Ford wielding a very hair metal pink BC Rich guitar on the front cover.

July 27, 1984: Pantera release their second album, *Projects in the Jungle*. Song titles include "Blue Light Turnin' Red" and "Only a Heartbeat Away."

1984: Hollywood-based London reform. Both Slash and Izzy Stradlin would pass through its ranks, as would future Cinderella drummer Fred Coury.

1984: Giuffria issue their Andy Johns–produced self-titled debut. The band's leader is Angel's Greg Giuffria, he of the flowing, Rick Wakeman–like locks. Other notables in the band are Craig Goldy, Chuck Wright, and David Glen Eisley.

May 15, 1984: Kick Axe release *Vices* on Pasha/CBS to positive reviews. Originally formed in Saskatchewan in 1976, they moved to Vancouver in '78. *Vices* shares that Spencer Proffer/Pasha sound with Quiet Riot, W.A.S.P., and Icon.

LARRY GILSTROM (GUITARIST, KICK AXE):

Vices is a very powerful album. It was the combination of many, many years of the band wanting to get a record deal and once we got that, we got to go down to Hollywood and record under some great circumstances. But it seemed to me that when we were doing our first album, a lot of the staff there were getting paid in currencies other than money. The song "Vices" was written right in Hollywood when we were recording and it was basically about what we saw going on around us [laughs]. That was inspired by just that very close surroundings of rehearsing in SIR and recording in Pasha. And we wrote that with Spencer, at his house, and we were just making it up.

Kick Axe's Raymond Harvey and George Criston

Kick Axe's Larry Gillstrom

1985   **1986**   **1987**   **1988**   **1989**

58

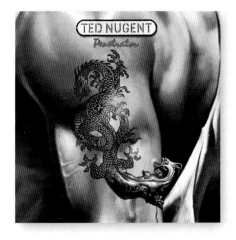

January 1984: Ted Nugent issues a blatantly hair metal album called *Penetrator*, replete with keyboards and high-tech production.

January 9, 1984: Van Halen release *1984*, their last album (of the '80s) featuring hair metal's finest template, David Lee Roth, at the mic. The LP marks perhaps the apex of the band's glam mania, with hits like "Jump," "Hot for Teacher," and "Panama," each accompanied by iconic glam videos.

TED NUGENT:

Everybody was talking about music trends and influences and looking for different angles and things. Where I should have been like AC/DC—I should have gone in there and just made the most blatant Ted Nugent record I could have possibly made. But I'm a team player and when people on my team who I respect recommend things that might be discomforting to me, I'm a giving and open person, and of course it was the stupidest thing I could have ever done [laughs]. So in my old age, I'm less giving and I'm less tolerant [laughs].

DEREK SHULMAN (A&R MAN, ON JON BON JOVI):

When I first signed him, they were totally unshapened, non-shapened, as it were. And in fact, we had various discussions about how the band would be put together. Because effectively, when "Runaway," which was recorded . . . it was recorded by some session guys at The Power Station, where Jon kind of like quasi-worked with his second cousin. So when I first saw him and the band he had thrown together, it was really very raw. The thing that I saw in Bon Jovi, and Jon Bon Jovi in particular, Richie Sambora, who he had recruited, was first of all the yin and yang, the lead singer and guitarist, which is very, very important in the hard rock and metal world. But Jon had this incredible drive to succeed, and be better and become as big as he's become, if not bigger. And at that point in time, to be perfectly honest,

David Lee Roth

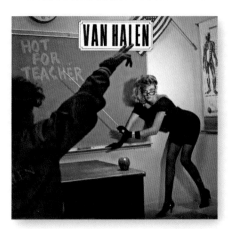

1980   **1981**   **1982**   **1983**   **1984**

his singing, you know, he was not sure where he fitted into the landscape. I kind of almost put it to him, does he want to be a pop star or a rock star? And he said he wanted to be a rock star. So there was a lot of shaping to be done. But he knew what his goal was—to be as big as he's become.

January 21, 1984: Bon Jovi issues their self-titled debut. Although an East Coaster, it nails more presciently the hair metal look and sound than many California acts. The album sells double platinum on the strength of the single "Runaway," the lyric of which is a typical "lost girl" tale perfect for the hair metal times.

Spring 1984: HSAS (Sammy Hagar, Neal Schon, Kenny Aaronson, and Michael Shrieve) represent an early attempt at a hair metal supergroup. It is Sammy's last high-profile billing before his hiring by Van Halen. Typical of the times, the band score a hit with a cover, namely "A Whiter Shade of Pale," a proto–power ballad now turned more deliberately so.

NEIL SCHON (GUITARIST, HSAS):

Sam and I talked about doing the project, and I had met Kenny Aaronson before, and Michael Shrieve. Michael had played in Santana when I was in the band, and Kenny was playing with Billy Squier at that time, and I thought he sounded great. So I called those guys up and said, do want to do it? And they flew out and we just started writing. Actually, we wrote on the spot, all of us together, and Sam and I sort of wrote everything, and we came up with about an hour's worth of material. We wrote for a couple of weeks, we rehearsed for about a week, and then we went out and just played a few live shows that we did and recorded it live and went back in the studio and doctored some stuff. But most of it is live. And then Sam went back on tour and I went back on tour. I believe we had about 300,000 units out there. So hopefully it would be close to gold right now.

1985   **1986**   **1987**   **1988**   **1989**

BOBBY DALL (BASSIST, POISON):

We would always say that our influences were the '70s, but with this band, you have four definite distinctive different personalities. Bret could very easily be in Lynyrd Skynyrd by way of example. CC Deville could be Billy Idol, any kind of power-pop thing. Rikki Rockett would be in the New York Dolls or Gary Glitter, and I would be in AC/DC if I had a choice [laughs]. So you put the four of us together, and we're four very strong personalities and no one backs down. And I think that's the magic. But we were all influenced by all the music of the '70s, the Van Halens, the Aerosmiths, the Cheap Tricks, I could just go on. And no matter what our influences were differently, all of us definitely liked bands that were showmen. And I think that's what comes through, especially in our live show.

RIKKI ROCKETT (DRUMMER, POISON, ON SLASH TRYING OUT FOR THE BAND):

For a couple of days we kind of worked with Slash. Slash is awesome; he just wasn't right for our band. God knows what would have happened to rock. Isn't it funny that things pivot on small events? But he loved Poison. And then he really hated us, once Guns N' Roses started, because he always felt betrayed by us passing on him. And I talked to him about it after and I said, "Aren't you glad it turned out the way it did? How can you even be mad about this?" He was mad because we pick CC instead of him, like, how could you do that? It was an ego thing. And I said, "It's not because you sucked; it's because you didn't make sense for what we were doing."

KEVIN ESTRADA (L.A.-BASED PHOTOGRAPHER):

Warrant moved here, Poison moved here. Even Mötley—Nikki moved here from Seattle. He's one of the forefathers of that whole movement, you know. David Lee Roth moved here but not specifically to make it as a rocker. Axl Rose, him and Izzy moved here. In Hollywood itself, at that point, I would say eighty percent of the bands were from out of state. There was a magazine out here called *The Recycler*, and it was a free kind of classified magazine. If you opened that up back then all you saw in the music section was tons and tons, hundreds, thousands of listings of people looking to put a band together. They just moved here to be the next Warrant or to be the next Poison.

KIM FOWLEY (MANAGER, RUNAWAYS):

So we have Mötley Crüe begetting Quiet Riot begetting Poison. And Poison, there's a story of how they came to L.A. and came to my living room first. I heard the demo, and they didn't have any place to sleep. So where did I park them? At Tommy Lee's sister's house, Mötley Crüe. Published by Kim Fowley. That's where they got their first free meal.

1980   **1981**   **1982**   **1983**   **1984**

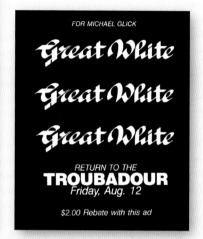

March 6, 1984: Poison arrive in L.A. from their hometown of Mechanicsburg, Pennsylvania, to seek their fame and fortune.

March 21, 1984: Great White issue their self-titled debut album. The sound is still very much of a heavier, more rhythmic and chunky heavy metal style that characterized the early days of hair metal.

March 23, 1984: Ratt's *Out of the Cellar* is released on Atlantic. The album is an instant hit and goes 3x platinum. The album is produced by the controversial Beau Hill, and contains "Round and Round," "Back for More," and "Wanted Man." The model on the cover is Tawny Kitaen, future wife of David Coverdale.

1985　　　**1986**　　　**1987**　　　**1988**　　　**1989**

STEPHEN PEARCY (VOCALIST, RATT):

Me and [guitarist] Robbin [Crosby], we lived in Ratt Mansion West, which was a one-bedroom apartment with three guys sleeping in it, and the road crew in the front room, and it was, you know, a hell house, a fun hell house. And there were things like me and Robbin driving in his beat-up old car and then hearing actually "You Think You're Tough" on two of the major rock radio stations in L.A., for the first time. And that would have to be the beginning and the best of all, of many, highlights. But the minute we went in to do that record, Beau had some good ideas, but he was a staff producer. We went in to record three songs and it was like, "Tell us how you like the guy." Well, it turns out we liked him. And we were off and running. While he was in there recording somebody's basic tracks, there was me and Robbin in the lounge, getting laid, partying, preparing for our session [laughs]. But it worked. The sound, I would say, *Cellar*, I wrote primarily the songs, but everybody cowrote. But they would bring their songs to me and I'd mold them into tunes and we'd get together and bounce ideas around. I think at that time, our songs were truly ours.

BEAU HILL (PRODUCER):

I was bludgeoned upon Ratt and forced upon them by Doug Morris, the president of Atlantic. I had met Doug about three weeks prior to going to California, and I was broke, struggling, a musician, wannabe record producer. Doug came to California when I was mixing a record and sat with me while I mixed it, and he obviously liked my work, and three weeks later, when I was back in New York, in my illegal warehouse-converted room, I got a call from Doug's office, and he said, "Listen, I'm thinking of signing this band Ratt, if you'd like to produce them." So I went to California with Doug and we saw Ratt play at the Beverly Theater. And I sat there and I saw two thousand kids losing their mind, and I went, "Sure, gosh, I'd really love to do it." Now, the guys from Ratt, being like most people, they were like, "Who in the hell is Beau Hill?" a), and b), "We don't want him and we think he's an idiot" [laughs]. And the list just goes on and on and on from there. The guy that they wanted was Tom Allom. That's who Pearcy wanted. So they were very unhappy with having me forced down their throat. But nonetheless their manager, Marshall Berle, who was Milton Berle's nephew, somehow persuaded them to accept this edict from Doug, and he really wanted the band to be on Atlantic, and I guess Atlantic had given them a reasonable deal, for back in those days, and that's it.

1980   **1981**   **1982**   **1983**   **1984**

PRODUCED BY DIETER DIERKS FOR BREEZE MUSIC

SCORPIONS come screaming back, following up their million selling Blackout with a new scorcher, "LOVE AT FIRST STING." WATCH FOR SCORPIONS TOUR BEGINNING IN MARCH

Manufactured and Marketed by
PolyGram Records
1984 Polygram Records, Inc

BAD BOYS RUNNING WILD
Photo by Claude Gassian

March 27, 1984: Scorpions issue *Love at First Sting*, a very Americanized record, quite glam in the sense of offering self-evident party songs and simplicity at every turn of riff. Scorpions are fully set to participate in the commercial pop metal times to come. The album includes party tracks like "Bad Boys Running Wild" and "Big City Nights," but the main track is the textbook "Still Loving You," which cements the Scorpions as a power ballad band, although only a handful of their biggest hits lean this way, which, really, is the case with every other hair metal band. *Love at First Sting* goes 4x platinum.

RUDOLF SCHENKER (GUITARIST, SCORPIONS):

[*Love at First Sting*] was the best balance we ever had between the rock songs and the ballads. To be the perfect thing was "Rock You Like a Hurricane" on the rock side and "Still Loving You" on the slow side. I think *Love at First Sting* would have sounded much better if we didn't go right to digital. Because we were one of the first bands to use digital. We made a mistake by going digital to digital to digital. Sometimes the guitar sound is very thin. We didn't use the compression of the tape. Somehow we didn't get a really big guitar sound. We had to record on digital, but it wasn't the best because it was one of the first machines, a 3M or something. And we had to go to analog to get the compression and then back to digital. I'm not very happy with it.

1985   **1986**   **1987**   **1988**   **1989**

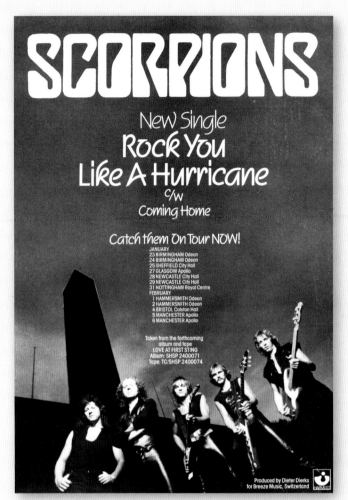

Scorpions' Rudolf Schenker

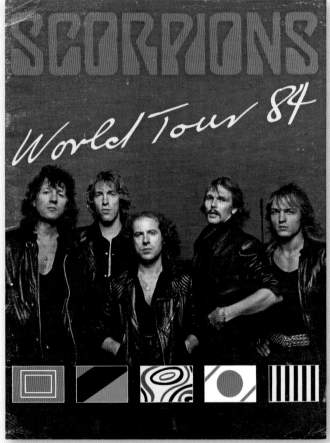

1980　　　　1981　　　　1982　　　　1983　　　　1984

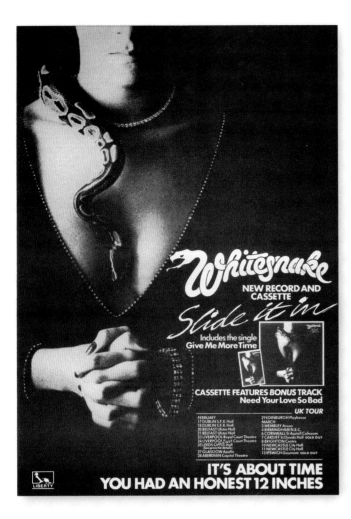

DAVID COVERDALE (VOCALIST, WHITESNAKE):

Slide It In was the first album I did under my own steam, the first one after getting rid of the ex-manager and revamping the band. There are actually two albums: one the US copy, one the European copy. [Guitarist] John Sykes came in to audition after we recorded the album. He actually came in to audition while we were recording it and [drummer] Cozy Powell didn't like him at all [laughs] and it didn't work out very well. But I kept the flame going for him and ultimately, obviously I call the shots because it's my band and I said I have to override you. I feel very strongly that he can take us to another level. He's a very powerful guitarist, a very talented young man, no question at all. But we had a lot of problems as time went on in terms of his attitude. His attitude, I felt, was very disrespectful to a lot of people I was working with and I also found out it was going on behind my back. And it got worse and worse and worse. There was a kind of resentment that he wasn't as well-known as I was at that particular time. Instead of having the patience to realize that he's going to get the keys to the treasury down the line, it was just intolerable to work with him in that atmosphere.

April 1984: The US release date of Whitesnake's *Slide It In*, a transitional hard rock/glam album on which David Coverdale begins to transform the band. The album goes 2x platinum in the US.

1985 **1986** **1987** **1988** **1989**

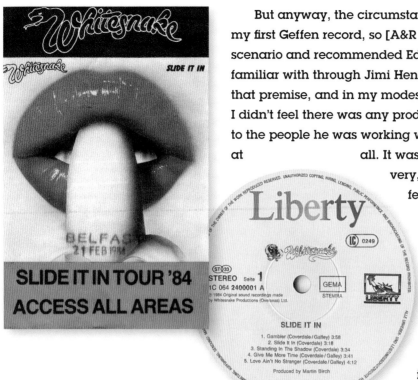

But anyway, the circumstance was *Slide It In* started out, this was my first Geffen record, so [A&R man] John Kalodner came into the scenario and recommended Eddie Kramer, whose name I was totally familiar with through Jimi Hendrix. And I was very, very excited on that premise, and in my modest opinion, I felt he was an imposter. I didn't feel there was any producer overview. He was very alienating to the people he was working with. The other musicians didn't like him at all. It was very disappointing. It was running very, very late and I was headlining a huge festival, Donington, *Monsters of Rock*, and the album wasn't ready for it. So I was like, well, let's put an EP out in England, like three or four songs. At least there was enough material for that. And while we were mixing this, he had to fly back to New York, and I was going, "This is just ridiculous." Where his focus was, I don't know, but it certainly wasn't on the record.

DAVID COVERDALE (ON THE HUMOROUS SIDE TO HIS SONGWRITING):

Slide It In . . . a lot of those songs I wrote in a place called San Lucia in the Caribbean, and having a very good time. Actually that was one of my least blues albums, least blues in the "My missus has disappointed me and broken my heart yet again" lyric. My wife and I at that time were getting on very, very well and we were very physically active [laughs], which was certainly promoting a lot of those tunes. "Slow an' Easy" I had written basically to replace a song called "Lovehunter" because I was bored sick singing it. And it was going to be a vehicle for my then slide player Micky Moody. And "Slide It In" literally was just a bit of tongue-in-cheek. One of the things that I had developed with Whitesnake . . . okay, long story short: I'd worked with Deep Purple, which were a deadly serious rock band, you know, and that's how they were perceived. And, you know, I like a good laugh, Martin. And I would write songs, once I got Whitesnake up and running, I would write songs like "Wine, Women and Song," "Would I Lie to You" just to get in your pants, "Slide It In." These were all tongue-firmly-in-cheek, end-of-Saturday-night, knees-up, sing-along songs. And it was only the narrow-minded female, militant female feminists [laughs], who couldn't see the joke. But you know, when I was in concert, the loudest voices I would hear singing the *Slide It In* songs were women. It's basically a bit of fun. I've got my deadly serious tunes, as you can testify, but a lot of them are just definite rock 'n' roll a-wop-bop-a-lu-la Little Richard knees-up songs.

1980   **1981**   **1982**   **1983**   **1984**

TURN THE POWER UP

Twisted Sister

STAY HUNGRY

➤ **Stay Hungry** ➤
The most Twisted Sister yet!
Featuring the single
"We're Not Gonna Take It"
As Seen On

On Tour: Summer '84

Produced by Tom Werman for Julia's Music, Inc.

On Atlantic Records & Cassettes

Twisted Sister's Jay Jay French, © Rod Dysinger

April 27, 1984: Twisted Sister issue as an advance single "We're Not Gonna Take It," which typifies a simple, almost juvenile form of hair metal that helped sell the genre to increasingly younger crowds.

May 10, 1984: Twisted Sister issue their smash hit *Stay Hungry* album, featuring heavy metal fight songs "We're Not Gonna Take It" and "I Wanna Rock," both with iconic MTV hair metal videos featuring the band's premeditated yet fully juvenile twist on glam ten years in the making.

MARK MENDOZA (BASSIST, TWISTED SISTER):

Tom Werman didn't want to do "We're Not Gonna Take It." He heard it and he said there's just no way you guys are doing this. He actually didn't want most of those songs on the record. He wanted us to do songs from other bands, get other writers. We fought that with him to the point where we may not have recorded that album. Although he's a good guy and we got along with him well, I don't think his production qualities were right for us. The album came out sounding okay—it's not a great-sounding record. I think it's wimpy. It sounds small. Twisted Sister live was huge, monstrous. And these guys never saw us do anything live.

1985   **1986**   **1987**   **1988**   **1989**

July 1984: Y&T issue their sixth album, *In Rock We Trust*, which finds the band shifting their previously traditional heavy metal sound to the new realities of the hair metal marketplace. Their new producer is Tom Allom, who was instrumental in simplifying Judas Priest's sound for that band's successful assault on America.

JAY JAY FRENCH (GUITARIST, TWISTED SISTER):

[*Stay Hungry*] was a big-budget record. It was like, you have to make the record of your life. We did it. There's some great songs on that record. It was a lot of fun. That sold about four and a half, five million worldwide.

DEE SNIDER (VOCALIST, TWISTED SISTER):

You Can't Stop Rock 'n' Roll is my favorite record overall. *Stay Hungry* is *Stay Hungry* [laughs]. It's the biggest selling album we had, it has the most famous songs that I wrote, and the most successful, and I adore them for that. But I did not like Tom Werman's production values. The concept of Tom Werman is that he was a hot producer they would put with metal bands, and he had a long track record and a glorious history of successes. But I just thought he tamed it too much. Instead of getting more and more powerful . . . you know, we wanted to do what Max Norman was doing with Ozzy, we wanted to do what Martin Birch was doing with Iron Maiden. . . . Martin Birch produced Black Sabbath too. I remember playing *Heaven and Hell* and saying, "This is what we want," and Werman would go, "Well, they've just got the bass cranked up on this thing. No, we're not doing that." But *You Can't Stop Rock 'n' Roll* is my favorite, but on *Stay Hungry*, really, it all came together.

DAVE MENIKETTI (VOCALIST AND GUITARIST, Y&T, ON *IN ROCK WE TRUST*):

[Tom Allom] was trying to be like the best producers are, which was sort of bring his expertise to the thing, but don't make every band sound the same. He had this engineer with him, Andy Daigenol, who was an absolute brilliant find, because Tom lived at the time in Florida. And he grabbed this guy from one of the Florida studios. And Andy and him together ended up doing all these incredible things in the studio at a time where you're not using ProTools and things like that where you can do things digitally. You had to do everything by hand with analog tape and the crude effects units you had back then. They'd do all kinds of things. We would come back into the studio in the morning after having done tracking all night long or something, and Andy and him, "Look what we did at the end of this song, man! Check this out— we stuck Phil's bass in and dropped it three steps and then put it backwards through a flanger." It was like, man! Very creative, and I like that. That's the kind of stuff that makes a record have its own flavor, above just the songs and the performances. But yeah, you would show up and it would be like a party or something, or any number of things. So I would say one of the most fun sessions we ever did was *In Rock We Trust*.

1980   **1981**   **1982**   **1983**   **1984**

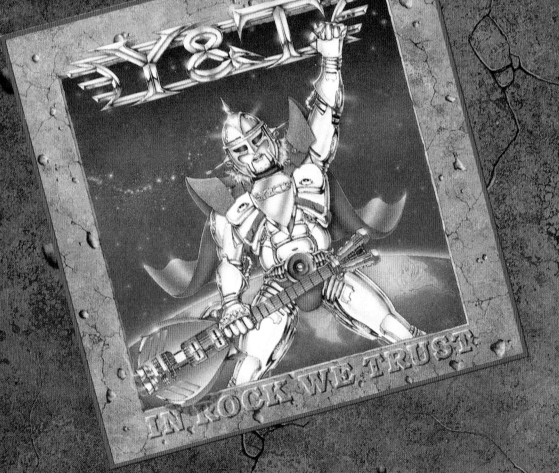

TRUST US!

The good guys of heavy metal are here to tell you twisted brothers and sisters that the quiet riot is over. The new Y&T album "In Rock We Trust" screams with a brilliance that even a deaf leopard could hear. So get this motley crew in gear and don't stop runnin' till you've felt the power and glory of an American rock anthem.

**"IN ROCK WE TRUST"
FROM Y&T** SP 5007

Watch for Y&T on tour. Only a rat would miss them.

1985   **1986**   **1987**   **1988**   **1989**

70

July 7, 1984: Ontario's Helix issue *Walkin' the Razor's Edge*, which features the "cheerleading for metal" hit "Rock You."

July 21, 1984: Stryper's debut EP, *The Yellow and Black Attack*, is released. Stryper begin their career opening for Ratt and Bon Jovi.

KEVIN DUBROW (VOCALIST, QUIET RIOT):

Bad production. Trying to repeat the same formula twice, and it didn't work. The only song I really care for on that album is "Condition Critical." We shouldn't have gone into the studio at that time. We weren't ready. We didn't have the songs. The producer ruined it, I think. It's silly. All the things that were clever about *Metal Health* turned silly on *Condition Critical*.

July 27, 1984: Quiet Riot issue the all-important follow-up to *Metal Health*. Entitled *Condition Critical*, the album goes on to sell three million copies worldwide (it's certified platinum in the US). Its big hit was another Slade cover, "Mama Weer All Crazee Now." It debuted at No. 15 on the US Billboard charts.

August 1984: Hanoi Rocks issue *Two Steps from the Move* in the US. It is the Finnish band's fifth album, with Hanoi Rocks being an underground glam influence for the likes of Guns N' Roses and others. Frontman Michael Monroe plays up the androgynous look quite extremely, while the rest of the band goes for a sort of New York Dolls/Aerosmith image.

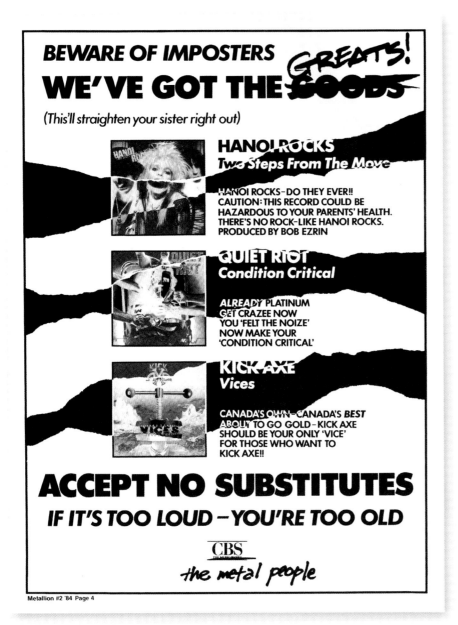

ANDY MCCOY (GUITARIST, HANOI ROCKS, ON WORKING WITH PRODUCER BOB EZRIN):

I loved Bob. From Bob, I learned a lot. Because you've got to remember, when we worked with Bob, I was only twenty-one, twenty-two years old, and he had been in the business for over twenty-five years already. So it was a big learning experience, how to arrange songs better and so forth. But you should have seen us live. It was better live than on the record. But I should be proud of the record, right? Those songs . . . "Underwater World" was written when I was so high on heroin you wouldn't believe it. Listen to the vibe of the fucking song—it's so obvious. "High School" was just an idea that became a great song. It's hard rock 'n' roll at its best—I heard that Aerosmith used to listen to it before they went onstage, to wind themselves up. "Don't You Ever Leave Me" was written when I was fifteen or sixteen, to my first teenage love. You know, you think it's going to last forever but first loves never last forever. And then "I Can't Get It" was written smacked out of my fucking head.

August 1984: Black 'N Blue issue their self-titled debut, featuring early hair metal anthem "Hold on to 18." The album, issued on hair metal–happy Geffen and produced by Dieter Dierks, now helping to commercialize Accept and Scorpions, also includes a cover of Sweet's "Action," linking this era of glam to the UK's from a decade previous.

JAIME ST. JAMES (VOCALIST, BLACK 'N BLUE):

We were probably signed based on how successful we were doing in the Los Angeles club scene. Wherever we would play, it was just packed out. They were lined up around the block trying to get in—we were really doing well. When we first got down there, there were maybe twenty people in the room. But we were signed after about six months. It only took a couple of months and it was starting to pack out. And basically there was a big buzz about the band and before we even got signed, there were people from Geffen who came up to see us and there were a lot of other labels calling saying, "Don't sign, don't sign, we want to talk to you." So there was a lot of interest and Geffen made a point to really try and snag us up quickly as they didn't want to lose us. It was an exciting time down there with all the bands that were going on. Technically, we were the third band out of that whole L.A. scene to get signed. Quiet Riot was first, then Mötley Crüe, then Black 'N Blue."

1980   **1981**   **1982**   **1983**   **1984**

Dokken kind of had a part in our story. Before we got signed, one of the things that helped us get attention also besides the live stuff is that we went into the studio and did a demo. And Don Dokken set us up with a producer, Michael Wagener. Actually, he was just engineering and Don was kind of producing. And this was before Don got signed. Don just took a liking to us and Don was pretty into the music scene by then. He had a deal in France and he was doing vocals for Scorpions, backup stuff. So he saw us in the clubs and thought these guys are really good. So he helped us get Michael Wagener. And I think he was partly responsible—between him and our manager, Garo—in bringing the tape to Geffen. And then our record was finally done, we get back to Los Angeles and within a matter of a couple months, we find ourselves out on the road with Aerosmith. And that's some of my idols there. Aerosmith was really big to me. And this is the first time we're out of smaller venues and playing the big arenas. I'll never experience that again, to be able to jump to that level. To be able to walk out and hear that roar.

The only one that ever treated us like crap was a guy named Alvin Lee [of Ten Years After fame], who has been around forever. We were supposed to play at a club with him in St. Louis on our way to the Kiss tour. They told us to set up on the floor in front of the stage, and we said fuck you and left. So we never even played with him. But that's an interesting story in itself because there were a lot of Black 'N Blue fans lined up outside the club. And I don't know why they were impressed with this guy. We

just said, we're not playing. But we walked down the road with these people who had bought tickets and after we signed all their stuff, it turned out there was this kid who had a band and he was saying how he had all this band stuff. And we said, "Where do you rehearse?" "Out of the basement." We said, "Okay, get everybody together, we're going to go play our set in your basement." And so we did. Took everybody out of the line and went to this kid's basement and played our entire set for them. And it's probably the coolest show we ever did.

1985   **1986**   **1987**   **1988**   **1989**

W.A.S.P.'s Randy Piper

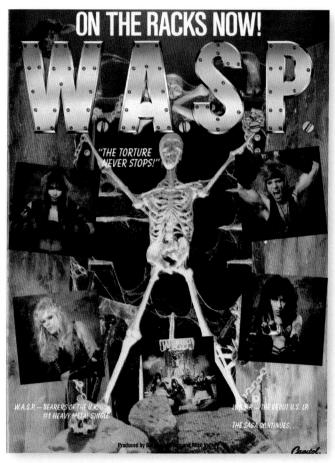

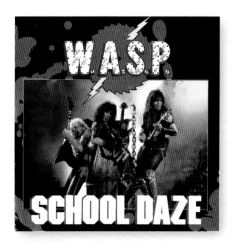

August 17, 1984: Blackie Lawless and the band of his vision, W.A.S.P., issue their self-titled debut album. The band is quickly associated with Mötley Crüe as part of a dark, decadent strain of hair metal. The opening track on the album, "I Wanna Be Somebody," epitomizes a central tenet of hair metal hopefuls: attaining fame.

BLACKIE LAWLESS (ON "I WANNA BE SOMEBODY"):
Musically I never thought it was one of the strongest songs that we did but I understand the sentiment, and the sentiment is what pushed me in the first place to do the song. Because I really thought that there's got to be a lot of people who feel like that. It's a very simple idea, one that had not been said before but I'm sure a lot of people were thinking it. To me I've always thought that a song title, or an idea of a song, was probably worth as much, if not more, than the song itself. If it's a sentiment that people can latch on to, I think that's real important. But that first album, there are a couple of words that come to mind and I'm trying to think of how to phrase it in a sentence. I guess I would call it beautifully crude, because there is an anger to that record. The best records I ever did were the ones where I stopped caring about what anybody else was thinking, where I refused to let what others were thinking creep into my psyche. That was one of them. And you think, well, you should have learned something [laughs]. You do, but sometimes you stray from the course. Twenty years later, you're going to stray from time to time. So yeah, I would say beautifully crude.

1980   **1981**   **1982**   **1983**   **1984**

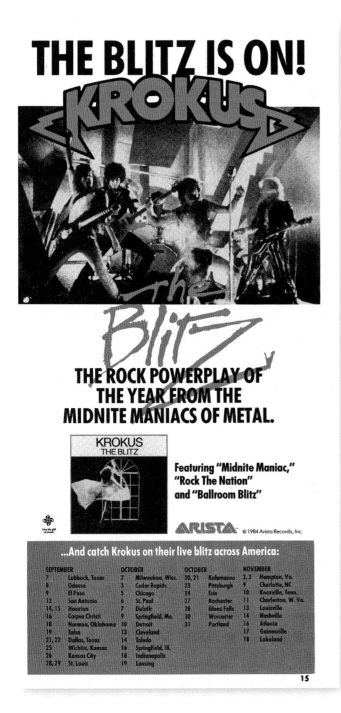

August 22, 1984: Switzerland's Krokus follow up their considerably heavy trad metal *Headhunter* album with a hair metal play and ploy called *The Blitz*, produced by Bruce Fairbairn. The album goes gold, just like its predecessor.

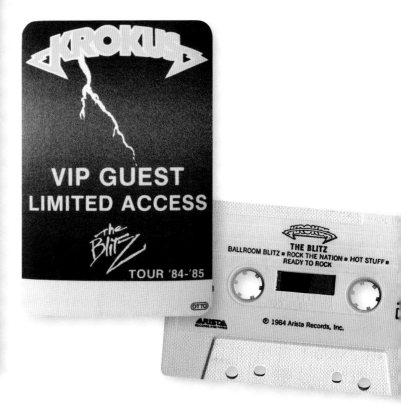

MARC STORACE (VOCALIST, KROKUS):

You must keep in mind, we were on tour with Def Leppard at the height of their success. And they didn't sing "Night Wolf," they sang "Photograph." In comparison, really wimpy stuff, sweetheart stuff. And we thought we'll try [to] meet halfway. And the scene was changing anyway and we were told by people around us that this was the direction to go in, kind of tone it down, color it up a bit. That's really what was happening. We made a mistake there, obviously. We should have kept the raw image. The songs we wrote were okay, but we shouldn't have gone so far with the production, the softening up of the Krokus sound. We went too far.

1985   **1986**   **1987**   **1988**   **1989**

76

September 13, 1984: Kiss repeat *Lick It Up*'s platinum success with *Animalize*, the cover of which features animal-skin patterns that would become popular in hair metal fashion. Moderate hits from the record include "Heaven's on Fire" and "Thrills in the Night."

Gene Simmons

1980   **1981**   **1982**   **1983**   **1984**

1985   **1986**   **1987**   **1988**   **1989**

September 13, 1984: Dokken issue *Tooth and Nail*, which goes platinum. George Lynch, after Eddie Van Halen and Randy Rhoads, becomes the third most recognized California shredder. The album is produced by one of the ubiquitous hair metal producers, Tom Werman. The poppy "Just Got Lucky" is a minor hit, as is power ballad "Alone Again."

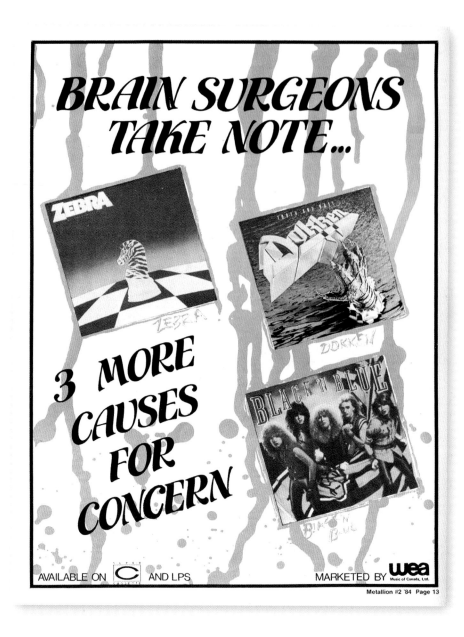

GEORGE LYNCH:

There's one thing, you take any one of those *Tooth and Nail* songs, [drummer] Mick Brown had a pretty big hand in the lyrics. You can always tell Mick's lyrics because they're always very Vegas-friendly. "Turn on the action, turn on the night, gonna roam the streets and start a fight. I'm like a wildcat at midnight, I'm like a stick of dynamite, evil senses flowing over me, gonna roam the streets and start a fight." "Just got lucky, believe your dirty lies, I've been hypnotized. . . ." I mean this shit, it's pure Vegas lounge. It's so funny. I always thought it would be funny to just go to Vegas on an off night and just do that, just go in there and dress like Elvis or whatever and just do Dokken Elvis style.

DON DOKKEN:

Everybody knows the song "Breaking the Chains," everybody heard the song, but nobody bought the record. I mean, it's death—it really tanked. We did an arena tour, it sold 100,000 copies, Elektra wanted to drop us. They said forget this band, they aren't going to go anywhere. Our managers had to beg them to keep us on the label. They said, "We'll give you one more shot." So we were up against the wall. So that's why I came up with the title *Tooth and Nail*. If we're going to make it, it's going to be with a fight. So we wrote twenty-five songs and narrowed it down to those eleven best. But that was the whole thing. Elektra wanted to drop us. They said the band tanked and we don't want to do it and we begged them to give us another chance.

We went through two producers. George didn't want to do two of the songs on the album, which became the hits, "Into the Fire" and "Alone Again." He didn't want to do the songs and I said you gotta do the songs, and we compromised. It's kinda funny, you know? He didn't want to do those songs—totally against it. But that was *Tooth and Nail*. It was our peak. It was a tough album. Even though it was our second chance and our last chance, the drug abuse is pretty heavy on the album. Not only us, but the producer and the engineer. There was just really a lot of drug abuse on the album. And we were in Hollywood doing the album, chicks, drinking, I was drinking. It was a tough record, and that's why I named the album *Tooth and Nail*. I told the band I wanted to call it that because this is it, if it doesn't go, it's over. There wouldn't be a Dokken.

And you know, it didn't go. We released "Into the Fire," didn't go. Then we released "The Hunter" and it didn't really go and then we did "It's Not Love" and it didn't really go, and then they did a video for "Alone Again." They didn't want to release it and I threatened to quit the band if they didn't release it. We did the video live and it finally popped. We were stuck at 450,000. It didn't go gold. We did three. We spent almost half a million dollars in videos and it was standing. And on the last part of the tour, after playing for a year, we did "Alone Again" at the Palladium in L.A., a live concert of "Alone Again" and I actually cheated the vocals in the dressing room and sang the vocals. You see me live on "Alone Again" and that's not me onstage. I'm actually in front of a black cloth, cheating it out. It looks like I'm live though. I walked off the stage, sweaty, in my bandana and my blue eyeliner and I did the vocals. But that took us from 450,000 to 1.1 million. "Alone Again" put us over the top. After a year of touring, it had stalled. But in those days, the record company would go and do another single, another single, another single. Now it's like, you put out a single, you've got two weeks, oh, didn't go, over, next band. We did four videos on the album. They kept banging it and banging it and banging it and finally it took. But now you get one single, two weeks, you're fucked.

1985   **1986**   **1987**   **1988**   **1989**

October 1984: Pasadena, California's Autograph issue a debut album called *Sign in Please*. Hit single "Turn Up the Radio" helps send the album gold.

November 1984: Keel, led by Ron Keel and hotshot guitarist Marc Ferrari, issue their debut on Shrapnel. *Lay Down the Law* isn't much glammier than the *Steeler* album Ron famously cranked out with Yngwie Malmsteen, but the look is party metal all the way.

November 1984: Molly Hatchet issue *The Deed Is Done*, their first in a fairly hair bandwagoneering direction. Many southern rock acts tried to cash in on this sound, including Blackfoot, .38 Special, and, to a lesser extent, Lynyrd Skynyrd.

DON DOKKEN
(ON WHETHER GEORGE LYNCH WAS EXPENDABLE):

I never thought that at that time. I didn't think he was expendable. I actually believed that without George there could be no Dokken. I mean, the record company told me that, the manager told me that. They said without George, you guys are finished because he's such a big guitar hero. So I said okay and I had to deal with it. I don't know what the hell made me think that. I got the record deal without him, I wrote the songs without him, I don't know what the hell I thought. Everybody was expendable. I thought the whole was bigger than the pieces. And I think in the '80s the whole was bigger than the pieces. George was a very big part of Dokken and he wrote some great stuff. And in the '80s, the guitar hero thing was much more valid. I mean, Van Halen couldn't survive without Eddie Van Halen. I think I had a bad reputation in the press then because I had low self-esteem. Some people don't understand that. Sometimes when you're a singer and you're looked up to and adored by millions of people, I can be totally insecure. And people say how can that happen? How can you feel insecure when millions of people love you and have your poster and girls have your eight-by-ten and have fantasies about you?

It's very easy. I was in therapy over it. I was very mentally beat-up. I thought I was totally handling it. This guy, George, is fucking with my mind but I've got it under control. But after a couple of years I didn't. The therapist told me that some people thrive on other people's misery. So the more beat down I got, the stronger he got. Sometimes I'd get sick on the road, with a cold or the flu, and my voice would be hurting, I would notice that he would have a really good show. He played really good that night and would be rocking out on stage. He'd be up front, really kicking ass. And then when I'd have a really good show and be up front rockin' all night, he seemed to shrink back and not be very aggressive. And I'd go, this is really strange. If I'm having a good show, then everybody else should feed off my energy. But when I would have a good show, he would back off. He would thrive off of my downfall. And that's not healthy.

DAVE HLUBEK (GUITARIST AND VOCALIST, MOLLY HATCHET):

The Deed Is Done, I thought that was the record that changed us. We were trying to do what people wanted us to do. We were listening to people around us in the business who can't pick a hit to save their ass. And they said, "Listen, get in tune with this period of time. The world is changing, the musical atmosphere is changing." And what happened is we got away from our roots and the band suffered because of it.

1980   **1981**   **1982**   **1983**   **1984**

LOU GRAMM (VOCALIST, FOREIGNER):

As far as something that I'm not too crazy about, I like just about everything, but maybe some of the things on the album after *Agent Provocateur*, in which I had very little input, and was basically just under [guitarist] Mick [Jone]'s direction in what to sing and how to sing. We were very much at odds, and it was just a labor for me. It was very soon after that album was released—and it really wasn't that successful at all—that I'd departed to make some strides in my own career.

MICHAEL MONROE (VOCALIST, HANOI ROCKS):

Our drummer died and the band wasn't prepared to go on. First of all, it was a great blow to the band. When he joined, Razzle, we were kind of down and going through a bad period, and when he joined it just brought life to the band again. His sense of humor and his character . . . everybody was very important to the band, but especially him. If [bassist] Sami [Yaffa] or [guitarist] Nasty [Suicide] would have left, we might have continued. Then Sami left anyways. Sami left the band, after that Razzle died, and then Andy and Nasty went. I'm not saying I was more together than them, but everybody was into self-destruction. There was too much hassle. We talked about some guys, but I knew it was over. I finally said, let's leave the nice memory of the band as it was and not ruin anything by trying to cash in and make a quick buck, hiring some other guys and pretend to be Hanoi Rocks. Let's close this with integrity. After Razzle died, we played two farewell gigs, January 4th and 5th at the concert hall in Helsinki, House of Culture. The second night, I think four or five songs were broadcast all over Europe. There was this TV show called *Europe A Go Go* and they showed four or five songs. One of them was "A Million Miles Away," the ballad, and I dedicated it to Razzle, and it was too soon after the accident. I had trouble singing it. It was too painful.

ANDY MCCOY (GUITARIST, HANOI ROCKS):

We did New York, like four or five times around the East Coast—that was our make-it-or-break tour of America. And you know what happened, how it ended—tragically. We were like a hair away from becoming one of the biggest bands in the world. But destiny or timing wasn't on our side.

December 7, 1984: Foreigner issue their fifth album, *Agent Provocateur*, which finds the band abandoning their warm, organic sound for hair metal. The smash single is a power ballad called "I Want to Know What Love Is." By the mid-'80s, bands formerly considered "arena rock" or "corporate rock" became indistinguishable from hair metal bands or became hair metal versions of what they had been (e.g., Heart and Cheap Trick). *Inside Information* (1987) and *Unusual Heat* (1991) would mark a big decline for Foreigner in quality, the band using and abusing many bad hair metal recording techniques and other clichés of the genre.

Vince Neil

December 8, 1984: Hanoi Rocks drummer Razzle is killed in a car crash. The driver is Vince Neil of Mötley Crüe. Mötley Crüe's bad boy image intensifies, while Razzle's death marks the end of Hanoi Rocks, one of hair metal's unsung pioneers.

December 31, 1984: Def Leppard drummer Rick Allen loses an arm in a car accident. It is important to the hair metal story in that the band kept him on, blending his playing with tricks of technology, proving that hair metal albums could be made by machines.

1985   **1986**   **1987**   **1988**   **1989**

1985

YOU GIVE HAIR METAL a bad name. Already, before it really takes wing, hair metal appears to be dead. Well, not really, but look at the following evidence or examples of bands screwing up. Van Halen self-destruct and David Lee Roth issues a shark-jumping EP of jokes. Mötley follow the exciting Shout at the Devil *with the flaccid* Theater of Pain. *Kiss, riding high on two hit albums, go with* Asylum, *which does okay but lacks the buzz of the previous two firecrackers. Quiet Riot continue their fade into obscurity, half because of Kevin DuBrow's big mouth. Def Leppard can't make a new album. W.A.S.P. issue* The Last Command. *Most fantastically, Twisted Sister follow the anthem-cornered* Stay Hungry *with a flop called* Come Out and Play. *Dio, Scorpions, Judas Priest, Black Sabbath, Blue Öyster Cult, Y&T, and Aerosmith are all on various trajectories of decline. Only Dokken and Ratt seem to be doing well: Ratt with the sophisticated* Invasion of Your Privacy, *Dokken with the not so substantive hair metal strains of* Under Lock and Key. *Not sure what to make of 1985, but one concept might be that it's a housecleaning year in which some of the dead wood is chucked, leaving a vacuum for . . . well, we know there are some big hair bands around the corner, and most of them are barely old enough to belly up to the bar.*

1980   **1981**   **1982**   **1983**   **1984**

BILLY CHILDS (BASSIST, BRITNY FOX):

It seems like mostly everything on the East Coast came out of the New York metropolitan area for the most part. There wasn't much out of the Boston area. There were a couple of bands out of Philly. But I wouldn't really call it a scene like they had on the West Coast. We kind of viewed it as . . . the whole East Coast was kind of a scene. Baltimore had a couple of really nice clubs, Hammerjacks in particular. Philadelphia was really only two hours from Baltimore, as we have a couple of clubs in Philly, and you had most of it going on in New York and also New Jersey. But that was pretty much our region. I don't know if it really continued on south much further than that. I'm sure for some people it did, but the regions become more isolated, and you're not dealing with a megalopolis-type situation. The East Coast bands seemed to have, although similar in look, I thought, a dirtier, grungier sound, actually. There was less of that homogenous '80s sound with the East Coast bands. I thought there was more of that in L.A. I think a lot of your East Coast bands were pretty talented. I mean, if you look at bands like Kix, they were just a really good band, as was Cinderella.

BILLY CHILDS (ON BUCKING THE TEMPTATION TO MIGRATE TO L.A.):

We saw Cinderella get signed and it seemed to us that Philly was a pretty good place to be sitting. And no, we never really talked about it. There were some guys who moved out West, and there were some guys that just decided to stay on the East Coast. It's a little more real, a little harsher, but yes, it's definitely more real. We are those kind of guys. . . . The longest we spent in L.A. at any one given time was during *Bite Down Hard*, and we were there for probably about five or six months. Cinderella stayed pretty much based in the East Coast. Now I think a couple of them live down in Nashville area.

1985: Pantera's third album, *I Am the Night*, is the last with Terry Glaze on vocals. The arrival of Phil Anselmo is another nail in the coffin for hair metal.

1985: London, always the bridesmaid and never the bride, finally issue an album, entitled *Non Stop Rock*, on midsized indie Shrapnel. Their lineup comprises Nadir D'Priest (vocals), Lizzie Grey (guitar), Brian West (bass), and Fred Coury (soon of Cinderella, drums).

1985: Kick Axe issue *Welcome to the Club*, which finds the band shedding pretty much any vestige of a glam sound or feel.

1985: Britny Fox form in Philadelphia, featuring two ex-Cinderella members.

1985: D'Molls and Vixen move to L.A. from Chicago and Minnesota, respectively.

1985   **1986**   **1987**   **1988**   **1989**

January 28, 1985. David Lee Roth issues his *Crazy from the Heat* EP and it's an instant novelty hit. The glitzy show-tune cover song concept lends added credence to the idea that Dave, and by extension hair metal, is more style than substance.

1985: L.A. Guns issue an indie EP called *Collector's Edition No. 1.* Only Tracii Guns from the classic lineup is part of the band at this point. Michael Jagosz has already replaced a previous singer, Axl Rose.

1985: Jon Bon Jovi discovers Cinderella playing the Empire Rock Club in Philadelphia. Bon Jovi recommends that Polygram A&R rep Derek Shulman (ex–Gentle Giant) come see them and a deal is struck.

1985: Black 'N Blue issue their second album, *Without Love*, a more melodic album than the more traditional, meat-and-potatoes metal of their self-titled debut.

JAIME ST. JAMES (VOCALIST, BLACK 'N BLUE):

The next one, it's a great record and it actually could be my favorite. Our producer, Bruce Fairbairn, and our engineer, Bob Rock, are a little more American musical kind of guys. The thing they had been doing up 'til then was Loverboy. It's a little more melodic than the first one, and that's okay because I'm like that. It was fine with me. Some people love that album and some people think it's their favorite and some people think it's a little bit too much of a departure from the first one. But there are a lot of cool tunes on there. And it was great working with those guys, and even Mike Fraser, who was our second engineer, who went on to engineer the Aerosmith stuff. Compared to Dieter Dierks, I think they tried to get a little more involved in bringing in outside songwriters and Dieter didn't do that at all. He took what we had and he would work with it because Dieter is very musical. These guys brought in Jim Vallance who is up there in Canada, Vancouver, big songwriter with Bryan Adams and he helped cowrite a couple of things. And I think Bruce Fairbairn in particular, he works more with the record company, like, "What do you want?" They were more into a "give the record company what they want" kind of attitude.

Our second hit was "Miss Mystery," and that was our MTV video and all that stuff. "Miss Mystery" actually did pretty well, got a lot of radio airplay. But actually everybody remembers "Hold on to 18" more. And the radio stations, during the metal shows will play that one more now, the specialty shows . . . although "Miss Mystery" at the time probably did better at radio than "Hold on to 18." But it's not the one people remember.

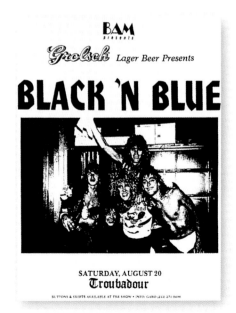

Black 'N Blue's Tommy Thayer and Jaime St. James.
© Rod Dysinger

Looking back, we weren't influenced by the hair band thing because we were before the hair band thing, or we were in the beginning of that, let's just say. There were a lot of bands that way that came along in the '80s, but we were ahead of all that. And the first album really shows that. It's a pretty hard-driving record. But the second one, like I say, brings on maybe a little bit different influences.

March 26, 1985: Keel issue their Gene Simmons–produced second album, *The Right to Rock*.

JAIME ST. JAMES (ON THE EXTENT OF THE BAND'S FAME):

We were in all the rock magazines. I can't think of anything huge. Oddly, and stupidly, enough, one of my favorite things was when we were in the *TV Guide*, when we were on Showtime. Hey, Black 'N Blue is in the *TV Guide!* In terms of covers, we were part of covers, but I don't think we were ever the main cover. But a lot of posters of Black 'N Blue, that came in these magazines. But we weren't big enough to get us a full cover.

RON KEEL (VOCALIST AND GUITARIST, KEEL):

I remember our manager used to carry a briefcase full of cocaine, and it was a bargaining chip. You know, if you want your record played on the radio, we'll send the program director and the DJ to Hawaii with the cocaine and a couple of prostitutes. "You'll get some airplay, dude!" And then you're all over the radio. You know, back then it was a little more honest. It was cocaine and whores instead of stocks and Mafia hits.

1985   **1986**   **1987**   **1988**   **1989**

March 27, 1985: Bon Jovi issue their sophomore effort, *7800° Fahrenheit*, which eventually stalls at platinum, lacking a huge hit single.

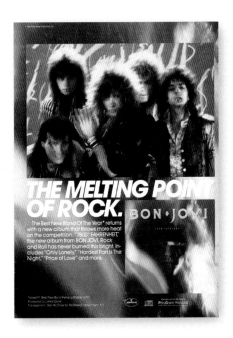

Richie Sambora and Jon Bon Jovi. © *Rod Dysinger*

When *7800° Fahrenheit* came out, we put Bon Jovi on the front cover and it helped. He was a virtual unknown, had that minor hit with "Runaway." And believe me, when you put Def Leppard on the front cover, we took a gamble. We weren't sure they were going to come back after *Pyromania*, and we put them up when the following album came out, and the publicity people and the management company were very, very grateful.

1980   **1981**   **1982**   **1983**   **1984**

NIKKI SIXX:

We toured for thirteen months for *Shout at the Devil*. The band has always been extremist, eccentric. We did more drugs, fucked more girls, drank more alcohol, got into more fistfights, blew more bands off the stage and it was full-on all the time. When we got off the road we were millionaires, drug addicts, alcoholics, sex addicts, and fuckin' rock stars. And we made an album that is that. [*Theatre of Pain*] is drug-, alcohol-, and pussy-influenced. I mean it's harsh. And I think some of the focus was off because of that. But there are some brilliant moments at the same time. "City Boy Blues" is great. But it was a mess—it was what it was. It was like a haze.

May 15, 1985: Stryper issue their debut full-length, *Soldiers Under Command*, presenting a hyper-glam image with a stripey theme. Musically, it's novelty Christian metal but very glam of sound, featuring high vocals, meticulous harmonies, and big hair and makeup for miles. Produced by Michael Wagener, the album goes gold, exposing an appetite for a Christian message amid the debauchery.

June 21, 1985: Mötley Crüe issue *Theatre of Pain*. Despite its critical drubbing (arguably deserved, given its lackadaisical writing and performances), the album eventually sells 4x platinum.

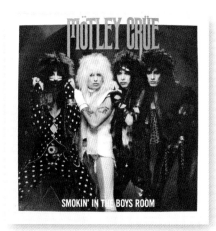

1985   **1986**   **1987**   **1988**   **1989**

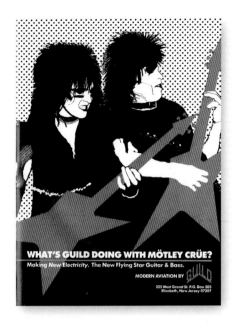

WHAT'S GUILD DOING WITH MÖTLEY CRÜE?
Making *New* Electricity. The New Flying Star Guitar & Bass.

MODERN AVIATION BY **GUILD**

225 West Grand St. P.O. Box 203
Elizabeth, New Jersey 07207

Summer 1985: *Metal Edge* magazine debuts, championing the glam scene clear through to 2009, when it and heavier sister publication *Metal Maniacs* cease publishing. Also, by this point, *Circus* magazine goes near relentlessly hair metal.

VINCE NEIL:

If you notice, we changed every year. We only had a dark image for *Shout at the Devil*—that was it. And then when people started doing that, we completely went the other way with the glam thing on *Theatre of Pain*. And then when people started doing that, we went toward the street look with *Girls, Girls, Girls*. We never, ever stayed the same. We just wanted to stay steps ahead of everybody else.

BEN LIEMER:

Theatre of Pain was being recorded in L.A., I think in Rumbo Studios which Captain & Tenille owned, or the Captain owned, and Mötley was there, interviewing. And I first came in and Vince was doing punches, vocal overdubs, and I watched Mick Mars work, and Nikki had just come back from vacation in Mexico. And as each guy showed up, the energy level went higher and higher, and the reason they showed up was that the magazine was coming. It wasn't me, [it was] the magazine. And I didn't have to do anything—the magazine was respected. All I have to do is not fuck up, not be an asshole, and be a normal person and talk to these guys like people, and it will all work out, and I basically did. That's how I worked it. And as we got friendlier and friendlier, I was allowed to go to Nikki Sixx's house. He drove me in his four-wheel-drive Jeep, up the canyons of L.A., the back roads, while holding onto the rollbar— there wasn't even a third seat—with the girl from his management company, sort of publicity contact, sitting in the front. Did the interview in his house. So that's the kind of level of access we were getting. Where other people weren't.

BEN LIEMER (ON *CIRCUS* SWITCHING ITS FOCUS TO HAIR METAL):

The reason was dollars and cents. Without question, I think we got the best reaction to those sorts of articles. There was a feedback loop that we used, basically, in every issue. There was a little questionnaire, a box about an inch by inch but it was the most important part of the magazine. And almost every publicist missed it. But it was a readers' poll. What groups do you want to hear more about, basically. So fill it in, send it in, great. If they wanted Mötley Crüe for fourteen months in a row, we did it. And, in fact, that's why they were in there month after month after month. That's what the fans wanted. You don't think we got frustrated sometimes?! I interviewed every single member of Twisted Sister, Dokken, Mötley Crüe, Ratt, Megadeth, and I think even possibly Queensrÿche, and other bands in there too, but those are the ones that spring to mind, every member. You know when you interviewed the drummer three times in one year, after a while, it was like, we weren't talking to Nikki anymore or Vince. Give us Tommy.

1980   **1981**   **1982**   **1983**   **1984**

BOBBY BLOTZER (DRUMMER, RATT):

You know, coming off the *Cellar* tour, and how long that tour was, I mean, I can't even imagine doing a tour that long now. It was like two hundred and fifty-five shows that year. We were out something like fourteen or fifteen months straight. Playing Japan was included in that, and then we went to Hawaii and got these condos on the beach and started to write *Invasion of Your Privacy*. We were there two or three weeks. Primarily, our manager was cracking the whip right off the bat. It was like, "Dude, just settle down." So for the first week, everybody just did their thing. And then we set up a porta-studio in one of the rooms and basically wrote the record, man. Then we flew back to L.A., recorded it at Rumball, and had a great time. I really like that record.

DON DOKKEN:

Stephen [Pearcy] had an identifiable voice. It might have been bad, but let's face it, when you heard it, you knew it was Ratt. . . . I remember in the '80s, there was whole slew of bands getting signed with some really good singers. But in my opinion, they just sounded like some guy—close your eyes and you could be in Las Vegas. No offense to them, they sounded great, they sang great, they had great chops, they could sing super-high, had great control, had powerful voices, they looked great, they're handsome, they had great stage presence but they didn't have that God-given identifiable tone. They just sounded like a guy that got cranked out of the school of vocal rock singers. And that was these bands' downfall. They didn't have anything identifiable. It wasn't a matter of being good or bad or good-looking or having some kind of personality, they just didn't have a unique sound.

STEPHEN PEARCY (VOCALIST, RATT):

Running around saying that we were saints . . . fuck no, we weren't saints. We were fuckin' drug addicts, partying rock 'n' rollers, and that's when I created the three P's: pussy, party, paycheck. I want people to know the good, bad, ugly, the beautiful, the terrible everything. I ain't holding back. You know, these guys go out, because they were married at the time, you know, shit happens, man. When someone hands you a platinum card and says, "Hey, go get whatever you want." Well, all right, I want that hooker on the twenty-fifth floor and I want a bunch of dope and don't bother me and I'm going to go play all fucked-up and have a great time." It's rock 'n' roll, man! Nobody is a saint.

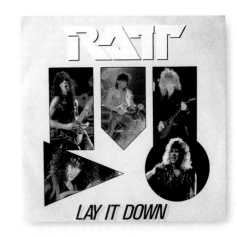

July 2, 1985: Ratt issue *Invasion of Your Privacy*. It goes 2x platinum.

1985   **1986**   **1987**   **1988**   **1989**

July 6, 1985: Heart release a self-titled album that's very glammy in look and sound. It eventually goes 5x platinum. The two albums before it, *Private Audition* and *Passionworks*, didn't even reach gold, affirming the success that a hair metal direction could bring to bands from a previous generation. The biggest hits are the power ballads "These Dreams" (Martin Page/Bernie Taupin) and "What About Love" (Brian Allen/Sheron Alton/Jim Vallance).

August 1985: Loverboy release *Lovin' Every Minute of It*, another double-platinum album for the pioneering Canadian melodic hard rockers.

August 15, 1985: Dio issue their *Sacred Heart* album. It is somewhat panned as a second-guessing hair metal play, and the opinion is enforced by the gaudy costuming the band adopt for the album's tour.

BEAU HILL (PRODUCER):

Okay, [Ratt] fired me after every record. And they did it in what I thought was kind of a cowardly way. One that particularly resonates with me, I think it was after the first record, we already sold three million copies and these guys went, "Well, if it sold three, and we hadn't had that idiot Beau Hill, we would've sold ten!" And so I get a call from my attorney one day and he says, "Hey, have you read *Billboard*?" "No" "Oh. Well Ratt fired you." And they fired me in the press, which I thought was a pretty sleazy way to do it. And then I got another call from [Atlantic president] Doug Morris, and Doug said, "Don't even think about it, don't even worry about it, because you've turned these guys into a hit act, and there's absolutely no way that you're not going to do the next record." So I did it. And it was kind of weird, because after every record, they fired me. Yet I still did four records.

JAIME ST. JAMES:

There were a lot of parties. Loverboy was recording in the next room and asked me to sing on [*Without Love*]. I remember a grueling ten hours, all through the night until five in the morning on a song called "Lovin' Every Minute of It." I did backups for ten hours on that. It was a Mutt Lange song, so they were real particular about making it perfect. And there are a whole bunch of backgrounds throughout that song and I'm one of the main voices on it. They must have overdubbed me a hundred times. Maybe not that many, but quite a lot.

VIVIAN CAMPBELL (GUITARIST, DIO, DEF LEPPARD):

Sacred Heart is just a steamin' pile of poo, as far as I was concerned. I mean, it was just horrible to make. That's when things went tragically wrong, not just with me but with [drummer] Vinny Appice and [bassist] Jimmy Bain too. There was a lot of tension in the studio. No one wanted to be there when Ronnie was there. We'd come in and do our parts and leave. There was no cohesive vibe in the band at that stage, because things had really started to go wrong from a business point of view. We were feeling very betrayed and whatnot, so no one had the enthusiasm for it. I mean, Ronnie wanted total control. He is a control freak, but at least on the first two records we were all standing behind him, giving our opinions. And like I say, for that record, we just weren't there. Our hearts and souls weren't in it, nor were our ears.

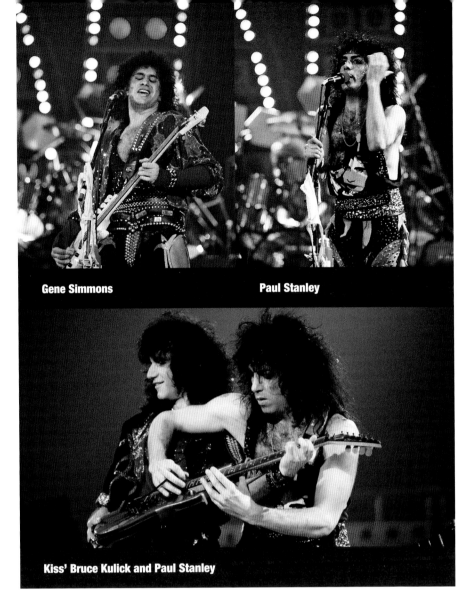

Gene Simmons Paul Stanley

Kiss' Bruce Kulick and Paul Stanley

August 24, 1985: Texxas Jam, an annual tradition since 1978, features Victory, Grim Reaper, Bon Jovi, Ted Nugent, Night Ranger, Scorpions, and a reformed Deep Purple. Scorpions are riding the high of their hair metal–leaning *Love at First Sting* album. Night Ranger are playing as a hit proto–hair metal band, while Bon Jovi are clearly a manufactured spot of product on the rise.

September 16, 1985: Kiss issue *Asylum*, which goes gold. The album sleeve depicts the band in glam pastels, with many of the songs on the record indicative of the boy-meets-girl party rock of the day. The album garners some singles action from semi-ballads like "Who Wants to Be Lonely" and "Tears Are Falling."

September 30, 1985: Mötley Crüe float "Home Sweet Home" as a single from *Theatre of Pain*. The rote, conservative, melodramatic power ballad, along with its similarly maudlin video, represents for many the worst ills of the hair metal industry.

VINCE NEIL:

We had the momentum of being on the road for so long, and without the success of *Shout at the Devil*, without that, I don't think it would have done so well. And with MTV being so supportive of "Home Sweet Home" and "Smokin' in the Boys Room." I didn't really like that album that much at all. The songwriting was just terrible except maybe for "Home Sweet Home." And I think Tom Werman did a great job on *Shout at the Devil*. I don't think he did a good job with *Theatre of Pain*. It was way too slick and it just didn't have the balls to it that the other one had.

BEAU HILL:

The guys from Ratt and the guys from Mötley were very, very close. Robbin [Crosby] and Nikki Sixx were actually roommates when we did the first record. And Mötley was the band that I was always having thrown in my face, from the guys in Ratt. It's like, "Dude, Tommy doesn't do this." And "Tommy didn't do that." And "Nikki wants this," and, "Hey, why don't we do what Nikki did?"

1985   **1986**   **1987**   **1988**   **1989**

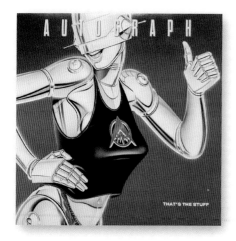

Autograph's Steve Plunkett.
© Rod Dysinger

October 1985: Sophomore effort from Autograph, *That's the Stuff*, will make the news again in 2001 due to the similarities between its cover art and that of Aerosmith's *Just Push Play*. In the meantime, their tour with Mötley Crüe and Heart is fitting, Autograph sounding somewhat like a cross between those two bands.

DON DOKKEN:

Under Lock and Key was our shining glory. It was a very polished album. We were focused. We had a taste of success, a little bit of money. We went in the studio and said, "Gee, we have a chance to be a big famous rock band." We actually stopped fighting for about four months to do that record. You know, Michael Wagener, to his credit was a very good organizer. He's like, "Okay, today we do drums, then we do bass, then guitars." And I stayed out of the studio. George [Lynch] didn't see me, I didn't see him. He wasn't around for vocals, I wasn't around for guitars. We stayed out of each other's hair. It was a slick and polished album, big production, big harmonies, poppier songs like "Will the Sun Rise" and "In My Dreams."

MICK BROWN (DRUMMER, DOKKEN):

Oh God, everything was so cool then. It was so damn exciting. We had better tour buses. We had a hidden camera at the back of the bus and the guys used to make porno tapes with their girls. Oh god, it was drugs and booze and all the chicks were hanging around, and the money started coming in, and big arenas, better drum stuff, bigger, everything was full-on ten in motion. It was brand new and all going a hundred miles an hour. It was a pretty exciting moment.

BEN LIEMER:

The twisted history between Quiet Riot, Dokken, Ratt . . . people were switching bands, essentially. [Bassist] Juan Croucier was in a lot of these bands in the early days. And so people came and went, and they would jump ship, and they would get in the band that they felt [was] going to succeed. Some of these bands are not exactly the greatest friends all the time, amongst the bandmates themselves. Some of them were marriages of convenience. Dokken fought and did whatever they did and they succeeded, ultimately. . . . I mean, that's how George Lynch and Don got along, but there was respect there ultimately for musicianship, and out of that tension came some decent work.

1980   **1981**   **1982**   **1983**   **1984**

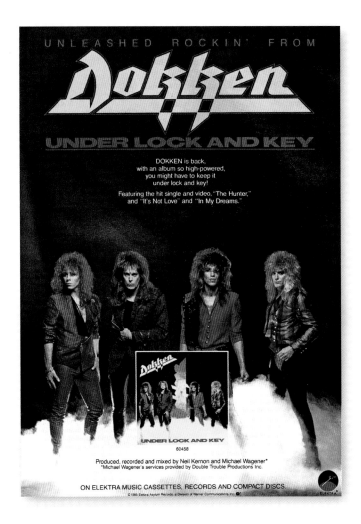

November 9, 1985: Dokken issue *Under Lock and Key*, which goes platinum. On the cover, the band goes for an upscale glam (or possibly truly glamorous) look.

November 9, 1985: White Lion's debut, *Fight to Survive*, is issued as a quasi-indie.

MIKE TRAMP (DANISH-BORN VOCALIST, WHITE LION):

I came to America based on fucking Van Halen. I liked the sound of Journey, Kansas, and Cheap Trick is one of my favorite bands of all time. And I'm the biggest Thin Lizzy and Queen fan that ever existed. That could be debated of course. But when Van Halen came on, and Roth strutted on stage, it was clear in my life that's where I wanted to be. And when I came to America, and formed White Lion with Vito, that became not so much. Because even though Vito's style has a lot to do with Van Halen and he was influenced by them, our music and songs did not have a lot to do with Van Halen. But they were, without a doubt, the band who were looked up to. And I would say about the time we reached the middle with *Pride*, and touring with AC/DC, and I was the competition to Roth, Roth had left Van Halen at that time. But now I had become Mike Tramp, one of the persons you competed against.

1985   **1986**   **1987**   **1988**   **1989**

94

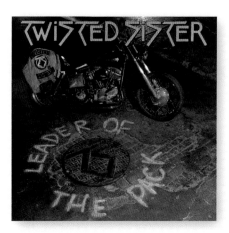

November 9, 1985: Twisted Sister issue their *Come Out and Play* album, which represents the band running out of steam, and, arguably, preoccupied with the commerciality of the hair metal genre.

MIKE TRAMP (ON THE MEANING OF GLAM IN THE '80s):
I've never walked in this territory we're talking about now, but I know in my consciousness that it exists. With Poison, there's a certain style of playing that is a little bit on the sloppy side. And that to me represents much more of the glam, in that category. A person walking into a room and seeing like a two-hour special on MTV—videos, Warrant, White Lion—they're calling everything glam, because we've got big fucking hair, we've got hairspray. But White Lion never considered themselves glam, because glam is also a bit of a lifestyle and a bit of an attitude and so on. We were a New York basement band, and it was a whole different attitude we grew up with. I think being a glam band has a lot to do with the attitude when you are walking around in the day too. In New York we were pretty much street kids in the daytime. We just put on some stuff when we went on stage. And glam had the tendency to go a little bit more female, a little bit more lace and stuff like that. Lace never entered White Lion. That's my defense, your honor.

MIKE TRAMP (ON THE LACK OF GLAM ON THE EAST COAST):
People forget, there are really only two bands that made it from the '80s out of New York City, which is Twisted Sister and White Lion. And you really realize that had a lot to do with the climate and the look of the '80s. It's just that, you know, in a blizzard, your fucking hair and your high-heeled boots and your tight pants and little T-shirt, just doesn't keep the weather out, man. Whereas on the Sunset Strip, you can be dressed the same way all year around. New York, we were shoveling snow, man, to get out of our freezing-cold, fucking basement. And it also had a lot to do with our sound and our attitude, and just the overall way that we lived quite a bit away from each other.

Twisted Sister's Dee Snider. © *Rod Dysinger*

THEY'RE READY TO COME OUT AND PLAY FOR YOU.

THE ALBUM
"Come Out And Play"

THE SINGLE
"Leader Of The Pack"

THE VIDEO
"Come Out
And Play"

PRODUCED BY DIETER DIERKS FOR BREEZE MUSIC

LOOK FOR TWISTED SISTER ON TOUR WITH SPECIAL GUEST, DOKKEN, STARTING JANUARY '86.

TWISTED SISTER TOUR DATES

January 8–Binghamton, NY/10–Portland, ME/12–New Haven, CT/14–Pittsburgh, PA/15–Rochester, NY/16–Toronto, ON/18–Philadelphia, PA/19–Glens Falls, NY/21–Worcester, MA/22–Largo, MD/24 & 25–New York City, NY/28–Cleveland, OH/29–Chicago, IL/30–Detroit, MI/31–Milwaukee, WI **February** 3–Minneapolis, MN/4–Cedar Rapids, IA/5–Kansas City, MO/8–Houston, TX/9–San Antonio, TX/10–Dallas, TX/12–El Paso, TX/14–Denver, CO/16–San Diego, CA/17–San Bernadino, CA/19–Los Angeles, CA/21–San Francisco, CA/22–Sacramento, CA/25–Portland, OR/26–Spokane, WA/28–Seattle, WA **March** 2–Salt Lake City, UT/4–Omaha, NE/5–Des Moines, IA/7–St. Louis, MO/8–Cincinnati, OH/9–Indianapolis, IN/11–Buffalo, NY/12–Providence, RI

TWISTED SISTER ON ATLANTIC RECORDS AND CASSETTES.

1985   1986   1987   1988   1989

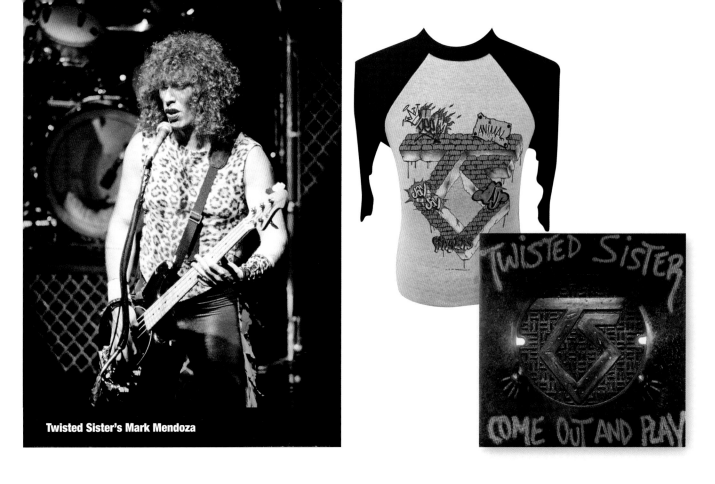

Twisted Sister's Mark Mendoza

JAY JAY FRENCH (GUITARIST, TWISTED SISTER):

Produced by Dieter Dierks. [*Come Out and Play*] was our most ambitious record. We worked forty-seven days straight, no break. He did drive us crazy but it was great. We drove ourselves crazy too. We had a time limit to work under, and we just worked. But Dieter had an amazing capacity to work constantly.

DEE SNIDER (VOCALIST, TWISTED SISTER, ON WORKING WITH DIETER DIERKS):

Dieter was great! He tended to overproduce, which he did with our record. His intentions were good, though. He would work you and work you and work you until he got it exactly right in a truly German fashion. But the more layers you put on something the smaller it gets, not the bigger it gets. The person he really put through the ringer was his assistant, his engineer. Because he had things routed and processed to the nines and it was very difficult for the guy. He'd come in with his diagrams of what he wanted and he knew what he was talking about, but it was just insane how he saw things being processed. And I think ultimately it made the record small-sounding not big-sounding, which was part of the problem with "Leader of the Pack." I remember hearing it on the radio. It just kind of fell out—it didn't jump out at you. On a radio station you need records that pop. "We're Not Gonna Take It" jumped. When it was on in the background, it jumped out at you—you just heard it. "Leader of the Pack" didn't.

1980   **1981**   **1982**   **1983**   **1984**

JAY JAY FRENCH:

The songs on that one were much more difficult. I thought it was very satisfying. It didn't sell well really, which disappointed me, although it was almost a million. Because we really put our heart and soul into it.

DEE SNIDER (ON COVERING "LEADER OF THE PACK"):

That came from the glam influence of Twisted Sister. I think it was the late '70s when I got the idea of playing it as a cover. And it went down really well with our audience, coming from the campier sort of mentality we had. In my ultimate lack of wisdom I thought, "Oh man, this would be the ultimate slick move for *Come Out and Play*, release this song, which will appeal to the core fans, while crossing over to the masses. And it wound up just the wrong song at the wrong time with the wrong production and the wrong video. And instead of expanding our popularity geometrically, it just killed us, really. And I have nobody to blame but myself on that one. But I had my reasons why I thought it would work.

STEVE RILEY (DRUMMER, W.A.S.P.):

I was pretty fortunate because I was involved in both of the big waves that came out of L.A. in the '80s. The first wave was with W.A.S.P. and Quiet Riot and Mötley Crüe and Ratt. And I was involved with that and it was a really, really wild time. I knew W.A.S.P. was a great band. They had just signed and I went to see them and it was just really wild because I had gotten hired to do an album with Gene Simmons producing—it was the Keel album. Keel needed a drummer and I joined right before they did the album. I had already known Gene Simmons from the '70s out here, and he produced the album and the album was sounding great! And I got a call right there in the Record Plant from Blackie asking if I wanted to do the W.A.S.P. world tour. And when I joined W.A.S.P. I knew it was a great band. It was before everything got all screwed up with them and before his head got too big for everything. And the band could just about blow anybody off the stage. We opened up for Kiss, Iron Maiden, all of them, and we were on fire. In fact, all these guys in L.A. Guns, that's how I met them. They were big fans of W.A.S.P. and they used to come to all the shows. I just have really good memories of W.A.S.P. other than the fact that the original four could have stayed together and not have Blackie disband it the way he did. Because it never had the same strength as the original four. I mean, I am like a stickler on that, bro. I believe the original is always like, you can never match it. And he hasn't matched it. But I've got some great memories of W.A.S.P.—it's just toward the end that it got kind of funky.

November 9, 1985: W.A.S.P. issue their second album, *The Last Command*, which includes moderate hits "Wild Child" and "Blind in Texas." The album reaches No. 47 and sells more than a million copies worldwide.

W.A.S.P.'s Blackie Lawless

1985   **1986**   **1987**   **1988**   **1989**

November 9, 1985: Y&T issue *Down for the Count*, a simpler, more melodic album in search of commercial success in the hair metal world that the band helped establish. It proves too little too late. "Summertime Girls" is the hit single and a shameless hair metal play at that.

November 9, 1985: Helix issue their fifth album, *Long Way to Heaven*, which gets panned for eschewing the tough music and black leather look of past presentations.

December 1985: Blue Öyster Cult issue the critically panned *Club Ninja*, a poppy album replete with hair metal characteristics. It is their first and last attempt at it, and a contributing factor in their breakup. Unlike Heart, Cheap Trick, Kiss, and Alice Cooper, BÖC would not be cashing in on a style of hard rock they helped innovate.

BLACKIE LAWLESS:

The Last Command should have been beautifully crude like the first one. But there's the influence of an outside producer, Spencer Proffer, who came in and tried to make us something we weren't. That sound came out of that specific studio, the people working on it. I mean the first W.A.S.P. album sounded a lot different from *Metal Health*, but like I say, it was a combination of the equipment . . . the equipment wasn't that great, to be honest with you. And we got every ounce out of it that we could and so did Quiet Riot. It's funny, if you look at the products that came out of there, there was some really interesting music. So it just goes to show, you have to have the best equipment in the world. It was professionally adequate but it certainly wasn't what I've got right now. And "Wild Child" . . . most of that was written really before W.A.S.P. ever got a record deal. Originally, I was going to give the song to Nikki to let Mötley Crüe do it, but we knew Vince couldn't sing it because of the range of it, so I kept it. And good thing for us that we did.

1980   **1981**   **1982**   **1983**   **1984**

CONGRATULATIONS
1985 CIRCUS MAGAZINE
READERS' POLL WINNERS!

MÖTLEY CRÜE
BEST ARTIST!

MÖTLEY CRÜE
BEST Concert

MICK MARS
BEST Guitarist

NIKKI SIXX
BEST Bassist
and
BEST Songwriter

THANKS FOR USING

ERNIE BALL

THE *PLAYERS'* STRINGS!

1985   1986   1987   1988   1989

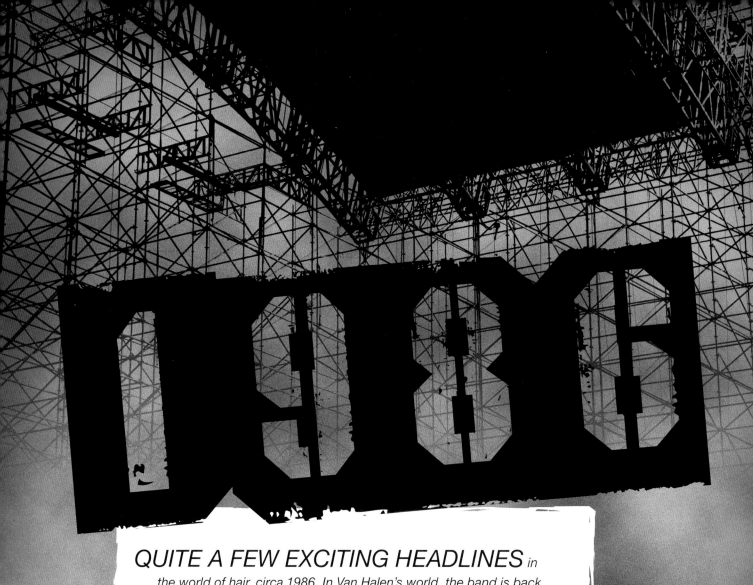

QUITE A FEW EXCITING HEADLINES in
the world of hair, circa 1986. In Van Halen's world, the band is back
with a new front man in Sammy Hagar, who helps edge the band into
the hair metal world with all of his syrupy sentiments on smash hit LP
5150. Meanwhile, Diamond Dave goes loud and proud as a solo artist,
putting together a Technicolor band of flash and excess so bright that it
is almost a parody of hair metal. Alice Cooper returns from near death
with a new record label and a shameless hair metal direction, from
his assembled band of young shredders through all the production
excesses one could possibly handle. The next buzz band, Guns N'
Roses, gets signed, partially because there's a misguided view that
they are somehow an "authentic" band above the goofiness of hair.
And then well within the definition of hair metal that's attracting all this
denigration come two new baby bands, Cinderella and Poison, both
with debut albums that upset the apple cart but good. Moving more
pancakes is Bon Jovi who finally explode with Slippery When Wet,
ushering in the golden era of hair metal, the fruition of all that money
spent on soft-focus, slow-motion videos sparkling with pixie dust and
other white powders.

1980   1981   1982   1983   1984

JAIME ST. JAMES (VOCALIST BLACK 'N BLUE, ON *NASTY NASTY*):
Gene was real involved. Part of the reason we wanted Gene to work with us is that he was really protective of the band. The band comes first, we want them to sound like themselves, although we'll try to please the record company. He's a hard-working guy—he doesn't fool around. It was a lot of fun being in the studio with him. We always had a lot of laughs. But he's very honest, sometimes brutally honest. He doesn't mess around. We would sit in preproduction at rehearsal and he would be there every day. We're talking about months and months of work. He'd be in there with us during the writing and try and maybe help guide something here and there. When he's committed to doing a project, he's in it one hundred percent. He was a good guy to have on your side, that's for sure. You've got to remember, even before we did *Nasty Nasty*, we were on tour with Kiss. That was the main tour we had for the *Without Love* album. I actually got Peter Criss to come into the studio to sing on that record, and Gene and Peter hadn't talked in years. Peter was actually scared, but I talked him into it, and of course, once he gets to the studio, not much singing happened. Him and Gene just sat and talked and went on and on for hours.

1986: L.A.-based vocalist and future MTV VJ Riki Rachtman and Faster Pussycat's Taime Downe open The Cathouse in Hollywood.

1986: Kick Axe issue *Rock the World*, which sees the band returning to a heavier, if still not very glam, metal sound. It will be the last album for the band until a reunion album in 2004 called *IV*. *Rock the World* is a major-label record in Canada, but is issued in the US on the Mercenary indie.

1986: London's second album, an indie called *Don't Cry Wolf*, features the same lineup as the first except that Fred Coury has left to join Cinderella, replaced by one Wailin' J. Morgan.

1986: Electronica band Datacian change their name to Love/Hate and harbor a Goth image inspired by The Cult's *Love* album.

1985   **1986**   **1987**   **1988**   **1989**

1986: Black 'N Blue issue their third album, *Nasty Nasty*. The band falls prey to the tendency toward overproduction so prevalent in the hair metal era (the fact that mentor Gene Simmons gets the production credit is neither here nor there).

January 28, 1986: Black Sabbath issue *Seventh Star*, ostensibly a Tony Iommi solo album. Whatever the case, it's the closest Sabbath would ever get to hair metal, featuring Glenn Hughes on vocals, songs about relationships, and even a power ballad called "No Stranger to Love" with a power ballad video to match.

March 1986: Great White issue their third album, *Shot in the Dark*, which includes "Face the Day" in homage to Australia's "baby AC/DC," Angel City.

March 1986: Guns N' Roses sign with Geffen Records, garnering a $75,000 advance.

TOM ZUTAUT (A&R MAN, ON GUNS N' ROSES):

They came over to my house and we just spun a bunch of vinyl, all our favorite things, and it ran the gamut from Aerosmith to Thin Lizzy to Sex Pistols to UK Subs and all these more obscure British punk bands, all the way to Elton John. Axl was a big Elton John fan and Bowie fan. So there was a bonding over music, but it wasn't necessarily just over Aerosmith. The Aerosmith story that probably got sort of distorted by the time, wherever you heard that from, was that they went over to Chrysalis Records and the guy at Chrysalis Records in A&R didn't know who Steven Tyler was. So the band was kind of astounded by that, so they just kind of said to the girl who did A&R and wanted to sign them that they could never sign to a label where the head of A&R didn't know who Steven Tyler was unless she took her clothes off and walked naked down the street from her office to Tower Records on Sunset, and they would sign with her, because it would prove that she was a bold person.

TOM ZUTAUT (ON THE MAGIC OF GUNS N' ROSES):

What the Rolling Stones were to the Beatles, Guns N' Roses were to all the '80s metal bands . . . they were basically like a dangerous bunch of drug addicts living a true, hedonistic, fuck-everybody-and-everything, sex, drugs, and rock 'n' roll lifestyle. And they were in it just to destroy the establishment in any way they could—physically, mentally—with their music, whatever it was. But they carried over a lot of punk ethic, so it was that mix of metal, hard rock, and punk that made them different and that's why it was so infectious. The machinery was cranking out metal like Anheuser-Busch was cranking out Budweiser. It was just one unidentified metal band after another with one-hit wonders, and when Guns N' Roses came out, they were the dangerous bad boys and people just flocked to it.

JOHN GALLAGHER (BASSIST AND VOCALIST, RAVEN):

The guy who signed us was really a dance guy, like a disco guy, and he wasn't really an A&R guy. But he really liked us and got us our deal with Atlantic. When we started the next album we really wanted to do really hard accessible songs, which is really a part of what we are. It just got exaggerated too much. And they were being really hard on [producer] Eddie Kramer to make this super commercial. And funny, you listen to that album and you listen to the album *Turbo* by Judas Priest, and they're almost identical. There's even that same kind of guitar synthesizer that we used, which is wild. To a point, we were like insulated in this bubble of touring and doing records. I don't think that could even happen these days with the Internet. You've got such an instant rapport with your audience. But back then, it didn't really matter, because people would say, you know, the album sounds really commercial, but we would do the same stuff live, and it was just killer.

1980   **1981**   **1982**   **1983**   **1984**

SAMMY HAGAR:

We started working on [*5150*], and I walk in and Eddie
is sitting down at the keyboard, and he plays [sings the
intro to "Why Can't This Be Love"]. And the sound of it,
he was playing the keyboard through his guitar amp.
He didn't even bother putting it into anything else. He
had his regular guitar setting and I heard that sound,
and I just went, "Fuck, yes! That is just totally cool!" And
I just jumped all over that. There was a lot of inspiration
going on. When something inspires you, boom, you
hear it. It ain't like no work—you don't even need a
pencil and paper, man. You just grab the microphone
and say, "Roll tape, because this is going to come out!"
And whether or not you use that first take or not is one
thing, but you've got that idea, and you go home and
listen to the magic, and that's the way we wrote those
songs. It was kind of like the Montrose situation—it
was very, very spontaneous and very Instamatic. It
was just Pow! And those songs were done and we just
started writing fresh. The only thing Eddie had, at the
end of that record, he had this piano thing that became
"Dreams," but it wasn't even near anything but Eddie
beating around on the piano with a couple of parts
[sings it], that little intro. But it wasn't a verse. It would
be hard to say that that song was even a song. But Mick
Jones heard that, the producer, and said, "I think you
guys need one more song." We thought we were done
and we were ready to go on tour . . . that's what a great
producer does to you. And we said, "Ah man, come on,
we've been in here for two weeks [laughs]." Once again
that was a pretty fast record. It was actually six weeks
total. So [Jones] and Eddie stayed up all night one
night, and Eddie just played him all these cassettes he
had, laying around on the floor of the studio. And Mick
heard that piano thing and said that could be a great
song.

March 1986: NWOBHM heroes Raven follow Saxon's ill-informed lead and try their hand at the new "commercial" rock, issuing *The Pack Is Back*.

March 1986: Ted Nugent issues his second and arguably last hair metal album, *Little Miss Dangerous*. Ted completes the circuit, with every last big American band from the '70s trying their hand at hair, with varying degrees of success.

1985   **1986**   **1987**   **1988**   **1989**

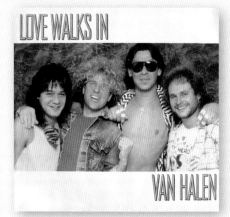

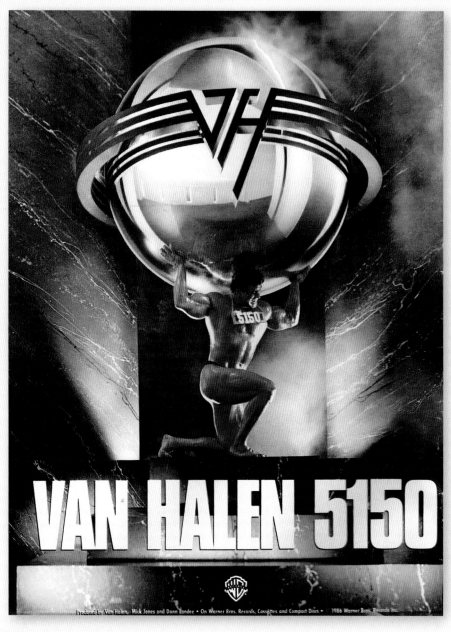

March 24, 1986: Van Halen issue *5150*, their first with Sammy Hagar. The glam look continues, but with a hint of upscale preppy new wave à la Rush. "Love Walks In" is the band's first true schlocky power ballad, with "Why Can't This Be Love" and "Dreams" being up-tempo examples of the form.

April 14, 1986: Judas Priest release *Turbo*, widely considered their bandwagoneering glam album, with songs like "Parental Guidance," "Locked In," "Private Property," "Wild Nights, Hot & Crazy Days," "Hot for Love," and "Rock You All Around the World." Priest partied it up by adding a little red leather to their black and fixing up their hair, especially guitarist K.K. Downing and drummer Dave Holland.

1980   **1981**   **1982**   **1983**   **1984**

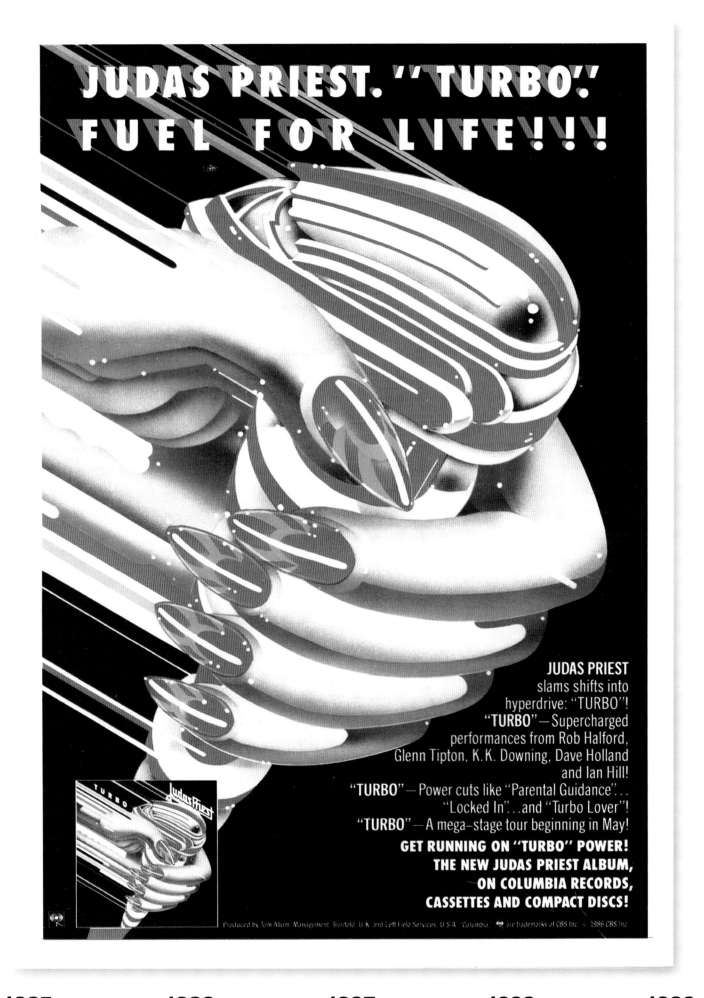

1985   1986   1987   1988   1989

April 30, 1986: Keel issue their third album, the Gene Simmons–produced *The Final Frontier*, which scores a minor hit with a cover of Bruce Springsteen's and Patti Smith's "Because the Night."

Gene [Simmons] did some wonderful stuff for us, business-wise. He wielded a lot of power. He would walk into a meeting with me to MCA Records and he would tell them what they are going to do. I remember one day we were over budget on the *Final Frontier* album, and we didn't have a huge budget to begin with. We were, you know, ten grand over budget or something, which, in the scheme of things wasn't really much in terms of the money they were spending back then. And Gene just told them, "I'll write you a check for the amount that you've invested into Keel right now, and I will turn around tomorrow and I will sell this record to another label for three times that amount. How is that?" And they shut up and let us go over budget as much as we wanted to. Plus, at the time, MCA was used to just taking a picture of the artist and putting it on the album cover—very cheap graphics and packaging. And we constructed the *Final Frontier* album cover, by John Taylor Dismukes, which is a classic piece of rock art. John actually airbrushed the New York City skyline, with the Twin Towers, the Statue of Liberty holding a Keel sword in her hand, and this Keel logo that looks like a spaceship coming up out of the New York harbor, and it was really an elaborate beautiful piece of work—it cost 15K. And Gene walks in with the actual piece of art, the painting that John had done, in front of the president of the label, the board of directors, and sits this piece of artwork on the easel there in the office, and he says, "This is your album cover. It's going to cost you fifteen thousand dollars." And nobody said anything, man. They just paid it because he had that kind of power.

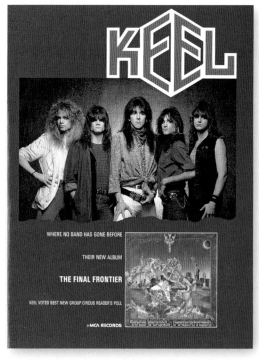

1980   **1981**   **1982**   **1983**   **1984**

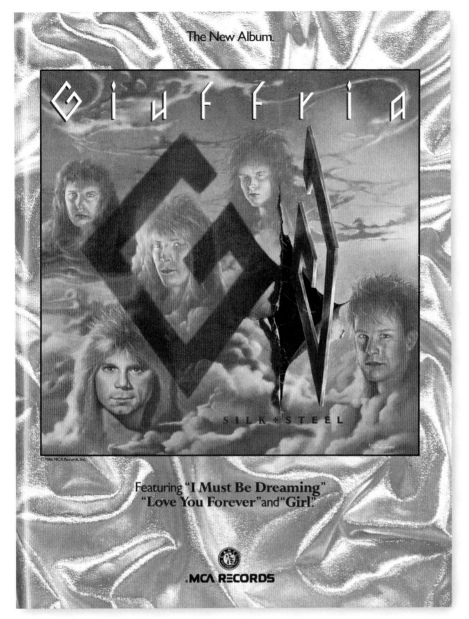

The New Album.

SILK ★ STEEL

Featuring "I Must Be Dreaming"
"Love You Forever" and "Girl."

.MCA RECORDS

Giuffria's Craig Goldy.
© *Rod Dysinger*

May 1986: Giuffria launch their second (and last) album, *Silk and Steel*, featuring one of the most hair metal–bound titles and cover arts of all time.

May 26, 1986: Swedish rockers Europe issue their third album, and very much their first hair metal effort, *The Final Countdown*, which sells 3x platinum. There are two smash hits: power ballad "Carrie" and the title track, soon to be a sporting event staple on par with "We Are the Champions." "Cherokee" and "Rock the Night" also garner radio play.

May 27, 1986: Journey release an ill-received album called *Raised on Radio*, pretty much abandoning their heritage sound for hair metal. It goes 2x platinum, but the band wouldn't record again for ten years.

June 1986: Danish/American consortium White Lion issue their debut *Fight to Survive* album in the US on the Grand Slamm label.

1985   **1986**   **1987**   **1988**   **1989**

Krokus' Marc Storace

Krokus' Fernando von Arb

June 16 1986: Krokus, formerly AC/DC-soundalikes, continue to try their hand at hair metal with the Tom Werman–produced *Change of Address*, featuring a novelty cover of Alice Cooper's "School's Out."

MARC STORACE (VOCALIST, KROKUS):

Everyone around us was talking about crossover Top 40. And we were fighting against it then. On the demo, you can hear songs from *Change of Address* before they were smoothed out to the extent that they were. And obviously, coming on with all the carnival costumes we changed to, that was also a big mistake. A lot of this was going on, though. You couldn't get in *Creem* magazine unless you came up with some new outfits and this was also wrong. It had nothing to do with music anymore.

BILLY SHEEHAN (BASSIST, DAVID LEE ROTH):

[*Eat 'Em and Smile*] was a real band approach. We did it in Dave's basement, hanging out, drinking beers, putting pieces of songs together, doing riffs, having a riot, laughing our asses off, going out afterwards into Hollywood and tearing it up. All that shit.

1980   **1981**   **1982**   **1983**   **1984**

The New Album × Produced By Ted Templeman × Featuring The Single "Yankee Rose"

On Warner Bros. Records, Cassettes And Compact Discs ©1986 Warner Bros. Records Inc.

July 7, 1986: David Lee Roth issues his solo debut, *Eat 'Em and Smile*. Dave and his hotshot band adopt a hyper hair band wardrobe and shred just as extremely.

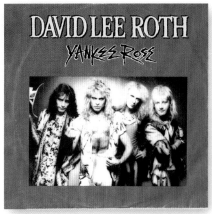

BEN LIEMER (ON INTERVIEWING ROTH):

I would always throw in some questions that were not just about the party and sex and drugs and touring. I said, "Dave, you're a bright guy, you come to New York, what do you like doing?" And he says, "I tuck my hair under my baseball cap and turn it around backwards and put the sunglasses on and a trench coat, and go off to the Museum of Modern Art or something like that." You know, his dad is like a Beverly Hills ophthalmologist. His band, they could play every note under the sun, but when Billy Sheehan played with David Lee Roth and Roth got him with Steve [Vai] and he pulled them in and said, "Okay, if you repeat that part five times in a row, then we'll make a bridge. . . ." I don't think Dave is the greatest songwriter in the world, but he knew to sit on them and keep them under control and focus that progressiveness into songs.

1985   **1986**   **1987**   **1988**   **1989**

July 19, 1986: The annual Texxas Jam features Bachman-Turner Overdrive, Keel, Krokus, Loverboy, Dio, and Van Halen. Keel is by this point a gritty, somewhat traditional hair metal band from the first wave, and stuck in first gear. Loverboy, very much like Night Ranger, who was on the bill the previous year, is at the time a hair metal pioneer still enjoying success. Krokus had evolved their sound to try to make it as a hair metal band. At the top of the bill, Van Halen is now very much a hair metal concern, having replaced David Lee Roth with Sammy Hagar.

July 23, 1986: Bon Jovi issue "You Give Love a Bad Name" as an advance single from their third album. It becomes a massive hair metal anthem.

August–December 1986: Guns N' Roses work on what will become the biggest album of the hair band era.

August 2, 1986: Cinderella release their debut, *Night Songs*, on Mercury. It goes 3x platinum and rises to No. 3 in February 1987. The band's first tour finds them and Poison backing Japan's Loudness. Drummer Fred Coury joins Cinderella from the infamous London, an L.A. band with no records but a bunch of members who go on to greater fame.

RIKKI ROCKETT:

The contrast [between Poison and] Cinderella is that even though they are from the same place we're from—I mean, they are literally from the same state—they are a little more blues-based than we are. We're a little more Ramones-injected, I would say. We're a straight glam band. We are. We're that post-punk, post-glitter, post-hard-rock-injected kind of thing.

BOBBY DALL
(BASSIST, POISON, ON THE BAND'S ÜBER-GLAM VISUALS):

You know, you stick your head above the crowd, someone's definitely going to throw a rock at it. And we always had the slogans that we're true to what it is that we felt—you know, love us or hate us, you're never going to forget us. And in life, as in anything, you can make millions of people love you, and you can make that much or more hate you [laughs]. That's just the way life goes. And there are people, critics or whatever, who will always want to take a jab at that first record cover with the real glam faces. I don't take any offense in it but it's definitely been there.

1980   **1981**   **1982**   **1983**   **1984**

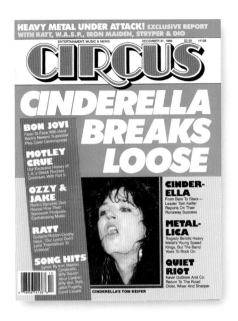

Cinderellas's Eric Bittingham.
© Rod Dysinger

August 2, 1986: Ex-Kiss guitarist Vinnie Vincent issues the self-titled debut from his band Vinnie Vincent Invasion, featuring "Boyz are Gonna Rock."

August 2, 1986: Poison issue their debut album, *Look What the Cat Dragged In*. The androgynous rocker look is taken to its furthest extreme and the music is positively juvenile. Arguably, the album simultaneously represents the birth of hair metal proper and its death knell. Featuring the tracks "Talk Dirty to Me" and "I Want Action," the album has sold 3.5 million copies worldwide.

RIKKI ROCKETT:

Look What the Cat Dragged In was actually a glorified demo. We did it so fast but we put a tremendous amount of effort into it and we were very rehearsed for it, but still, the technology wasn't what it is now. You couldn't do as much in a short period of time as you can now. We sold 30,000 when we were on an independent, Enigma, and then Capitol picked up three acts—us, Stryper, and The Smithereens. The first attempt didn't work. They released "Cry Tough" as a single and a video and it really flopped. We got rotation once a day on MTV on that for about two weeks and then it got dropped. So we thought it was over with that record. We were looking at the next record. And then we got the Ratt tour and we said, "Look, we need another single to go out there. Please let us do this." And they gave us a video and a single, not much of a video budget. So instead of looking for continuity and pulling the wool over everybody's eyes like we had this huge budget, you see what the outcome was. We just said, "Let's turn on the cameras and let's just go, and I don't even care if a camera guy gets in the shot. Let's change clothes every other frame so there is absolutely no continuity or integrity whatsoever. Let's just make it fun and turn it into a party. The song's a party, let's make the video a party. You know, who are we trying to fool here?" And it worked. People got it and understood and it was fresh. But a lot of that kind of thing started to dissipate as the '80s came to a close, that essential fun aspect. Nothing ruins rock 'n' roll more than somebody overplaying. And I never saw so many bands come along and go, "Wow, Poison did that, but we can do it better because we've got a guy who is going to play fifty notes a second instead of two." [laughs]

1985   **1986**   **1987**   **1988**   **1989**

O.K., BOYS AND GIRLS,
IT'S TIME TO TAKE YOUR

Poison

LOOK WHAT THE CAT DRAGGED IN

THE DEBUT ALBUM
Featuring
CRY TOUGH
AVAILABLE NOW ON CAPITOL/ENIGMA

1980   1981   1982   1983   1984

BEAU HILL (PRODUCER, ON RATT'S *DANCING UNDERCOVER*):

The third record, which had "Dance," which was my least favorite—I had a conversation with Robbin [Crosby] when we finish that record, and I said, "We do not have a single. And we're going to ruin the band's career if we release this record." And he agreed with me. He said, "Yeah, we've got an album full of filler—we don't have a single." So Robbin and I sat down and we wrote "Dance," which was the single, and that was the song that compelled [*sic*] that record platinum as well. There was a lot of strife and conflict on that record. I don't want to paint it as just a horrible experience. It wasn't, because as hard as the records were, we also had some hilariously funny, great times. But there was always that kind of underlying resentment that I got shoved down their throat. And I think also, when we did *Dancing Undercover*, I don't think it was particularly popular when I made the announcement that I don't think we have a single.

JAIME ST. JAMES (VOCALIST, BLACK 'N BLUE):

[Black 'N Blue] had done *Without Love*, the slick, produced album with [Bob] Rock and [Bruce] Fairbairn, and believe me, that was a great album, and I can tell you that Jon Bon Jovi and Richie Sambora came up to me one night at the Rainbow in L.A. and said, "Hey, the whole reason why we used those guys for *Slippery When Wet* was when we heard your record." And that was huge.

DEREK SHULMAN (A&R MAN):

[Jon Bon Jovi] could appeal to females as well as males. But to get him back into the rock world, it was a definitive, how can I put this? It was a deliberate thought process of putting them with the heaviest bands possible, so he could get his rock chops down. So we put them out with Scorpions, Kiss, with the hard and heavy male-oriented crowds, so that his fan base would have the male appeal as well as his obvious good looks and all the other parts. And when MTV came along, that was very important. For his appeal to the female crowd. So he was always very aware of where his appeal was. And when he struck out on his own to do solo things, and then became getting involved in country, he knew that his pop appeal, if you like, was as strong as his rock appeal.

August 9 1986: Ratt issue *Dancing Undercover*, their third Beau Hill production. It goes platinum, but there's a sense that Ratt are already beginning to be seen as yesterday's news.

August 18, 1986: Bon Jovi issue *Slippery When Wet*, which goes on to be the biggest selling album of 1987, eventually hitting 12x platinum and 28 million worldwide sales.

Richie Sambora and Jon Bon Jovi. *Phil Dent/Redferns/Getty Images*

1980   **1981**   **1982**   **1983**   **1984**

RON KEEL:

The tour with Bon Jovi that we did was incredible—*Slippery When Wet* in '87. We ended up getting the tail end of that tour, which was the northeast United States, which was Bon Jovi's strongest market. I mean, New Jersey, New York, Pennsylvania . . . Bon Jovi was unstoppable at the time. We were doing three and four nights at the Garden and the Meadowlands. And that was also when the band, Keel, was exceptionally strong. We were supporting what I thought was one of our best efforts, the self-titled album, which had some very strong songs on it. So that whole tour was a dream come true.

JERRY DIXON (BASSIST, WARRANT):

We were together, before we got signed, about three and a half years, playing clubs, doing the Hollywood scene, flyering and demoing, and then about a year later we went in and did the first record. But before that, Jani was out in Ohio, and before that he played for another three years, maybe four years. So everybody combined. I was in different bands, so we played the club scene probably for five or six years collectively before we got signed. But we were all still pretty young when we finally got hooked up in the band. And our sound. . . [guitarist] Joey [Allen], [guitarist] Erik [Turner], and I were very heavy on Iron Maiden and Black Sabbath, believe it or not. And the other guys, they were into Boston and Cheap Trick, more mainstream pop stuff like that. We kind of mixed those two together and created the Warrant sound. As for the look, I've been in Warrant since I was fifteen years old, so we just kind of followed, kind of fell into it, and it was just our vibe. We did what we did. We didn't get posters out and go, "Okay, this is the new look this month" [laughs]. It's kind of a natural thing, if you can call that natural—just glam up. The main reason why a lot of bands took things that far was the competition factor. Back in those days, you had the Sunset Strip, you had seven clubs all right next door to each other, so it was the more outrageous your band could be, if one guy was going to have this band, and your guy can do it one bigger and one louder, with a bit more attention, you drew more people. So it was a really competitive environment, to outdo the other band. The more outrageous you got in your look and your music and your show, the more attention you got—you're trying to steal the people from Faster Pussycat's show next door.

KEVIN DUBROW (VOCALIST, QUIET RIOT, ON *QR III*):

Confused. Too much keyboards. I don't know. It's just a mish-mash of everything. It's a mistake that I've often seen other people make, trying to follow a trend. Whenever you try to follow a trend you're always late. And we were trying to follow that Bon Jovi keyboard-type thing, and it didn't work for us. *QR III* did just under gold—about 410,000.

September 1986: Warrant, although formed in '84, jam at Hollywood's Db Sound with singer Jani Lane, who subsequently joins the band and becomes a major contributing songwriter.

September 8, 1986: Quiet Riot issue *QR III*. Bassist Rudy Sarzo is replaced by Chuck Wright. The inexorable decline of Quiet Riot's commercial fortunes continues, with this album not even going gold. There is no cover version attempt at a hit single.

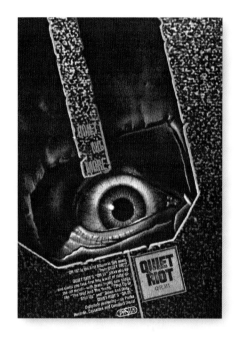

1985   **1986**   **1987**   **1988**   **1989**

Quiet Riot's Carlos Cavazo. © *Rod Dysinger*

Quiet Riot's Kevin DuBrow. © *Rod Dysinger*

SPENCER PROFFER (MANAGER, QUIET RIOT):

Condition Critical is pretty much the brother album of *Metal Health*. In terms of just, they just wrote other songs and we made a consistent record but didn't want to deviate too much. But the problem was, Kevin had alienated a lot of people at radio and out in the touring community, which caused a bit of a lack of support for the next record. I actually think that *Condition Critical* is a better musical album, but it was just, they had kind of peaked with the first one, because of some problems that Kevin had with certain personalities in the community. And it kind of wound up backfiring on him. You see the opposite with Jon Bon Jovi and Doc McGhee's management of Jon Bon Jovi. Jon was an opposite kind of artist. He didn't alienate people, and that's why he's relevant today. He's one of the most dignified, smartest, most gracious guys out there to artists, radio, video people, and Kevin was kind of a little more belligerent. So I think what exploded Quiet Riot was not the music. *QR III* was just more of the same but a little more colorful. We added a keyboard player, John Purdell, and actually "The Wild and the Young" was a great track with a fantastic video. Very much a George Orwell–produced video, which we all conceived. But they had lost the moment, while Mötley Crüe went out there and tore it up. But at least we started the thing. I was kind of heartbroken, because when you see bands that could just sustain longer, it's how they communicated with their audience. And Mötley Crüe did a great job out there, and Doc did a phenomenal job managing them, with his partner Doug Thayer. It was hard to harness Kevin on the road—and his mouth.

1980   **1981**   **1982**   **1983**   **1984**

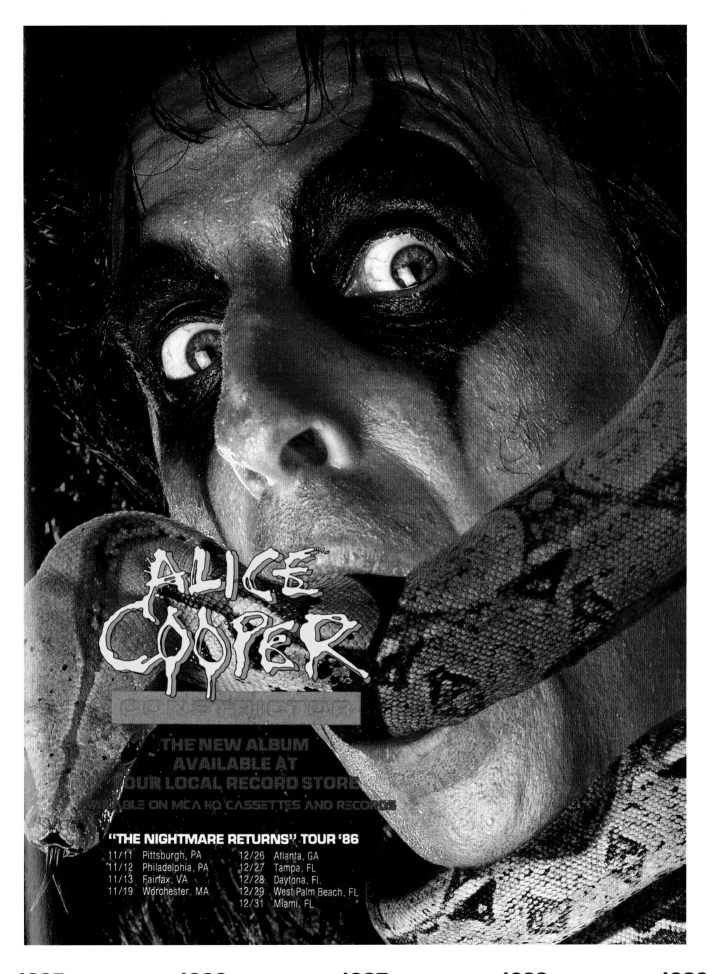

ALICE
COOPER
CONSTRICTOR

THE NEW ALBUM
AVAILABLE AT
YOUR LOCAL RECORD STORE
AVAILABLE ON MCA HQ CASSETTES AND RECORDS

"THE NIGHTMARE RETURNS" TOUR '86

11/11	Pittsburgh, PA	12/26	Atlanta, GA
11/12	Philadelphia, PA	12/27	Tampa, FL
11/13	Fairfax, VA	12/28	Daytona, Fl.
11/19	Worchester, MA	12/29	West Palm Beach, FL
		12/31	Miami, FL

1985   **1986**   **1987**   **1988**   **1989**

September 22, 1986: Alice Cooper returns from a three-year retirement that followed three weird, new-wavy albums recorded while high on crack cocaine. He comes back clean and sober, as a no-nonsense hair metal shock rocker with *Constrictor* on a new label, MCA. Most of the album is a cowrite with guitarist Kane Roberts, who is also in the band as Alice's right-hand man. The front cover features Alice in makeup with his snake wrapped around his neck and face.

ALICE COOPER:

The thing about *Constrictor* was that I had just sobered up. I had never been Alice Cooper on stage sober. What do you think that first gig was like? Me putting on all of the gear, getting ready to go onstage and realizing, what if Alice doesn't show up? I'm going to be out there in front of these people without the alcohol. What if Alice just doesn't show up? Well, the first night we played, Guns N' Roses opened for us and I had this new band with Kane Roberts and Ken Mary and Kip Winger on bass—a great band. And what I wanted to do was come out with an album that had no ballads on it. It was just pure heavy Alice. You know, it was heavy metal, but I called it "heavy Alice." It wasn't really metal like Metallica or Megadeth, but I had this new sound and I had the new image. If I look at Alice now, back in the *Billion Dollar Babies* or *School's Out* days, I see a character that was a whipping boy. I look at his posture and he's humped over. I look at the fact that he gets his head cut off and he gets hung. He was always society's whipping boy, and that's the way alcohol made me feel. He appealed to the outcasts of the world. And now Alice was this incredibly vicious villain who stood straight up, who wore all black leather, and he was now this character that was an arrogant Captain Hook. And he looked at the audience with disdain, as if "You are the great unwashed and I am of course Hannibal Lecter" [laughs]. And it was a new way of me performing Alice. I didn't feel beat up anymore. I needed to prove to the audience that there was a new generation Alice here.

BEAU HILL (PRODUCER, ON WORKING ON *CONSTRICTOR*):

It was just Alice, and he didn't really have a band. And he had a cowriter, Kane Roberts. He and Alice had spent a great deal of time writing this record, and Alice got a new deal on MCA, and that's how they got me in. I introduced Alice to Kip Winger, and Kip played bass on the album, and then subsequently Alice hired Kip to go out and tour that particular album. Alice was so easy to work with. He was such a gentleman and such a riot. He was really open. It was like, "Okay, how about we try this?" "That's great, let's do it." I was an Alice fan when I was a kid, and so this was a real privilege for me. He had already come back from the edge of all of his various abuses that he was so notorious for. The weirdest thing that he did is that he'd like to fall asleep on the couch and watch what he referred to as splatter movies, stuff like *Halloween* and *Friday the 13th*, all that kind of stuff. He was a very gracious person to be around, and any time we were out walking on the street, he would stop and sign autographs.

1980   **1981**   **1982**   **1983**   **1984**

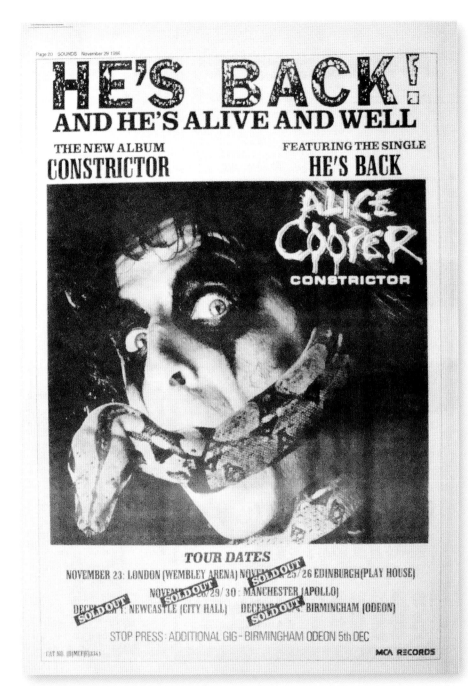

HE'S BACK!
AND HE'S ALIVE AND WELL

THE NEW ALBUM
CONSTRICTOR

FEATURING THE SINGLE
HE'S BACK

ALICE COOPER CONSTRICTOR

TOUR DATES

NOVEMBER 23: LONDON (WEMBLEY ARENA) NOVEMBER 25/26 EDINBURGH (PLAY HOUSE)

NOVEMBER 28/29/30 : MANCHESTER (APOLLO)

DECEMBER 1: NEWCASTLE (CITY HALL)   DECEMBER 4: BIRMINGHAM (ODEON)

~~SOLD OUT~~ ~~SOLD OUT~~ ~~SOLD OUT~~ ~~SOLD OUT~~ ~~SOLD OUT~~ ~~SOLD OUT~~

STOP PRESS : ADDITIONAL GIG - BIRMINGHAM ODEON 5th DEC

CAT NO. [D]MCF[E]3341

MCA RECORDS

ALICE COOPER:

I did not want to come out with anything with the soft underbelly to it. I wanted Alice to come out there and punch the lights out. I saw all these bands. I saw, you know Kiss. I knew who Kiss was; we helped invent Kiss. We told them where to buy their makeup. They were no shock to me. And I said, "I need to blow these guys off the map." And to me, attitude-wise and show-wise, we did. Kiss were a different thing from us. Kiss were comic book, where Alice was still the master of theater. And I was the master of surprise. This was much darker than anybody in Kiss. The one thing about *Constrictor* is that I took metal, and to me, made it a little smarter. The arrangements, the guitar playing of Kane Roberts . . . he is the most underrated guitar player of all time. The fact that he looked like Schwarzenegger really detracted from his guitar playing. I mean, people did not listen to him. They'd listen to the album and say, "Who played the guitar on this? It's incredible! Is it Eddie Van Halen? Is it Steve Vai?" "No, that's Kane Roberts." He was a genius guitar player, on both those albums [*Constrictor* and 1987's *Raise Your Fist to Hell*]. And if you listen to those albums, there's a lot of early Alice melody lines. I learned my lessons from Bob Ezrin. I never wrote songs that didn't have great melody lines. It's just now I was attacking it differently. I was attacking it with a much more aggressive guitar, bass, and drums.

1985   **1986**   **1987**   **1988**   **1989**

TOM SCHOLZ (FOUNDER AND GUITARIST, BOSTON):

The Boston sound just sort of follows me around. I can't seem to do anything in the studio that doesn't end up somehow having those identifying marks on it—it just sort of happens whenever I start working on music in the studio. I do kind of like distortion, I must admit. You know, overdriven guitar is probably the most expressive instrument that has ever been invented by mankind. I might have to give violin a close run on that. But I think overdriven electric guitar is probably tops. You can play one note a thousand different ways on a guitar, and every different way produces a little bit different result as far as the emotion goes that you get out of it.

September 23, 1986: Boston, a proto–hair metal original, returns after an eight-year absence with *Third Stage*. The band's perennially melodic hard rock sound fits in well with current tastes and the album sells 4x platinum.

September 26, 1986: Boston issue "Amanda," a rote hair band power ballad, as the first single from *Third Stage*.

Late 1986: Skid Row forms in Toms River, New Jersey.

October 1986: Bad Company enters the hair metal sweepstakes. Four years past their last album with Paul Rodgers on vocals, the band issues *Fame and Fortune*, featuring, as Rodgers' replacement, Brian Howe, who last made a hair metal record with Ted Nugent.

BRAD DELP (VOCALIST, GUITARIST, BOSTON):

I really credit Tom with coming up with the Boston sound. I think it's the notion of, he always liked heavy guitars. A lot of people refer to it as "Boston guitars" or the "Boston guitars sound." As you probably know, later he even came up with a [guitar amplifier] he called the Rockman. And that in itself is quite an accomplishment. And then incorporating vocals, he was always partial to a lot of harmonies. And I think at the time we came out, a lot of times it was a choice between the two. You either had the Beach Boys, something with a lot of harmonies, or you had the heavy Led Zeppelin-ish straight ahead rock 'n' roll. I think Tom somehow managed to combine the two of those, certainly on the first album. If you look at "Peace of Mind," songs like that, they have an awful lot of vocals on them but they have the heavy guitars as well.

BRAD DELP:

[W]hen we went out in '87 with the *Third Stage* tour, we did the entire first album as a setpiece—we did it right from start to finish.

1980   **1981**   **1982**   **1983**   **1984**

October 26, 1986: Stryper put together second full-length, *To Hell with the Devil*, which goes platinum. "Free," "Calling on You," and "Honestly" become big MTV videos.

October 31, 1986: D'Molls sign with Atlantic.

October 31, 1986: Bon Jovi issue "Livin' on a Prayer" from *Slippery When Wet*.

November 8, 1986: W.A.S.P. issue their third album, *Inside the Electric Circus*, the band's third and last record to go gold.

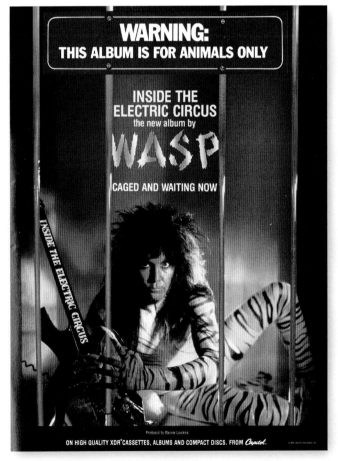

1985   **1986**   **1987**   **1988**   **1989**

1980　　　1981　　　1982　　　1983　　　1984

JEFF KEITH (VOCALIST, TESLA):

Mechanical Resonance was great because that's your first effort. You're always proud of your first effort. But then again, you're trying to figure out who you are and set your boundaries. A lot of people go back to that album, and it's got "Modern Day Cowboy," all kinds of great tunes. We just watched some videotapes my mom had the other night of City Kidd which was the name of our band before Tesla. Oh my God! The clothes we wore and the things we did. That was [bassist] Brian [Wheat] and [guitarist and songwriter] Frank [Hannon] and me and these particular videos we were watching go all the way back to 1983, when we worked with Ronnie Montrose and all that. It's embarrassing, but, hey, it's another stepping stone, back in the early days. You watch the stuff and you go, "I'm little bit embarrassed about that!" But, hey, those are the things you do to get where you're going. When Tom Zutaut signed us to Geffen, that was our name, City Kidd. But we knew we didn't want to go with that name, and that's when we came up with Tesla. Our management at the time helped us come up with that. We were halfway done with *Mechanical Resonance* when we came up with that name. But we knew we didn't want to be City Kidd with two d's. We knew that.

TROY LUCCKETTA (DRUMMER, TESLA):

["Modern Day Cowboy"] was our first single, so it means a lot to me. That was the track that actually broke us with radio, got us on the David Lee Roth tour. Because he had seen the video and he thought the band and the song kind of stuck out a little bit over the other bands at the time, and he picked us for his tour. It was a song that opened all the doors for us. That was the tune that just kind of said, "Hey! Here we are! Who are these guys? We're Tesla."

December 8, 1986: Sacramento's Tesla issue their debut album, *Mechanical Resonance*, on MCA. The album will be certified platinum three years later.

December 16, 1986: Guns N' Roses issue their debut, a four-song EP called *Live ?!*@ Like a Suicide*. It's a ruse, from the crowd noise lifted from Texxas Jam to the fact that its indie imprint, UZI Suicide, was really Geffen.

1985   **1986**   **1987**   **1988**   **1989**

1987

BON JOVI'S Slippery When Wet *shows the industry what could happen if the stars aligned in the much derided genre of "pop metal." In 1987, the stars align all over the skies over Hollywood Hills. At midlevel, Great White and White Lion continue to press on, as did Dokken, who keep their fan base happy with* Back for the Attack. *Moving up the ladder, Mötley Crüe reestablish dominance with* Girls, Girls, Girls, *not much better of an album than its predecessor, but who cares? Drink and drug now, for tomorrow may never come. Climb that stairway to heaven, and there you have Aerosmith finally getting clean and cluing in to hair metal trickery, breaking the bank with famous comeback album* Permanent Vacation. *Def Leppard finally closes sessions on their* Hysteria *album, releasing it to a public who doesn't seem to mind that the whole thing sounds like it was made by robots—illiterate ones at that. And then in one of the strangest stories in this great year for hair metal, washed-up old-timer David Coverdale replaces his entire band with a retooled Whitesnake and takes over the world with his self-titled album full of hefty anti–hair metal rock balanced against some of the most egregious power ballad moves and grooves known to man dressed like woman. And then there's Guns N' Roses, who, no question, caused a ton of decadent excitement with their* Appetite for Destruction *album. Even if they don't quite fit the theme, their sales actually taking off in 1988 . . . and in '89, and '90, and '91, and. . .*

TONY HARNELL (VOCALIST, TNT):

We were the third band on Doc McGhee's roster, after Bon Jovi and Mötley Crüe, which is why we never made it big. They were both a lot of work and he didn't have much time for us. So we were with him for only one album, and then we pretty much instigated a break with him after the touring was over with. And then we were with Mark Puma, who managed Twisted Sister, Kix, and Zebra. I think *Tell No Tales* did about 500,000 or 600,000 on its own, and [1989's] *Intuition* did about 300,000 or 400,000. All the albums together, total, we probably did about a million and a half. But on the *Tell No Tales* front, we were at the point where we worked up to about 250,000 in the US and were really ready to crack, and Polygram decided to pull the plug and not release what I really thought would be the thing that would have pushed us over the top, which is one of the ballads. We've always been a great ballad band. Our ballads were always really special and not the same as the other bands. It was always just a really beautiful side to the music, and no one outside of the real hardcore fans of the music ever heard those ballads. Because all the bands were releasing ballads and going gold off of them at the time.

KEITH OLSEN (PRODUCER):

A power ballad is really good because it's a way of having a rock 'n' roll band be accessible, because radio was not going to play anything other than the ballad. So, gee, okay, what do we have to do to get exposure, to get people to actually want to go out and buy it? Because remember, the media is the message.

DAVID COVERDALE (VOCALIST, WHITESNAKE):

"Here I Go Again" I wrote many, many years ago in Portugal, before people in America heard it in '87 or whatever, and it was actually about the breakup of my first marriage. I wrote that in 1980, '81, so that's pretty old. It's interesting. That turned into a huge anthem, fist-punching-the-air stuff, which is interesting because it isn't that kind of theme. But whatever. I've had enough people talk to me or write to me and say how helpful or beneficial the song was to them in a particular crisis in their lives. And that to me, as a writer, is success, when you can connect like that. And that was a problem I had with Whitesnake. A lot of the stuff was becoming so overtly pompous, catering to big rock stadium scenarios. You'd get the sentiment of the song in the beginning and then the group would explode in and I was just riding the gods of electricity, let alone trying to put any sort of emotional content into it.

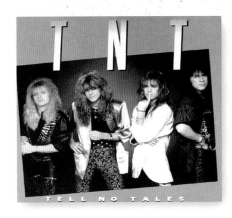

Early 1987: The classic Skid Row lineup is in place, with the addition of long-haired Canadian Sebastian Bach.

1987: Norway's TNT make a play for hair metal domination with their third album, *Tell No Tales*.

February 3, 1987: Whitesnake issue a remake of their own song "Here I Go Again" as an advance single. It goes on to become one of hair metal's biggest power ballads.

1985 **1986** **1987** **1988** **1989**

February 18, 1987: Poison issue the quintessential party rock anthem "Talk Dirty to Me" as a single from their debut album.

March 1987: Autograph release their third record, *Loud and Clear*. Ozzy and Vince Neil cameo in the video for the title track. It's followed by an official breakup in 1989.

March 3, 1987: Bon Jovi score a third smash hit from *Slippery When Wet* with "Wanted Dead or Alive."

BOBBY DALL (BASSIST, POISON):

["Talk Dirty to Me"] was actually the song that got CC DeVille the job in the band. We had just lost our guitar player after moving to Los Angeles. We had been out there for about a year, and our guitar player had left, and we were auditioning guitar players in L.A. Amongst them was Slash, CC, and the third guy was the guy who filled in for Joe Perry in Aerosmith. Those were the three guys we had narrowed it down to. And obviously the Aerosmith guy and Slash, I had the utmost respect for, but CC DeVille came through the door and he's this obnoxious, rude, Brooklyn loudmouth [laughs], in-your-face kind of guy. And he played a little ditty for us and that song turned into "Talk Dirty to Me." So that song originated with CC DeVille and I think it's one of the quintessential rock 'n' roll songs of our genre. You know, Poison gets slagged for having the makeup or whatever, but if that song had been done by . . . what was the band out of England? If that song had been done by the Sex Pistols, it would've been a punk anthem. And the fact it was done by Poison maybe took a bit of respect away from it.

IAN ASTBURY (VOCALIST, THE CULT):

Electric was very interesting because it was one of Rick Rubin's first records. It was very educational for both of us. We were very much part of the Def Jam family at that time, like around the Beastie Boys, LL Cool J, Run-D.M.C. We were staying in New York and we did it in 1986 at Electric Ladyland Studios, and we actually recorded the album twice. That was the second time we recorded it. We recorded the album in England in the summer of '86 and we didn't like it, so we went to New York to do it. The first time it was recorded with Steve Brown, who did the *Love* album and we thought it was kind of wimpy. When we hooked up with Rick, I mean, Rick was really into AC/DC. I was more into the Stones, actually. But Rick was really into AC/DC so we kind of ended up with that really kind of riff-oriented thing. I mean, to me punk was always about evolving and changing. The thing about *Electric* was, if you consider when it came out, recorded in '86, and out in early '87, there was no one else making records like us. It was pre–Guns N' Roses, pre–Jane's Addiction, pre-Soundgarden, pre- all those bands. We were the first one to do it. We were the first ones to make the transition from truly an alternative, independent band into a

1980   **1981**   **1982**   **1983**   **1984**

mainstream alternative act, bordering on like a hard rock act. And because of that, we suffered the slings and arrows of anything that is visionary. We get it all in the back and then everyone else reaps the rewards. That's what happened on several occasions.

TOM ZUTAUT
(ON FELLOW GEFFEN A&R MAN JOHN KALODNER):
His skill was basically taking existing bands and reconfiguring them. So he would get this guy from this band and put him in this band and it would be like a supergroup, like Asia. Aerosmith was a mess because Steven Tyler and Joe Perry hated each other, and John was involved in getting those guys back together and getting them reenergized and reinventing Aerosmith. And ultimately he turned them into a pop band. John had a great ear for rock music that could cross over into pop formats and sell millions of records. And he would introduce a Diane Warren to Aerosmith and they would have a huge song that was in a movie. And he resurrected Cher's career, even though she's not metal. He had this real knack for taking people who are washed-up and over with and reinventing them. Like Whitesnake, for instance, was a band who had a couple of obscure records in England and nothing was happening. And John was able to make them one of the biggest bands in the '80s by sort of reinventing them and working with them to find better songs and cowriters and make better records with better producers, and not letting them record until they had enough good songs, and basically helping mold them into a more commercial sound from their more rootsy blues sound.

April 6, 1987: Even intellectual post-punk band The Cult succumb to the charms of shiny stadium rock, completely reengineering their sound for the big, dumb, lovable *Electric* album.

April 7 1987: Whitesnake's self-titled album finds Coverdale in full glam mode, with huge hair, all the posturing, the fashion models in videos, and bona fide power ballads in "Is This Love" and "Here I Go Again." To make the record, Coverdale fires his less photogenic British band for a new gang of world-beaters. The album goes 8x platinum in the United States.

April 9, 1987: Whitesnake issue blues behemoth "Crying in the Rain" as a single.

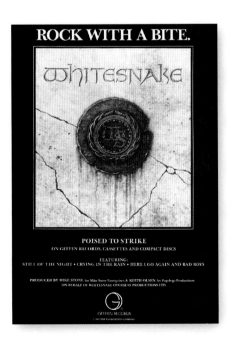

1985   **1986**   **1987**   **1988**   **1989**

NEIL MURRAY (EX-BASSIST, WHITESNAKE):

I think John would have basically said to David Coverdale, sometime in '84, early '85, there's a huge gap in the market in the States for a Zeppelin-type group, something a bit more hard-hitting but without being very kind of Van Halen-ish. So it was a fine balance, hearkening back and being up-to-date at the same time. Like "Here I Go Again" was mostly [ex-guitarist] Bernie Marsden's song from *Saints and Sinners*, which we did in '81 and it came out in '82. Once again Kalodner definitely decided that this was going to be a mega-smash if you re-recorded it. So we re-recorded it for the album and he still wasn't really happy with it so they re-recorded it again in what is more of a remix version but it was in reality a total re-recording with various session guys. And this was after myself and [guitarist] John Sykes had parted company with David. So the version that everybody knows is a very slick production and it certainly sounded great at that time. If you listen back to the original version, it sounds possibly raw and unfinished. But it's always been a really good song, and that's the most important thing you've always got to have. The production is always just the icing on the cake.

DAVID COVERDALE:

"Crying in the Rain" was a big old blues opus, and another one that was written after the breakup of my first marriage, again written in Portugal, for a contractual album I had to do to get out of my management deal. When I got out of Deep Purple, I had inherited these couple of managers because of extraordinarily long-term contracts and that has led me to believe at that time I had to make a choice between one or the other of the Purple managers. And the one I picked, I never felt comfortable trusting but I was never given any choice. I'll tell you exactly what it was. My daughter, who fortunately is incredibly talented musically, went through a period in her early formative years, four or five years old, of getting hit with bacterial meningitis, Kawasaki syndrome, all of these horrendous killer illnesses, and after that I realized, with all the unhappiness that I had professionally, and disappointment, that that was absolutely no reason to have my head in my hands with that "What am I going to do?" scenario. When you see a helpless child ill, really all you have is the talent of the doctors and prayers to God for her recovery. I came out of her illness with the balls to turn around and say this means nothing to me, I want out. And at that time I was in the middle of a record and nobody knew how to finish it, other than myself. So that was the only ace I held: to be able to get out of those contracts.

1980   **1981**   **1982**   **1983**   **1984**

TOMMY LEE (DRUMMER, MÖTLEY CRÜE):

Myself and Nikki wrote that song. At that time, we were touring so much and I think we must have visited every single strip club on the planet and we were like, "You know what? We gotta write about this. We have to write a song about that experience." And the title was, like, you're driving down the street and you always see "Girls, Girls, Girls" in neon lights and it's, like, "Okay, let's do it."

May 11, 1987: Mötley Crüe issue the title track to their *Girls, Girls, Girls* album as an advance single. The gritty rocker becomes infamous as the quintessential hair metal stripper tune.

1985   **1986**   **1987**   **1988**   **1989**

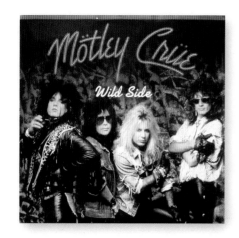

May 15 1987: Mötley Crüe issue their fourth album, *Girls, Girls, Girls*, which eventually sells 4x platinum, just like its predecessor.

Tommy Lee

NIKKI SIXX (BASSIST, MÖTLEY CRÜE):

Later, with [producer] Tom Werman, he kinda took on a bit of that Roy Thomas Baker. You know, all of a sudden he started producing all these L.A. bands and he started becoming quite hot. And we did [1985's] *Theatre of Pain*, which was really a fucking mess. It's just a pile of rubbish, the whole fucking record, with a few moments of maybe brilliance. And because he was the guy who did *Shout at the Devil*, he didn't really know how to control us, or to do what it is we needed to do to make the follow-up to *Shout at the Devil*. And *Girls, Girls, Girls*, he, by then, was just as fucked-up as we were. And that was just a fucking abortion, in my opinion. We really produced that record on our own, because it was more of a lifestyle record. We just kind of brought the lifestyle and put it on tape. With a band like Mötley Crüe, it's like trying to break a horse. You need to know when to let the horse kick and you need to know when to lay in and not let it get away with bullshit. There were times when we needed for him to have a stronger personality. Much as what Bob Rock had. Bob Rock was able to let us be a band, but at the same time be, like, "You know what? It's not good enough and we're not going to go home until it's done." That's what we needed after doing *Theatre of Pain* and *Girls, Girls, Girls*.

NIKKI SIXX:

[*Girls, Girls, Girls*] was a direct rebellion against *Theatre of Pain*. It's what "Dope Show" [*sic*] is for Marilyn Manson, against *Antichrist Superstar*. You can see the parallel . . . with what Marilyn Manson is doing now. They're doing the same thing. They are rebelling against themselves. I think we were getting so much heat for focusing more on the way we looked. So it was, like, *Girls, Girls, Girls*, we decided, you know what? Let's just go leather and motorcycles, because we were all into that. We were like a gang. And don't forget, there was high drug addiction at that time, although we all bottomed out at different times.

VINCE NEIL (VOCALIST, MÖTLEY CRÜE):

If you take those records out and look at them, what we went from, I'm wearing pink on the back of *Theatre*. And in a sense, *Theatre of Pain* was a rebellion against *Shout at the Devil*. I bottomed out near the beginning of *Theatre of Pain*, end of *Shout*. And Nikki was at the end of *Theatre*. No, it was the middle of *Girls*. We had just finished the U.S. tour, and we had to cancel the other part.

NIKKI SIXX:

And Tommy is right about the same time, near the end of Girls. Mick was the same thing. That's when we all kind of decided to reevaluate what the band was all about musically and emotionally. We'd been strung out and fucked up for ten years. Hard. Not kidding. It's like there's kidding. There's like . . . Poison? Like kidding, like, "Hey let's go have a party." And then there's, like, puking up bad smack at a five-hundred-dollar-a-night hotel room in New York City ten minutes before you have to go on stage.

TOMMY LEE:

["Wild Side" is] one that Nikki and I wrote. That was my first . . . I sort of brought in my new technology to Mötley Crüe. At that time, in 1984, is when I bought my first Macintosh and I was experimenting with recording direct to disc and using sequencers. So that [makes machine gun sounds] in that track, I sort of brought that in and I was trying to get Mötley Crüe to plunge forward, mine new territory with some sequencers and some electronics.

ROBB REINER (DRUMMER, ANVIL):

[Vocalist and guitarist Steve "Lips" Kudlow] calls the album a bit of the disaster because we had tainted the image visually, with our hair all done up and shit, all that red and black leather. I mean, three years earlier we had done *Forged in Fire*. That's what Anvil had meant at that point. And now we come out with *Strength of Steel*—it just didn't work. I think the music is actually quite outstanding on that album. It was the image that I think really fucking bothered Lips the most. Musically I guess we could have been heavier, not like we didn't know how to do that. But we chose to do this—that was the package. I don't want to say we were trying to go commercial, but that was our attempt at it.

DAVID COVERDALE:

"Still of the Night," a quick scenario: Many, many years ago I was going through my mother's attic in the north of England, and I was going through all these old work tapes from the Purple days. So I grabbed them and threw them in my bag and listened to them. A lot of it was crap, but it was very funny for me to hear the journey from the seeds of songs that became ultimate Purple staples. And I found a demo that Ritchie Blackmore had given me and I thought, well, that's an interesting riff. So I took that and changed it around completely to the point where it had absolutely nothing to do with the initial inspiration. But credit where credit is due. And then I presented my take on this riff to John Sykes, who put a great attitude on it and took it further as only he could. There is lot of Led Zeppelin comparison there, which I don't have a problem with, because Zeppelin was fucking

May 21, 1987: Speed metal pioneers Anvil try their hand at hair metal with *Strength of Steel*.

June 6, 1987: Heart succeed with a second hair metal album, *Bad Animals*, which goes 3x platinum in the United States. Outside writers are everywhere on the Ron Nevison–produced record.

June 7, 1987: Whitesnake issue "Still of the Night" as a single from their *Whitesnake* album. Although not particularly hair metal in character, the heavy metal anthem is nonetheless a huge classic of the times.

1985   **1986**   **1987**   **1988**   **1989**

June 17, 1987: Great White issue their fourth album, *Once Bitten...*, which sells double platinum on the strength of the single "Rock Me."

June 20, 1987: The annual Texxas Jam features Farrenheit, Tesla, Poison, Whitesnake, Aerosmith, and Boston, all new hair metal bands or old bands participating in the form.

June 21, 1987: New York's White Lion issue their major label debut, *Pride*, on Atlantic, after a few setbacks in their four-year history. It goes double platinum in the United States, remaining in the Billboard Top 200 for a full year. "Wait" proves a poppy metal hit; "When the Children Cry" is a quasi-ballad with a positive message that was a moderate hit. Guitarist Vito Bratta is recognized as a shredder, and the band is one of the rare East Coast experiences to participate in the hair metal era.

marvelous and continues to resonate. But the huge influence on that is one of my favorite songs from my childhood, "Jailhouse Rock," Elvis Presley, and another huge influence was the Jeff Beck Group, when Rod Stewart was singing with them. And part of the atmospheric thing was an inspiration from a track of his called "Rice Pudding." I tell you, I've played that song all over the world and nobody had a problem with it other than Robert Plant [laughs]. And of course a couple of years later I have Page playing it, going, "This is fucking hard!"

NEIL MURRAY:

That was definitely a kind of commission by John Kalodner and Geffen Records to write something that was going to be very Zeppelin-like. And it's certainly obvious from how that came out. But the annoying thing was then we got criticized for being a kind of Zeppelin soundalike, which wasn't the case at all. There wasn't much else on the record that sounded like Zeppelin. The whole album took an awful long time to record but certainly we could tell that that was going to be an important track. The whole center section of it at first was kind of going in the direction of "Whole Lotta Love," the whole freak-out psychedelic part. And it became slightly more structured in a sense. I came up with the very simple chord structure for that middle section which builds up and builds up. The whole thing had so many guitar tracks and keyboard tracks and redone vocal parts, it changed quite a bit from the original state until it actually got released.

JACK RUSSELL (VOCALIST, GREAT WHITE):

Those were great days, a lot of fun. We were playing huge arenas and getting platinum albums and Grammy nominations. But right now, where I'm at in my life, I look at my walls and see the platinum albums there, the Grammy nominations and compare them to what I'm doing now with my life, with my music—they're just stuff that collects dust. They don't mean as much as they used to.

MIKE TRAMP (VOCALIST, WHITE LION):

Pride had sold past three million, you know, just in America alone. But you never really get the true numbers. But, you know, we sold over a million records, and that was unbelievable, and then when it went past two million, then you started entering a completely different world. I mean, we toured with Kiss, Aerosmith, but touring with AC/DC was the best, because it was so consistent, always sold-out shows. And AC/DC was so fit as a band, they were unmovable, there was no doubt of who they were. There was no fighting the fact that they were AC/DC, the band they always had been. They weren't in fear of us or anything and it didn't matter how good we were, they came on and they played "Highway to Hell" and that said it all [laughs]. It just is what it is. I would stand out there every night and watch it.

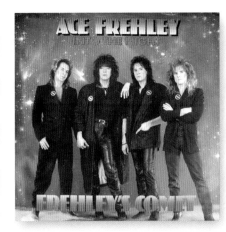

NOW THE FUR IS GONNA FLY!
FASTER PUSSYCAT is on the prowl.
Sassy, sexy, spittin' fire and kickin' ass.
Bluesy rock-metal that's gonna hiss its way into your head.

Faster Pussycat, featuring "Don't Change That Song,"
"Bathroom Wall" and "Babylon."
Produced by Ric Browde

HOWLIN' AT YOU...ON ELEKTRA SUPERIOR-QUALITY
CASSETTES, COMPACT DISCS AND RECORDS.

DUFF MCKAGAN (BASSIST, GUNS N' ROSES):

Paul Stanley from Kiss wanted to do [*Appetite for Destruction*]. But he wanted Steven [Adler] to add all these drums and wanted to change the songs and we were like "Fuck that," you know? And there was another guy, Spencer Proffer, that big drum sound. We had gone in and done some demos with him. He was a nice guy but he put Steven on a click track, number one, and we did "Night Train," I think, and it sounded so sterile. It didn't sound like us at all, his big drum sound and all that crap. So we didn't do that. And finally Clink came down to our rehearsals, and he was a guy who had engineered a couple of Triumph records and nobody had heard of Mike Clink. But he came down and recorded us on his eight-track and it sounded killer! He didn't try to change the songs; he didn't try to do anything. And he says, "Well, it sounds good. Do you want your record to sound anything like this?" And he just played us back. "Okay, perfect."

June 21, 1987: Keel issue their self-titled fourth album, the cover of which eschews the band's logo for a tough yet glam band shot.

June 21, 1987: Canada's Helix issue *Wild in the Streets*, their last with any major push in the United States. Capitol would drop the band after the album's poor No. 179 showing on the Billboard charts.

June 23, 1987: Sammy Hagar, a toiler at melodic hard rock ever since he left Montrose back in 1974, issues his only solo album while a member of Van Halen. *I Never Said Goodbye* (a.k.a. *Sammy Hagar*) naturally fits the hair metal world, particularly given Hagar's pioneering of the power ballad.

July 7, 1987: Ace Frehley issues *Frehley's Comet*. Frehley draws visual and stylistic comparisons to the Vinnie Vincent Invasion, hair band assemblage of another ex-Kiss guitarist.

July 7, 1987: Faster Pussycat issue their self-titled debut, beating Guns N' Roses by two weeks with a certain sleaze metal look and, frankly, a similar sound.

1985   **1986**   **1987**   **1988**   **1989**

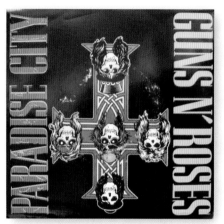

July 21, 1987: Guns N' Roses issue *Appetite for Destruction*, which goes on to sell 28 million copies worldwide. GN'R become the lead example of the scruffy, down 'n' dirty hair band look, alongside lesser examples like Skid Row, Love/Hate, Seahags, and Junkyard.

DUFF MCKAGAN
(ON RECORDING *APPETITE FOR DESTRUCTION*):

We didn't know enough about studios to know to put a fuckin' vibe into a studio. Really, our main concern was having some booze. You know, our main concern was getting songs down. We were really serious about our music. As long as we had a couple fifths of something. Food wasn't really an issue. We really didn't care about what anything looked like. We didn't have naked girl pictures up or anything like that. I think we had a bunch of nasty magazines and stuff. This was a really nice studio. We didn't know you could put up anything of your own there. Had we known that, you know, we might have done something.

SLASH:

I mean, *Appetite* is *Appetite* [laughs]. That's like a signature stamp of a band in a period or in a place where it was that. And it's pretty inimitable. It is what it is, and we're the only guys who could have done it. It was at that time, and we were all really young and it's got a certain raw aggression to it. I don't think the playing is really all that proficient on it, but it's got a certain kind of fucking aggressive, in-your-face sonic thing to it. It is what it is. So I'm a fan of it, probably not the way that other people are. It's just something that, when I hear it, it sounds cool and everything is in its place and, mistakes and all, it sounds good.

DUFF MCKAGAN:

[Slash] wears his emotions on his sleeve when he plays guitar. You know, there's a guy like Zakk [Wylde] who will just rip your head off. And Zakk is an amazing guitar player, no doubt about it. That goes without saying. Slash . . . like my wife, on the way back from Vancouver one night, she's saying to me, "What's the difference between a Slash solo and a Zakk solo?" And I said, "Zakk will rip your head off and amaze you with technical ability. There is perhaps nobody better at it. Of course, Zakk will let you know that. He'll be the first one to let you know that and that's all right, he's got confidence in himself. Slash is more, I don't know, more of a feel guy. Slash can make you cry with what he's playing."

1980   **1981**   **1982**   **1983**   **1984**

NUNO BETTENCOURT (GUITARIST, EXTREME):

I think the first band we really noticed that was kind of doing less of what maybe Poison and Warrant were doing was Guns N' Roses. I think Guns N' Roses were going back to the Aerosmith side of things, that version of it, which was definitely more punk and rock combined. I think that was the first hint.

NIC ADLER (OWNER, THE ROXY):

I was born the same year as the Roxy, so I've only always known it as rock 'n' roll. I've obviously seen it change over the years, but my first memories were Guns N' Roses, Mötley Crüe. I would get picked up from grade school by one of the girls who worked in the office, and she was Izzy from Guns N' Roses's girlfriend, so she would literally play the demo tape of *Appetite for Destruction* over and over. So those were my earliest memories on the Strip, was being a kid and watching Guns N' Roses sound check, I guess.

PHIL COLLEN (GUITARIST, DEF LEPPARD):

What we'd always done in the past, when [producer] Mutt [Lange] was involved, on *Hysteria*, *Pyromania*, and *Adrenalize*, is we would write the songs and go, "Okay, how do we make it better?" We've gotten a lot of flak for that, because sometimes it's taken us forever. You go back in the studio and you rewrite, and you have people knocking on the door, "Guys, what's going on?! Are you guys finished?" "No, no, we're making it better!" And that's the main thing really. It's not the time or the production, it's making the song right. And that goes for everything—the backing vocals, everything. Playing everything separately, because we don't play as a live band.

RICK ALLEN (DRUMMER, DEF LEPPARD):

When you listen back to when those records were made, I mean, it would appear to be that ProTools was made for Mutt Lange. Because he would dissect songs, and sort of hone the good parts of the songs, until the good parts were as good as they could possibly be. And that process itself can sometimes feel a little bit contrived.

PHIL COLLEN (ON HEAVY METAL):

We never really considered ourselves a heavy metal band. We've always considered ourselves a rock band in the tradition of like the Stones or Queen or The Who or Van Halen. So I think the guitars are important and the attitude. Like I say, you can be a pop group that plays a rock song, but that's not us at all. We're really a rock band that crosses over into the pop thing. I really do think there's a difference. Especially in the '80s, you had a lot of a pop groups that would put on a fuzz box and go, "Now we're a rock band." And it's, like, "No it's not real." We were, and are, a real, sweaty rock band that crossed over into the other side of it.

August 3, 1987: Def Leppard issue the long-awaited *Hysteria*, featuring an übersynthetic, soulless production that helped hasten the demise of hair metal (and which has not aged well). The album takes three years to make and, for all the wait, features vapid lyrics and every hair metal cliché in the book (and this from a British/Irish band). It sells 20 million copies worldwide.

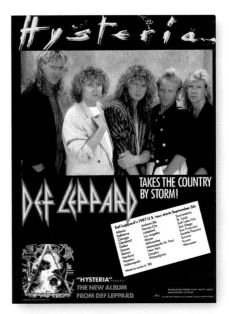

1985   **1986**   **1987**   **1988**   **1989**

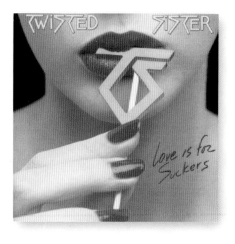

August 13, 1987: Twisted Sister, long past expiry date by not adapting to the evolving hair metal sound, issue their last album, *Love Is for Suckers.* Producer is hair metal stalwart Beau Hill.

August 18, 1987: Aerosmith come back strong, utilizing an uncomfortable number of hair band tactics but not succumbing totally to new trends. *Permanent Vacation* finds the band recording with Bruce Fairbairn in Vancouver and calling upon the services of a number of outside writers. Worst travesty, however, is the power ballad "Angel," which lacks so much Aerosmith charm it could have shown up on any number of big records from the era. "Angel" is cowritten by music guru Desmond Child. "Rag Doll," "Permanent Vacation," and "Dude (Looks Like a Lady)" are also somewhat hair metal–bound. Child cowrites elsewhere on the album, along with Holly Knight and Jim Vallance. The album goes 5x platinum.

DEREK SHULMAN (A&R MAN, COMPARING DEF LEPPARD TO BON JOVI):

They were very similar and very competitive in a lot of ways. Because they were at Polygram at the same time. . . . But whereas Def Leppard had incredible management, great songs, and had the Mutt Lange production, what [vocalist] Joe Elliott didn't have, and even though I thought they had great songs that were still very viable and vital, was the driving force that Jon Bon Jovi still has. I mean, not *had*, still *has*, and continues to have, and drives to be relevant in every decade, whatever it is. So I think they knew where they sat. But the drive was to get them beyond just being an '80s band. They wanted to be current in whatever era they were in, and not just current and try to be emo or whatever, be current in the Jon Bon Jovi guise.

PHIL COLLEN (ON *HYSTERIA*):

I think because we had experienced all the highs on *Pyromania*, and all the lows of, like, [drummer] Rick [Allen] having his accident during the *Hysteria* sessions, when that album came out it was a real relief. It had taken so long and we were really pleased with that. Again, we had taken it a stage further. It was combining different elements. Like, *Pyromania* was the ultimate rock album, I think. But [*Hysteria*] had different elements. There was stuff like The Police and The Fixx going around, and we introduced those kinds of guitars to it. We brought the clean guitars, the Andy Summers thing, which no one had ever done. It's right across the board . . . African Burundi drums on "Rockit." We've got crystal-clear guitars, and then the vocals, but done with conviction. It was kind of a standout album at the time, with a lot of other bands using the samples, the sounds, and all the technology. So again, we absolutely got that one right.

JAY JAY FRENCH (GUITARIST, TWISTED SISTER):

We were breaking up at the time. It was a horrible experience. There's my comment about that record [laughs]. I have no idea if I'm on that record or not, to be honest with you. I have no recollection. If you follow the history of most bands, you'll find that they struggle, and then they have their career album, and then, you know, decline. I have to think that MTV helped destroy the band to a degree. We became a caricature. The band lost focus of who we were, which was a great bar band, first and foremost. And it became, more or less, a vaudeville show after a while and lost its intensity.

DEE SNIDER (VOCALIST, TWISTED SISTER):

I agree with that, although I never heard him say that before. Kiss would never be the Kiss we know if MTV had existed. With Kiss, if you wanted to go see the band, you had to go see them in concert. You had a picture in a magazine, but if you wanted to go see what they were all about, you had to go to the concert. With Twisted Sister, we did a live concert which they showed eighteen times in a year, the Twisted Sister *Stay Hungry* tour. Comedians would say, about Johnny Carson, that going on Johnny Carson was the greatest thing that happened, but you had to burn your material the next day. Because it was played out. You couldn't go into a club and do the bit you did on Carson. Everybody saw it! So here we were, going from town to town . . . [MTV] gave you that exposure, that big amped-up launch, but they also totally exposed it. They pulled the curtain back and showed Oz.

JOE PERRY:

With *Permanent Vacation*, there was an energy around us. It kind of matched up, because here we were, old dogs, going fifteen, twenty years of being in the business, and I felt we were reaching a creative stride there, after all the trials and tribulations and all the personal bullshit we had been through. But I think [1989's] *Pump* is probably my favorite record because we were on a roll.

MIKE FRASER (ENGINEER):

Permanent Vacation was a lot of fun to do, just because I guess these guys are fresh out of rehab and sort of rediscovering themselves. I know they kept saying, "Wow, this is so great to be able to actually do music and to know what you're doing." [laughs] Because before they'd be in such a haze that people would just tell them, "Okay, go out there and sing. Go out there and play," and they didn't even know what they ended up with until they heard the record later. So I remember that being really exhilarating. I remember one night, Bob Rock and I, at the beginning of *Permanent Vacation*, I think it was a Saturday night or something, and these guys walk in in their long trench coats and stuff, and we thought, "Wow, how great to have Aerosmith here on a Saturday night, you know?" [laughs] But yeah, they'd have plenty of arguments amongst themselves. You know, Steven drove Joey Kramer nuts most of the time. But it was all part of the creative flow. There was never any harsh or bad feelings, as far as I remember. I guess Steven's a bit of a drummer, too, so he's always on his case. What was it, "'Rag Doll," over and over and over again, and then finally Steven says, "Well, if you don't get it this next take, we're using a drum machine." So we ended up using a drum machine [laughs]. But I think at the end of the day we had Joey go out and play over the top of the drum machine, just to get the more real toms and cymbals and stuff like that.

August 21, 1987: *Wildside*, Loverboy's last album before a long hiatus, and last on the glam gravy train, goes only gold (though inside of three months), whereas each of the band's albums thus far had been multiplatinum. (Of note, Mötley Crüe had a hit single called "Wild Side," also in '87.)

September 1987: Warrant record a demo tape in hopes of signing with Prince's label, Paisley Park. Columbia eventually signs the band. Before a record is made, the band play dates with D'Molls and Britny Fox.

September 5, 1987: San Francisco's Y&T issue *Contagious*, a very high-gloss, corporate-sounding, full-on hair metal album. They had been building up to this through 1984's dumbed-down *In Rock We Trust* and 1985's *Down for the Count*. The band's five albums from '76 to '83 explored various forms of more traditional hard rock, but now, on Geffen, the coats of shine intensify.

September 5, 1987: Alice Cooper issues his second corporate hair metal kiddie rock album, *Raise Your Fist and Yell*. Again, the album is cowritten with Kane Roberts.

1985 **1986** **1987** **1988** **1989**

September 18, 1987: Kiss issue *Crazy Nights*, which, despite its critical drubbing and weak production from Ron Nevison, returns the band to platinum status, proving that hair metal mania rewards all comers. Also indicative of the times, there are many cowrites with song doctors, including Desmond Child and Diane Warren.

October 3, 1987: Guns N' Roses issue *Appetite for Destruction*'s lead track, "Welcome to the Jungle," as a single.

October 12, 1987: Dee Snider announces his departure from Twisted Sister, two days after the last tour date for the *Love is for Suckers* album.

TOM ZUTAUT (A&R MAN):
I tried to stay out of it. To me, Aerosmith ceased to be a rock 'n' roll band when they started writing songs with Diane Warren. They turned into a pop band. And you could still go to the shows and have a good time and stuff, but I think when these bands started using outside writers, they were turning into pop bands, and that was the end of that. None of my bands ever did that. If they couldn't write a great song, I didn't let them make a record. I just kept them out of the studio until they had ten good songs.

RICK ALLEN (ON OUTSIDE SONGWRITERS):
It makes the record company feel as if they came up with the ideas. No, I mean, that's basically it. You go, "Well, if you can't make our songs hits, you're going to have to go find somebody who can." It's almost appeasing them. It's like going, "Okay, you guys feel as though you can't do it. . . ." It's weird to me, because we've done it so often in the past, and I think it's down to who's working with the company at that particular moment in time, and really, who's interested. If you don't have any interest from the top down, I think you're shit out of luck.

DUFF MCKAGAN (ON "WELCOME TO THE JUNGLE"):
That was a song written about a time when Axl had hitchhiked, either in a part of Queens or Brooklyn or maybe even the Bronx, where these little kids were swinging sticks at him [laughs]. He found himself in this place where he just shouldn't have been. And then there were some old guys, you know, like, "You're in the jungle, you're gonna die." He's like, "Fuck, let's get out of here."

JERRY DIXON (BASSIST, WARRANT, ON THE L.A. HAIR SCENE):
By the time we hit the scene, Ratt had already got signed, Mötley Crüe had already got signed, Guns N' Roses had gotten signed, Poison just got signed, and then we came out. So 1984, '85, it kind of sucked because we missed all that, but once all of those bands got signed, they were out of our hair. They were out making records and touring. It kind of opened the door for us to be able to do what we did and take that market share and go in and sell out all these venues. By the time we got signed, our first record didn't come out until 1989. Theoretically, we're not even an '80s band! We were like the last ones left, those beaten stepchildren going, "Wait a minute, we've gotta get signed!" Yeah. I think we were almost the last band of that era to get signed.

JERRY DIXON (ON GLAM FASHION):
From the neck down you looked tough, and then from the neck up [laughs], you look like a drag queen. You know, with leathers on [laughs]. It was looking for the best thing you could do at that point to draw people into your show. And you know, we found out. We did this flyer where we were in bathroom stalls and girls were on their knees,

1980   **1981**   **1982**   **1983**   **1984**

simulating oral sex, and that show sold out. And we started taking over the reins on the Strip. It was like, "Wow, okay," and then the light bulb went off. The more shocking you could be, the more people would come to your show. And if you didn't do anything, you might've been The Beatles, and nobody would've walked in to see you at that point. That's not what it was about. The vibe, it was a lifestyle, and it was just over the top—the most outrageous band won.

DON DOKKEN (VOCALIST, DOKKEN):

The "Back for the Attack" sessions weren't good, and I don't think that's a very good album. I think there were two or three good songs, which were the singles, and there was a lot of filler. It's a long album and there's a lot of masturbatory guitar playing. There was a lot of cocaine around. That's when the things started with, "I don't want Don in the studio." I submitted my songs from my house and they learned them, and I wasn't even around for rehearsals, and I wasn't around for the mixes either. We were already on tour with Aerosmith when they mixed it. One of the funniest things we ever did was our last night with Aerosmith. Aerosmith had that song "Angel," and we took George, which isn't something he would usually do because he is such a serious guy, and we . . . bought some wings at a prop shop and we gave him a pillow with feathers and we hoisted him up with a harness and when they sang "Angel," we hoisted him up and he was flying back and forth over the stage and throwing feathers down on the stage. And the guys in Aerosmith just totally cracked up. . . . But the funny thing was (a) that George did it, which we were all shocked about, but then (b) we left him there. [laughs] . . . So he was like, "Okay, we're done, you can let me down," and then we just left him up there. And the last song they did, "Dude (Looks Like a Lady)," we put [drummer] Mick [Brown] in a full-blown red sequin dress, in drag. Our makeup girl put him in drag, full-on make-up, high heels, the stockings, the whole nine yards. He looked just like a chick, boobs, bra, and I swear, for about five seconds when he was walking out, Steven Tyler thought he was a chick. And he went up and started grabbing and hugging Steven Tyler, and then I think Steven started to realize that that was one ugly chick.

DON DOKKEN:

Mick made a comment one night, kind of a naïve comment, [that] if you sleep with a good-looking girl, a model, you get AIDS, if you sleep with a ho backstage, you get AIDS. We were talking about that and I said, "AIDS doesn't discern between good-looking girls and fat, ugly chicks." And this is all around '85, '86, so that partly inspired the lyrics for "Kiss of Death." It's about the kiss of death. It's, "Oh, she looks bitchin', she looks beautiful, gorgeous. She says, 'I've never been backstage before.'" You take her back to the hotel room, and you get it.

November 27, 1987: Dokken issue *Back for the Attack*, their last studio album until a fragile reunion in 1995. "Mr. Scary," an instrumental guitar workout, becomes a signature shredder track and sticks as George Lynch's nickname.

November 27, 1987: W.A.S.P. issue a live album called *Live . . .in the Raw*.

1985   **1986**   **1987**   **1988**   **1989**

1988

NOT THE MOST EXCITING YEAR for hair metal releases. With most bands out touring and cashing in, the quality of many albums, not surprisingly, is on the wane. It's also time for sophomore releases from new world-beaters and ridiculed hair farmers Poison and Cinderella, as well as another light 'n' fluffy offering from Van Hagar called OU812. Scorpions issue an overworked let-down called Savage Amusement, very hair in its cynical motivation and execution. Dokken goes with a bloated live album and GN'R issues an odds 'n' sodser to keep the party going. And boy does it, the Gunners being the belle of the ball at this point—the point being an uneasy and wobbly "maturity" for the form, more like flabby middle age. Elsewhere, L.A. Guns and Winger issue debuts, each band being a Frankenstein's monster of hair metal conceits but with angles: L.A. Guns being punky, Winger being virtuosic.

Kingdom Come's Rick Steier. © *Rod Dysinger*

1988: Black 'N Blue issue their fourth and last album, *In Heat*. On the cover, the band is pictured from the chest up, naked, flowing locks everywhere, backlit by fire. Guitarist Tommy Thayer's next significant gig will be Kiss.

Early 1988: Love/Hate now have most of the songs that will comprise their seminal 1990 album, *Blackout in the Red Room*, but are repeatedly overlooked for a deal.

JAIME ST. JAMES (VOCALIST, BLACK 'N BLUE):

In Heat was probably our least successful [album], because by that point Geffen was not putting much effort into us. Just kind of put it out there and see what it does, kind of thing. But I think it's a strong record. We got a bit more back to production, rather than the raw thing. Once again, there are couple ideas that went awry. It's going to happen on every record where we try things.

January 4, 1988: L.A. Guns' self-titled debut is released on Polydor. After the gold success of their second album, this one gets dragged to gold as well. Much of the record is written by the band's previous singer Paul Black.

1988: New Orleans's Lillian Axe issue their self-titled album on MCA, which is much more thoughtful and musical than their pleasure-and-pain hair band name would suggest.

1988: L'Amour East, in Elmhurst, Queens, New York, ends its five year run as the hair metal capital of the East Coast, leaning toward the lighter metal in comparison to the more famous Brooklyn L'Amour.

PHIL LEWIS (VOCALIST, L.A. GUNS):

I went up to the mic and tested it, you know, "Check one, two." Tracii looked up from his guitar and said, "OK, you've got the gig." That was my audition. It was only when I came over that I found out the singer was a junkie at the time and he actually nodded off in the president of Polygram's like second or third meeting to get signed. And I mean, no one's going to go with that.

STEVE RILEY (DRUMMER, L.A. GUNS):

Tracii was really good friends with Johnny [Thunders] and always looked up to him, and I knew Johnny also. We definitely have a connection. That was basic raw, raw rock 'n' roll and we absolutely recognize them and loved them. Again, it wasn't super-popular or big chartbusters, but it was all stuff that we latched onto. If you take something from the New York Dolls and mix it up with Led Zeppelin, you can come in the middle and get a really nice feel for music.

PHIL LEWIS (ON MOVING FROM THE UK TO L.A.):

It was definitely a challenge. The music part, that was good, because in music, we all speak the same language. I was influenced by American music at the time anyway. The problem was, I'd been out of Girl for a few years and was doing a lot more technical stuff with Bernie Torme, and when I got the gig in Guns, they kind of wanted Phil from Girl, and I kind of moved on from that. It was definitely a huge culture shock. I arrive at LAX with two hundred bucks and a hair dryer and wondered where it's going to go from there. And I lived in a motel for the first couple of months. I just felt that I was the right guy for the gig. And I don't get homesick. Going from London to L.A. was interesting, but they're two metropolises and there are a lot of parallels. But when I started to see the heart of the country, then it became very, very obvious how different the people who I was singing to were from me [laughs].

1980   **1981**   **1982**   **1983**   **1984**

BILLY SHEEHAN (BASSIST, DAVID LEE ROTH):

Skyscraper was an overdubs studio album. For *Eat 'Em and Smile*, we played together in the same room—it was a band album, Ted Templeman produced it and it was really awesome. For *Skyscraper*, it was two twenty-four-track machines linked together, MIDI this, MIDI that, computers, overdubs, overdubs, overdubs. The band never really played together in the same room. The drums got laid down, and I'd come in one day and put on my bass parts, and then Steve came in and did his guitar stuff and then Dave did his vocals. It wasn't a band anymore. So to me, the album didn't have the same vibe. I thought the material could have been really good. If you would only take that material and add the soul of really playing it, I think it would have happened. "Hot Dog and a Shake," I love that song, but there's a few errors in it. First of all, the chorus has too many words in it. There are so many words going on it's impossible to sing, especially live, where things tend to be a little faster anyway. So a lot of that stuff was never really thought out when the songs were designed. For me, a regular ol' rock 'n' roll band, playing in bars . . . if that's what you all are, that's what you should be.

January 26, 1988: David Lee Roth issues his second solo album, *Skyscraper*, featuring feel-good hair band hit "Just like Paradise."

DOUG PINNICK (BASSIST AND COVOCALIST, KING'S X):

Out of the Silent Planet changed the rock world, if I could say that. Because as far as I'm concerned, our record was the first record that was pretty much a complete detuned album. And it had melodies over this detuned kind of thing. And then Soundgarden came out and they were doing pretty much the same thing. So it was a new thing and I think that inspired a whole new generation.

1985   **1986**   **1987**   **1988**   **1989**

144

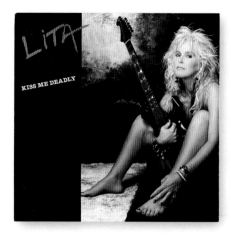

February 2, 1988: Lita Ford issues *Lita*, which features power ballad "Close My Eyes Forever," a duet with Ozzy. "Kiss Me Deadly" is also a hit.

March 25, 1988: Krokus ditch their logo but retain the hair metal, producing their *Heart Attack* album.

March 28, 1988: King's X issue their debut album, *Out of the Silent Planet*. The record is replete with hair metal harmonies and production appointments, but the intelligence of the writing indicates a restlessness within the community.

BEAU HILL
(PRODUCER, ON SEEING WARRANT FOR THE FIRST TIME):
Everybody was scouring California and New York, okay, let's find the next Ratt, and Warrant showed up. Their manager invited me out to a show in the Valley and—the same thing with Ratt—I went and the place was packed. There had to be a couple of thousand kids, and Warrant was on stage, and when I first saw them, they were a little bit corny from my perspective, because they kind of wore rock uniforms where the clothes were all coordinated. I absolutely loved [vocalist] Jani [Lane]. He was very personable on stage, and I always told him he missed his calling in being a Baptist preacher.

1980   **1981**   **1982**   **1983**   **1984**

BEAU HILL (ON WARRANT'S DEBUT):

We were in preproduction and I was listening to the guys, and I went to their manager, and I said, "Look, we're in the era of Warren DeMartini and Eddie Van Halen, the guitar gods, and these guys are not soloing at that level yet, and we need to bring someone in to do the solos." And I did. So I called a band meeting and I told them how I felt, and it was, you know, very open and very honest, and to their credit, they took it in stride, and I'm sure it wasn't a pleasant moment for them, but to their credit, they said, "Okay, we'll try it." And I brought in a guy that I had produced, his second record, a guy named Mike Slamer, British guy . . . and Mike and I had been friends for a long time, and when we were both on the East Coast, anytime I got in the weeds and I needed something done guitar-wise, he was the guy I would call. And I knew his personality would blend with these guys, because he wasn't an egomaniac, and it wasn't like he was going to demean them in any way. And indeed it worked out quite fantastically, because they loved him so much that he wound up teaching them guitar after the record was done. So he taught those guys all the solos that he did, and so that when they played live, they did a pretty damn good job of replicating what Mike did in the studio.

BEAU HILL (ON OUTSIDE WRITERS):

In a perfect world, it would be nice if the bands could write their own stuff. That's part of why you are good enough to be signed in the first place. But, having said that, being on the record side, think of it this way. Most bands have their entire lives to write their first record, then, because of the touring cycles and because the record company wants more product, then you have to come up with a stellar sophomore record, in like the blink of an eye. And so being able to have that breakthrough single became very difficult for a lot of groups. So, you know, you would go to a Diane Warren or a Holly Knight, and start picking through the bones of what they have to offer. And, those two women in particular, are unbelievably talented! I mean, they're just great. And if you are a good producer and you have a really great song, then it's incumbent on you to mold the song and make that architecture work for your act.

RICK NIELSEN (GUITARIST, CHEAP TRICK):

Back in the '80s, we did some stuff where there was definitely some keyboard stuff and some songwriting people that were brought in that, you know, we all cringed. But our manager and the record company people all said, "Oh, this is going to be terrific" and "Some of these [label] guys . . . you know they're going to work this harder because they don't like the other stuff you're doing." It's like, you don't want to do it, but we tried to do it right. But you know, once in a while you do need direction. But we look back now and say, we should've known better.

April–November 1988: Warrant work on their debut album, with producer Beau Hill, famed for his work with Ratt.

April 12, 1988: Cheap Trick get on the glam bandwagon with a pure power ballad called "The Flame," predictably not written by them. In fact, most of the album *Lap of Luxury* is cowritten or written by song doctors. "The Flame" goes to No. 1, and the album goes platinum. "Ghost Town," another ballad, is a cowrite with Dianne Warren.

1985　　　　**1986**　　　　**1987**　　　　**1988**　　　　**1989**

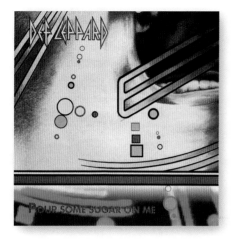

April 16, 1988: Def Leppard issue "Pour Some Sugar on Me," which becomes one of the biggest hair metal anthems of all time. The song, from the eight-month-old *Hysteria* album, reaches No. 2 on Billboard.

April 16, 1988: Scorpions issue the ill-received *Savage Amusement*, a sort of bad corporate rock redux of their smash *Love at First Sting* record, which had marked the band's big shift to dumb rock. The album goes platinum.

RICK ALLEN (DRUMMER, DEF LEPPARD):

["Pour some sugar on me"] was a line Joe came up with and he just kept singing this thing in the studio. And [producer] Mutt [Lange] got to hear it and really, they just based the whole song around the chorus. And the drum rhythm, we actually ripped straight from an LL Cool J song. It just seemed to fit. It's a bit of a silly song, but people seem to jump on it and love it. It was one of the songs responsible for *Hysteria* really going through the roof.

RUDOLF SCHENKER (ON *SAVAGE AMUSEMENT*):

The production wasn't as good as it could have been. Somehow that was one album too much for [producer] Dieter [Dierks]. Because we were very much of the team in the early days, and somehow Dieter had different ideas for *Savage Amusement*. For us it was always important to work as a team, but on that record it was more like a dictatorship. There was maybe too much of a Mutt Lange type of style. He wanted to be the second Mutt Lange, with more production and computer drums and stuff like that. We were not so happy about that, but we found a way to finish it.

MATTHIAS JABS (GUITARIST, SCORPIONS):

The one that took the most time, and wasn't that great anyway, was *Savage Amusement*. That took forever. It had also to do with the producer trying to be Mutt Lange. When Def Leppard took, I think, four years with *Hysteria*, everybody tried to stay four years [laughs]. It was like the battle of the producers and we were unfortunately in the middle of it. And songwriting-wise, it wasn't a great album and it took us like two and a half years. We wasted so much time that I don't even want to remember it.

1980 **1981** **1982** **1983** **1984**

DEREK SHULMAN (A&R MAN):

Dumbing down? Yes and no. I was there for [1982's] *Blackout*, and that was great straight-ahead hard rock. But if you see them play, they're an entertaining band. They're not Pantera, let's put it that way. Pantera was a purist metal/hard rock band, where there was a "fuck you" attitude. Scorpions never had the "fuck you" attitude about them. They wanted hits as well. And it was their idea to do "Rock You Like a Hurricane" and "Wind of Change," "Big City Nights." They wanted that.

ERIC BRITTINGHAM
(BASSIST, CINDERELLA, ON PRODUCER ANDY JOHNS):

Andy Johns, oh man, there's like a million stories with him. He's very eccentric, very passionate, a little too passionate at times [laughs]. He's like a madman, a mad scientist. But he's a great producer, barring none. In my books, he's probably the best engineer/producer out there. He was a maniac at times. He would come into the studio completely drunk off his ass and you're like, "Oh great, here we go," but by the end of the day he got some great shit.

DEREK SHULMAN (ON CINDERELLA'S GUITARIST):

Tom Keifer's an incredible musician and great guy, but unfortunately, even though they had fantastic success, which I was part of, they got tagged into this sort of hair band/glam thing, which was very *au courant* at the time. . . . I'll give you a very small vignette here. Tom, underneath it, wanted to be taken seriously, and should be taken seriously, as a great blues player. He sends me demos from time to time, and I put it on my computer and blasted it, and some kids in my office came in and said, "What is this?! This is unbelievable! Who is this? We should sign them." And I said, "Do you really like this?" These are guys, who are in their early twenties, and they're saying, "This is unbelievable, great blues-influenced rock." And I said, "Well, should I tell you who it is?" "Yeah, we've got to sign them." "They're Cinderella." And they looked at me and said, "Oh, er, right," and they walked out of the office. And that is indicative of what the stigma of the glam era and hair band era has done to Cinderella and Tom Keifer. Because they have so many more chops in them—it's not just based on their appearances and what they were.

May 17, 1988: Vinnie Vincent Invasion issue their second and last LP, *All Systems Go*, which generates two videos, a No. 64 chart placement, and 150,000 sales.

May 21, 1988: Cinderella's second album *Long Cold Winter* is released. Guitarist, vocalist, and leader Tom Keifer further explores his deep-blues roots. The album reaches No. 10 and goes 2x platinum. "The Last Mile" is one big power ballad, although another power ballad, "Don't Know What You've Got (Till It's Gone)" becomes the band's biggest hit, peaking at No. 12 three months after the album is released. "Coming Home" and "Gypsy Road" are also singles. The ensuing tour comprises 254 shows.

1985   **1986**   **1987**   **1988**   **1989**

1980   **1981**   **1982**   **1983**   **1984**

Your Mama Don't Dance

RIKKI ROCKETT (DRUMMER, POISON):

[*Open Up. . .*] shipped platinum. All US numbers. We've had our good days and our bad days in Europe. We tried for the first two years in our career to break Europe. It was very difficult. We'd play clubs and then a theater and all this is on the heels of playing large places in the US. Staying in shitty hotels, having half a crew. But we did it. We bit the bullet and said we really want Europe. We wanted them to get it. But at the same time there was that alt.metal thing happening over there. You were either a pop artist—I mean a one-hundred-percent pop artist—or you were true metal. You were either Duran Duran or you were Motörhead and there was no in-between. It was a very difficult market for us and in the United States and even Canada there is much more levity there. But then we ended up opening for Aerosmith at [England's] Castle Donington a few years later and finally we did make our mark in Europe. But it took a tremendous amount of effort and time.

May 21, 1988: Poison's second album, *Open Up and Say . . . Ahh!*, sells ten million copies worldwide. The ultimate glam band, here they are at the peak of glam. Includes "Nothin' But a Good Time," "Fallen Angel," and "Every Rose Has Its Thorn."

BOBBY DALL (BASSIST, POISON):

[Producer] Tom Werman was great. He's a master and he has a very unique sound. His approach is one that is a lot of fun. Tom isn't a real "drive you to the bone," "be on top of every minute detail" kind of guy. He's a little more hands off and hangs out with you. Back then, the band was very young, we were partying hard and Tom was one of the boys [laughs]. He was right there with us [laughs].

1985 **1986** **1987** **1988** **1989**

May 24, 1988: After a stopgap EP, Frehley's Comet issue *Second Sighting*.

May 24, 1988: Van Halen issues the second album of the hair band-ish Van Hagar era, *OU812*, which includes another shameless power ballad, "When It's Love."

JERRY DIXON (BASSIST, WARRANT, ON HAIR METAL'S "NOTHIN' BUT A GOOD TIME" CREDO):

It's just that era, and the thing that really makes it still stick, rock 'n' roll, in our era, it was just a good time. It wasn't anything heavy, it wasn't about politics. It wasn't about war or anything bad. It was just about going out and having fun, nothing major. And that appealed to a lot of people. I think it still does. People still come to the shows and almost relive that, and it takes them back to high school. Back to that entertainment that music should be. Music should take you away somewhere. I'm not saying that where we take you is the best spot, but it was just a good, no-brainer fun time.

ACE FREHLEY (ON *SECOND SIGHTING*):

Some of those songs are good, you know? Some of those songs are maybe a little too poppy. I maybe would've done them a little different today. I'm trying to get back into the mindset of my roots, you know what I do? I read my fan mail. I listen to what the kids say and what they want to hear. They really want me to play heavier stuff, and do wild stuff, which is an element in music that is lacking today.

SAMMY HAGAR:

We could do no wrong. And we didn't stop getting along until the very end. So *OU812* was the second record and it was still fantastic. We were coming off the first No. 1 record Van Halen ever had. We were very prolific and anxious to write and we went in with nothing. We just said, let's start recording today. We just made a date. We had come off a very lengthy tour for *5150*. Eddie had a bunch of riffs he was jamming around, I had a bunch of lyrics in notebooks that I had been thinking about and writing. And we just put them together and jammed in the studio. It was just complete simple magic. A great story here. Ed and Al picked me up from the airport when I flew down to start the record. I flew into town, I got in the car, and Ed and Al go, "You know, we kind of stayed up all night last night and we worked on this one little thing and we want to play it for you." And I'm going, "You fuckers started without me!" just joking around, because we were all buddy buddies, and they played me . . . it was just a piano and drums to the song "When It's Love." Before the song was over, I was singing "How do I know when it's love?" And by the time we played it over and over again, by the time we got to the studio, that song was written and done—lyrics, melody, everything. That's the kind of magic we had going. And that was the first song we wrote from *OU812*.

DON DOKKEN:

Monsters of Rock, it was embarrassing. I remember Eddie Van Halen on several occasions going and knocking on George [Lynch]'s door saying, "You know, you have to change yourself, George." He used to play the shows, even in front of 100,000 people, with his back to the

1980　　　**1981**　　　**1982**　　　**1983**　　　**1984**

audience. And he said, "I can't help it, I hate Don. I hate Don's guts, and I can't do it. How did you do it?" Eddie would say, "Lookit, I didn't like David Lee Roth, we fought like cats and dogs, but nobody knew about it on stage. We didn't wash our laundry on stage. For one hour and a half a night, we were the best of friends, because we owed it to our fans." Eddie would say, "You owe it to your fans, who paid hard-earned money, to go out there and kick ass for an hour and a half. And after you get off stage, you can hate Don's guts. But for an hour and a half a night, get out there and do your job." And that came from Eddie, who George really respected.

And I thought, cool! Now he's going to get out there and kick ass. And he went out there the next night and played his entire show with his back to the audience. And when I announced him for his guitar solo, the spotlight went to him and he was standing behind an amplifier hiding. I was so humiliated and embarrassed that I went and bought a bottle of Jack Daniels and just got completely shit-faced. So the next night it was Rudolf Schenker and Eddie Van Halen and Lars Ulrich that went to George's room and said, "What the fuck are you doing?" And George said, "I can't do it. Don says he's gonna quit the band. Why should I do it? Why should I even try?" It was the high point of my career, and it was a dream come true to stand on a stage in front of 100,000 people. It was the high point of my life and it was the low point of my life because it was humiliating and embarrassing.

And to watch Metallica go up on stage every day and just kick ass! I was going, "Oh man, this is so cool. And at the same time I thought that's what we should be. We should have been like Metallica. They were so awesome. And we would go on stage and I would think, "Man, we are half of what we were before on tour with Aerosmith, where we were kicking ass." And then here we were, just kind of going through the motions, just trying to make it through the set, just hoping George wouldn't do something horrible. And twice on the tour, he walked off on the encore. We would have a huge encore—80,000 people would give us an encore—and I came back on stage and announced the song, "In My Dreams," and turn around and made the cue, and I looked behind the stage and George is walking like a hundred yards off to the dressing room holding his guitar. Shit like that will kill you.

He was destroying himself. There was an awful and infamous saying that now the band laughs about, Jeff [Pilsen], Mick [Brown], and I. We played Giants Stadium in New York and the next day there's a review of the Monsters of Rock: "Scorpions, in true German spirit did a fine, regimented show. Metallica slaughtered the audience and attacked them with fury. And then Van Halen with their nonstop energy" . . . blah, blah, blah . . . and "Dokken hit the stage and sold a record number of hot dogs." Ouch. That hurt. Sold a record amount of hot dogs [laughs]. Oh man! And this is in the *New York Times*. And that shit went on every day.

May 27, 1988: The first date of Van Halen's Monsters of Rock Tour 1988, on which Van Halen took out a festival package consisting of themselves, Scorpions, Dokken, Metallica, and Kingdom Come. Scorpions were in full hair band mode, promoting *Savage Amusement*, while odd men out Metallica represented a changing of the guard.

1985　　　**1986**　　　**1987**　　　**1988**　　　**1989**

June 6, 1988: Philadelphia's Britny Fox, friends with Cinderella from back home and in business now for three years, issue their self-titled debut, on Columbia. The cover art displays the band in all their glam glory. The album goes gold (very close to platinum), peaking at No. 39 on the strength of Slade cover "Gudbuy T'Jane."

June 17, 1988: *The Decline of Western Civilization Part II: The Metal Years* documentary film is released, placing hair metal in a morally bankrupt, vacuous, dim light. The highlight is an interview with W.A.S.P.'s Chris Holmes, lounging in his swimming pool, guzzling vodka, his mom watching on from poolside. Also appearing in the film are Vixen, London, Odin, and Poison.

June 28, 1988: Stryper's *In God We Trust* is released. It will go gold. Poppier and more melodic than its predecessor.

BILLY CHILDS (BASSIST, BRITNY FOX):

Not to speak for the other guys, but I guess they would pretty much agree with me. I always saw us as somewhere slightly above average. Never saw us as a huge Bon Jovi–type band or anything like that. I saw us as a rock band. I didn't really see us as an '80s band. I thought we had an awful lot of elements of AC/DC to us, but there was also, because of our original singer ["Dizzy" Dean Davidson], who was an awful lot like Tom Kiefer, there was an awful lot of Cinderella influence in there. . . .

Well, we toured with Poison, the first headlining tour, which was a really great experience, really nice guys. With Poison, our first big tour, we were actually making twenty-five dollars a day per diem. We weren't even getting salaries. We toured with Ratt; they were pretty cool for the most part. Once again, nice enough guys. Alice Cooper, fucking beautiful guy. Great White . . . I would say that ninety percent of the people I toured with were definitely cool. There were very few assholes. You have to look at it this way, Martin, these guys are beginning to live their dream. They're playing these arenas, or sold-out clubs. They're on their first albums, and the guys are in a good mood. Most of the people I ran into were nice enough. Did a lot of touring with Joan Jett. Once again, cool down-to-earth chick. A lot of people don't understand that, but she really is.

1980   **1981**   **1982**   **1983**   **1984**

In 1987, the whole world went mad for Europe with over 6 million "The Final Countdown" albums sold. In 1988, Europe is back and they're *Out Of This World.*

The new, fully digital album from Europe.
Featuring the single and video, "Superstitious."

EUROPE IS "OUT OF THIS WORLD."
On Epic Cassettes, Compact Discs and Records.
Also featuring the sizzling tracks:
"Coast To Coast," "Open Your Heart" and
"Let The Good Times Rock."

Winger's Paul Taylor, Kip Winger, and Reb Beach.
© *Rod Dysinger*

ROD MORGENSTEIN (DRUMMER, WINGER):

We were on some very interesting tours with Kiss and Poison and Bon Jovi, so there were a lot of wild, crazy people out on the road. . . . I have incredible memories of just being on a tour bus and careening down the highway at seventy-five or eighty miles an hour with a hundred cars of fans keeping up with you, yelling and screaming and girls popping out of the moon roofs and pulling up their tops. All that wild, hilarious stuff that is like folklore now. You know what—I'm probably the most G-rated guy. Winger's probably the only metal band, between the four of us, that didn't sport one tattoo, so that could be our claim to fame [laughs].

BEAU HILL:

Kip is probably the single-most talented guy that I've ever known. He was greatly maligned by the rock press because he's a good-looking guy, and I feel that he was very unfairly maligned, vis à vis his bass playing and his writing. There were two things [*sic*] that happened to Winger that destroyed their career, in my opinion. The first one was when Kip agreed to appear in *Playgirl* magazine. The second thing that happened was not his fault. It was when Lars, the drummer of Metallica, in one of their videos, threw a dart at Kip's poster. And

July 3, 1988: The last annual Texxas Jam is a *Monsters of Rock* tour date, featuring Kingdom Come, Metallica, Dokken, Scorpions, and Van Halen.

August 9, 1988: Europe issue *Out of this World*, which features the very pretty Swedish band filling the front cover with nice hair. The record goes platinum, mainly on the back of *The Final Countdown*, which continued to sell steadily.

August 10 1988: Winger issue their self-titled debut album and somehow become a lightning rod for the growing anti–hair metal forces. *Winger* is produced by Beau Hill and issued on Atlantic, both iconic hair metal institutions.

1985   **1986**   **1987**   **1988**   **1989**

August 17, 1988: Guns N' Roses score smash success with "Sweet Child O' Mine," perpetuating the idea, fast becoming a cliché, that ballads help fuel sales of hair metal records.

August 23, 1988: Bad Company issue *Dangerous Age*, their second squarely hair metal record, and second fronted by Brian Howe. The album goes gold.

September 1988: Vixen's self-titled debut appears, on EMI.

then the third nail in the coffin was after all of these other things that happened, and Kip had kind of become the MTV punching bag, then Beavis and Butthead showed up and the nerdy kid in one of the cartoons was wearing a Winger T-shirt, and Beavis and Butt-head were wearing Metallica T-shirts. So Kip was being lampooned from one end to the other. This had absolutely nothing to do with his tremendous depth as a musician. I mean, he plays acoustic, classical guitar, he plays piano, he's a composer, he studied with a Juilliard professor in composition. So, as far as just depth of musicality and legitimate physical chops, Kip has forgotten more than probably anybody I've ever worked with.

DUFF MCKAGAN (ON "SWEET CHILD O' MINE"):
That's written about Axl's girlfriend at the time, ex-wife at the time, Erin. I'll tell you something about that song. We wrote the song really as a joke. Axl was serious about the lyrics, but we were like, "Fuuucck. A ballad? Come on." So you know that beginning guitar riff? It was absolutely written as a joke, at first. It was meant to sound funny. If you listen to it, it's goofy. But like everything at that point for us, it worked [laughs]. Everything worked. But it was really written as a goof, like a circus riff, because nobody wanted to do this thing.

SLASH (ON DUFF'S ASSERTION THAT NOBODY WANTED TO DO BALLADS):
Yes, but especially in the early days, or at that particular point in Guns N' Roses' career. Fuckin' we were so hard-edged that ballads just seemed so sappy. And still, to this day, it's a sappy song, but it's also coming from an emotional place for Axl that was very heartfelt and meant a lot. And over the years, I actually started to enjoy playing it. But I used to dread having to walk out to the front of the stage and start playing that lick. And for the longest time, I couldn't always play it right [laughs]. It's not the most conventional finger styling.

TRACII GUNS:
I remember even when we were in junior high school, Slash had this guitar teacher, and he used to always come up with these high riffs, chicken-scratch riffs, so when I first heard "Sweet Child O' Mine," I thought that's where that came from. It's a great song. Bought those guys mansions and drugs and cars and hookers.

SLASH:
Tracii wouldn't know where the fuck that came from [laughs]. No, it was just something I made up while I was sitting around with Izzy. And it's not an exercise, but it's just one of those kind of quirky little things I do when I'm fucking around. It just happened to be something I stumbled on that afternoon. So I was more just trying to perfect it, because it was a little more left field; it's not a predictable style

[laughs], guitar player kind of note configuration or whatever. So once I stumbled on it, I was trying to sort of perfect it. Izzy started playing the chords that went underneath it. And I sort of transposed a couple of notes to fit the chords, and then Axl heard us doing it, and all of a sudden he was onto something. And I hated that song [laughs]. It had nothing to do with any guitar teachers at all.

MARQ TORIEN (VOCALIST, BULLETBOYS):

We're not in the genre! We're not a genre band. We're not a hair band. We're a hard rock band. That's all we are. I mean, even if you look on the first BulletBoys album, no hair all sprayed up—jeans, T-shirts, that was it! We don't look like Poison. We were like this anomaly when we came up; we used to carry guns . . . a lot of hype too, but a lot of the hype was real. Bro, we lived it, we hung out with all of our greatest friends—Guns, L.A. Guns, Faster—because they were before us. And when we came up we were just very blessed to come out. Straight out of the box, we sold half a million [in] record time and it just kept going from there.

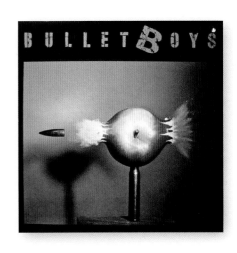

September 20, 1988: L.A.'s BulletBoys are touted as the second coming of Van Halen, with their Ted Templeman–produced self-titled debut, which hits No. 34 on Billboard and sells gold on the strength of "Smooth Up in Ya."

October 1988: Quiet Riot issue a self-titled album. The lead singer is Rough Cutt's Paul Shortino. It's the only Quiet Riot album to not feature Kevin DuBrow on vocals. As well, Chuck Wright is replaced on bass by Sean McNabb.

CARLOS CAVAZO (GUITARIST, QUIET RIOT, ON THE HAIR METAL SCENE OF THE LATE '80S):

When a lot of the L.A. bands took off, there was an overindulgence of signing bands—everybody and anybody—and that might be what helped to kill the '80s sound. But sounds change every ten to twenty years anyway, with a new generation of people; that's just the way it is. But there was an overabundance of those kind of hair metal bands, and they were maybe overdoing it with the hair and the shows. There was a good part of '80s metal and there was a bad part of '80s metal. I think too much of the bad part started coming out.

1985   **1986**   **1987**   **1988**   **1989**

October 18, 1988: Gene Simmons gets involved with Greg Giuffria as a producer. Greg ditches the Giuffria name and issues a self-titled album under the House of Lords moniker.

October 22, 1988: Ozzy Osbourne releases *No Rest for the Wicked*, which marks a bit of a heavier direction from the hair metal strains of *The Ultimate Sin*.

November 3, 1988: Ratt issue *Reach for the Sky*, which manages platinum, although it's considered a bit of a rehash. Beau Hill once again produces.

ZAKK WYLDE (GUITARIST, OZZY OSBOURNE):

No Rest, I just remember, I was telling my friends, "Oh man, I'm gonna do an Ozzy record." And I was going to do everything I could to fuckin' make it a fuckin' heavy album. Not some wimpy fuckin' . . . I wasn't going to be the one to ruin fuckin' Ozzy, you know what I mean? I don't want to be the guitar player who is known as . . . well, he used to be fuckin' heavy until this fuckin' jackass came along. And Ozzy was nervous. I'm nineteen years old. He's like, "Fuck man, I hope the fucking little fucking bastard can fucking do it," you know? He was more or less that way. He would be leaning over my shoulder just saying . . . he was more like leaning over my shoulder, where on *No More Tears* he was more relaxed. He didn't have to worry about my fucking ass.

ZAKK WYLDE (ON PRODUCERS KEITH OLSEN AND ROY THOMAS BAKER):

Roy actually did nothing on the fucking album. Did nothing. I remember thinking to myself, "This guy helped produce 'Bohemian Rhapsody' and The Cars' record?!" He didn't fucking do . . . the motherfucker showed up and met the band. He treated me like a real fucking asshole. So I've got no fucking sympathy for him. I was trying to do the best job I could. Keith Olsen was the fucking guy on that fucking record. He was the shit that made that record sound ass-kicking. As soon as he got in there and he doubled the guitars, everything sounded fucking great. Because he knew what the fuck he's doing. Roy Thomas never touched a fucking button when we were in there. Never even threw an idea out on the table. Not that we need them anyway. But he was just like . . . nothing. All I remember is him just ordering food all the time. That's all I remember him doing. I'm not joking.

JERRY DIXON:

I wouldn't say these producers didn't do any work, because they really created that sound. So it was important to have them. Did they get overpaid? Absolutely. That was another thing that killed most of our bands. The producer would demand $150,000 and three points from record one, but the thing was they didn't have to pay back their debt. You sold a record, they got paid—we didn't. Our money went to pay back all the debt for making the record and making the video. But you do what you have to do. That was the only way. Nobody in their right mind that was good was going to make a record for less than that. And you can't blame them, you know? They're probably all shit out of luck. They're probably hurting as bad as the whole music business is.

BEAU HILL:

After I got fired after *Dancing Undercover*, [Ratt] actually hired Mike Stone to do *Reach for the Sky*, and they went in and cut about six or

1980   **1981**   **1982**   **1983**   **1984**

seven tracks, and Stephen [Pearcy] put his vocals on it, and then they sent it to Atlantic for sort of preliminary approval, at which point I got a call from [Atlantic president] Doug [Morris], and the quote was, "These guys sound like a fucking Holiday Inn band. Would you please take the record over?!" And they fired Mike Stone, sent the engineer back to Australia and I said, "Okay, well, let me hear what we've got." And so I flew out to L.A. and went to the studio and listened to all of their masters, and that was a record that I probably did the most writing on. And similarly to "Lay it Down," I just heard Warren [DeMartini] jamming around, playing part of the opening figure to "Way Cool Jr." and I went, "Oh wow, that's really great, let's do something with that." Stephen and I just started piecing together the melodies, like we had on the previous three records. I mean, it got to a point where—and this was also another big problem—Stephen just didn't come to a lot of our preproduction rehearsals. His thing was, "Well, look, we're just going to write the melodies when we get in the studio, and I'll just do it there. Why do I need to sit around and listen to you guys thrash everything around in rehearsals?" Which pissed a couple of the guys off. It was like, "Why don't you make him come down here and make him rehearse?" And I'm like, "Come on, we're fine, we'll get through it." So it was constantly things like that—they were always peeling the scab off the wound [laughs].

November 15, 1988: Kiss issue a greatest hits album called *Smashes, Thrashes & Hits*. Its double-platinum status demonstrates the band's legacy and staying power, as well as its acceptance as worthy participants in the hair metal era. The band scores a minor hit with a new studio track added to the record called "Let's Put the X in Sex."

Gene Simmons. © *Rod Dysinger*

Paul Stanley. © *Rod Dysinger*

1985   **1986**   **1987**   **1988**   **1989**

November 16, 1988: Dokken issue their double-live *Beast from the East* album, which goes gold.

BEAU HILL
(ON '80S METAL AND THE ERA OF THE BIG-SHOT PRODUCER):

Doug Morris said, "You ought to be happy when they fire you, because your paycheck gets bigger when they have to hire you back." So, yeah, that's a fair assessment, that it became . . . I mean, the business was just so phenomenally healthy back then, and a lot of those bands wouldn't have done as well as they did without the collaborative efforts of their producers. The Mutt Langes and the Bruce Fairbairns . . . oh gosh, there were just so many.

BEAU HILL (ON HAIR METAL LYRICS):

The lyrics that came out of that particular time were pretty terrible. And I can say that because I contributed a fair amount of those terrible lyrics myself. They weren't very introspective. The thing that made that whole time fun was that it really was about sex and rock 'n' roll and sex and rock 'n' roll [laughs], which was the whole thing about Ratt. I mean, every single song was Stephen out there telling all these women, "Well, you may be lucky enough that I'll have sex with you."

DON DOKKEN:

A lot of fingers were pointed at me. I had a very bad reputation for a while in the press, like, "Don's a jerk, he's got a big ego, he's an asshole." And I just thought, whatever. People would see me at shows, backstage. I always had a sourpuss look on my face because I didn't want to talk to anybody. I was pretty grumpy all the time. I was miserable, absolutely miserable, because all this shit was going on with George and it was very frustrating. Here I have a dream of being famous and a rock star and I have a guitar player who is snorting lines of cocaine off the monitors in every song. And I don't do drugs myself. I'm antidrug. Or who is flipping me the finger when no one is looking, in front of ten thousand people? Yeah, I'm pretty pissed. And that went on for years. It was my own fault for letting him

1980   **1981**   **1982**   **1983**   **1984**

get to me. I should have just let it roll off my back, but I was hypersensitive about the situation, so I'd be very cranky and I'd go into an interview and I would be all pissed off. So I let it get to me. And that anger was perceived as arrogance.

DON DOKKEN (ON THE SOURCE OF GEORGE LYNCH'S ANGER): I asked him that, and you know what his comment was? I said, "What can I do to stop this? What can I do to make you happy?" And he said, "Change the name of the band." I think that had a lot to do with it. After the band broke up, [drummer] Mick [Brown] went with George. Mick said, "I was absolutely sure, Don, that you were the problem. You were the asshole, you were the jerk, you were all the problems in this band." And he realized he was wrong. Because I was always the one screaming and yelling, and I was. I was trying to keep the band going; I was frustrated. I was trying to take the band to where I thought it should be.

November 29, 1988: Guns N' Roses issue *GN'R Lies*, a live and acoustic odds 'n' sods album (half of which consists of the band's debut indie EP). It is one of the early examples of a rockin' hair metal band going "unplugged," a move that would become a *de rigueur* cliché career move for hair metal bands.

November 30, 1988: Guns N' Roses issue the single "Paradise City" from *Appetite for Destruction.*

DUFF MCKAGAN: I'd written the chorus for ["Paradise City"] one night when I moved to L.A., so it was before the band. I was living in this shithole. In 1984, after the Olympics, all the police had basically left Hollywood and it turned into this cesspool. The police and the city had come in and cleaned it up for the summer Olympics and once that was over, they just left. And for a while, it was just kind of a shithole. It's come back now, like every place has. You can walk through downtown Detroit now without a problem, whereas ten years ago, or maybe more, you wouldn't have walked in certain places. So I lived in this apartment and "Paradise City" was written about an imaginary place that I wasn't in at that point.

THE TWO THEMES OF 1989 *in the lifecycle of hair metal are both essentially positive. First, Guns N' Roses and their "dirty hair metal" proposal inspire quite a few bands to dress down, rough up their sound, and inject some blues and punk energy. These road rats in the cellar essentially rediscover the magic that was Aerosmith circa* Rocks. *Ergo, there goes Skid Row, Seahags, Dangerous Toys, Faster Pussycat, and Bang Tango. Next is the trend toward bands trying harder. Both Aerosmith and Mötley Crüe go to Bruce Fairbairn in Vancouver and pump out feel-good classics.* Dr. Feelgood *is the liveliest Crüe spin since* Shout *and possibly since their wholly irreverent debut.* Pump, *against all odds or expectations, is actually a ballsier, grittier, heavier record than* Permanent Vacation.

As an amalgam of these two ideas, even new bands eschew the growing joke that is hair metal and strive to inject some intellectual heft into what they do. Witness the funk-shred of Boston's Extreme, or the brooding yet soulful heft of Tesla, or the Beatles/Elvis Costello/Cheap Trick tinges played up by the wonderful Enuff Z'Nuff. To close on a sour note, hair metal gets its own Altamont: the highly hypocritical Moscow Music Peace Festival, done for all the wrong reasons and then rifled through by drugs and egos, is enough to make fans question their blind allegiances to these rock pigs.

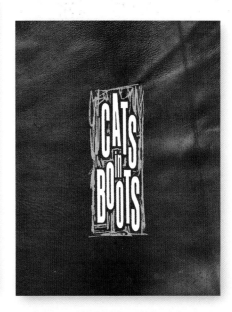

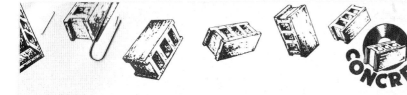

CATS IN BOOTS

Joel Ellis - Lead Vocals, Harmonica
Takashi "Jam" Ohhashi - Guitar, Vocals
Randy Meers - Drums, Vocals
Yasuhiro "Butch" Hatae - Bass, Vocals

Once Upon A Time...

There was a certain feline who wore oversized boots, who walked on his hind paws and talked as a human would, saving lives of ladies in distress while wooing them, the world over. His soul belonged to no one. That was Puss In Boots, remember? Let's now update that classic "tail": make a 360 degree turn, turn up the volume on your stereo just past "11", and add a dash of 80's streetsmarts, and you've got **Cats In Boots**, the explosive hard rock find on EMI, spinning heads with their debut album, <u>Kicked & Klawed</u>.

Not unlike that historical tabby of old, Cats in Boots are the troubadours of the streets, and the streets of the <u>world</u>. Life's a bitch all over. Whether it's Cleveland, Houston or the ever-glittering enigma of Hollywood, California, Cats In Boots have lived and are living the "rock 'n roll lifestyle", but with an unusually worldly outlook due to the talents of two members' hometown of Tokyo, Japan, the biggest and toughest city in the world. It takes guts to compete there, and it takes balls to defy the mold that hard rock seems hell-bent in shaping, but Cats In Boots have their claws drawn and are ready, willing and able to climb out of the alley and onto the arena stage.

The songs aren't pretty, the tunes aren't soft. Sure, they like the ladies, but to hear lead singer Joel say it, they "practice safe sex" (and you know 'Practice Makes Perfect'!). But just as fast as they rejoice in the joys of the female flesh, they look dead-on into the perils of drug abuse, prostitution, violence and peer pressure, class separation and untimely death. Ultimately though, from start to finish, <u>Kicked & Klawed</u> takes you on a fast car race that excites, ignites and burns you while it destroys any pre-made expectations you may have had about what rock from the street means.

CONCRETE MARKETING, INC. • FOUNDATIONS • FOUNDATIONS FORUM
1133 Broadway, Suite 204, New York, NY 10010 USA • Telephone (212) 645-1360 • Fax (212) 645-2607
Telex 4900000460 OBR.UI • Esi "OBRIEN-US" • MCI Mail "355-7729" • Delphi/Pan "CONMAN"

1989: Glam "shred" band Nitro issue *O.F.R.*, which stands for "out-fucking-rageous."

1989: San Francisco's Sea Hags issue their one and only album, on Chrysalis. It's produced by Mike Clink. (Kirk Hammett had produced their early demos.) The band's founder, Chris Schlosshardt, will die of a heroin overdose two years later.

1989: San Francisco's Jet Red issue a self-titled debut; years later, bassist Brad Lang will wind up in Y&T, also from the Bay Area.

1989: L.A.'s Cats in Boots turn in a credible major label debut (their second after an indie) in the dirty, sleazy, bluesy *Kicked & Klawed*.

1985   **1986**   **1987**   **1988**   **1989**

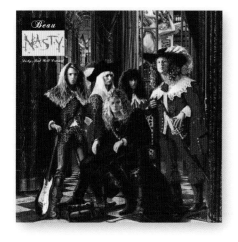

1989: Beau Nasty issue their perfectly named debut, *Dirty But Well Dressed*, produced by Beau Hill, with cover art indicative of an upscale Britny Fox look. Touring ensues with Loverboy to the light side of them and Love/Hate to the heavy.

January 24, 1989: Skid Row issue their self-titled debut, which goes on to sell 5x platinum. In keeping with their New Jersey roots, the band comes off as a grittier, more street version of hair metal, as opposed to most acts of the genre, who were either from California or had relocated there. The album generates hits in the anthemic "Youth Gone Wild" and the power ballad "18 and Life."

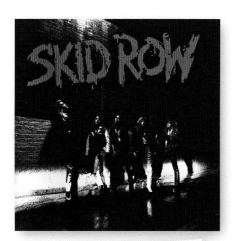

DAVE "SNAKE" SABO
(GUITARIST, SKID ROW, ON "18 AND LIFE"):

I was working in a music store in Toms River, New Jersey, which is where [bassist] Rachel [Bolan] and I had met, and I had these chords and whatnot that I would fool around with in the music store. And I said to Rachel, "I've got this idea for a song." Originally it was supposed to be about my brother, who went to Vietnam, and his name was Rick, but we couldn't just grasp that at the time. We couldn't wrap our heads around that particular story line. Whether it was too close to me and I couldn't contribute, I don't know why. So we just came up with this fictitious story based on true-to-life events. Once again, a lot of the lyrics come from Rachel, and he just has a way of making certain situations very poetic and yet have a strong message and an ability to connect with the audience. And that song in particular just seemed to connect because people have seen people go through that situation. So it was a pretty universal conjoining of band and fan.

RACHEL BOLAN:

The first album, I mean, there was anger and innocence in there. Being our first album, we had our whole life to write it basically [laughs]. And that's the album that put Skid Row on the map, and as proud of that album as I am, there's still things on there where I'm like, "Ooh, man, that's kind of cheesy." But we were young; we didn't know any better. When Snake and I first got together, we had three different guys in the band, a different singer, different guitar player, and a different drummer. So we hooked up, and kind of one by one we replaced them. And by the time, man, we must have had forty songs written. So the first album was pretty much fully written before the band was the band that it was on the first record. It was pretty much like it was on the first record, but there was a lot of other stuff that just seemed too derivative of bands. When you write that many things, you tend to run out of ideas. There was stuff that sounded like Van Halen, so those were weeded out. Plus you tend to know what the good songs are. You can tell when the band plays it, what lights everybody up at the same time.

DAVE "SNAKE" SABO (ON "YOUTH GONE WILD"):

We just wanted to express our rebelliousness. When you're growing up, your rebelliousness comes from different places. Whether you're slighted in school because you're different or the outcast or you're not socially adaptable. We've all gone through our own and trials and tribulations of being persecuted for how we look or our police systems. And we felt when we had gotten together that we had all gone through many similar situations where we were outcasts from the mainstream and that song was a reflection of those feelings.

1980   **1981**   **1982**   **1983**   **1984**

GEORGE LYNCH (ON SKID ROW'S SEBASTIAN BACH):

Great front man, and he's a ridiculously good singer. Whether or not you like that style is a subjective thing, but he definitely has pipes and he definitely has confidence in himself, and stage presence. He definitely demands being the focal point, which is what a singer should be required to do in the kind of cock rock that we play [laughs].

JERRY DIXON (BASSIST, WARRANT):

It's because we were so poor. We just thought that was pretty goddamn hysterical. Because this is five of the poorest bastards you can meet. So you know what? We're gonna call our record *Dirty Rotten Filthy Stinking Rich*. We came up with this concept for the guy on the cover and put it in the videos. So it was a kind of a paradox. . . .

It was a different world. It's hard to picture it now, but there were no downloads. It was all about radio, all about singles, all about MTV, and the way it went was, you would take your single, and then you went and still spent a shitload, a quarter-million dollars on a shitty video, gave it to MTV for free, and then you went around and bought golf clubs for program directors at radio stations, and gave them VCRs, did some golfing, and that's the way it worked. You would go on the road and just schmooze these people, and it just kind of snowballed. Once a certain amount of the big radio stations started playing something, all the smaller ones followed in the country, and you're off to the races. But it was a mess. Financially, what happened to all of us was really bad. And I'm glad I'm not alone [laughs]. But yeah, basically, it was all recoupable. Every single, every video, every limo they sent, every dinner you went to, every set of golf clubs they bought for a program director behind your back. Had we known . . . I guess, it wouldn't have been too hard to figure out. I think we did thirteen videos at an average cost of probably $200,000, and each record cost anywhere from $175,000 to $250,000. And then all the airline tickets, tour expenses, buses and the pyro, all of that, took the tour money, so at the end of the day, this is a bank loan basically.

January 31, 1989: Warrant issue their debut album, *Dirty Rotten Filthy Stinking Rich*. The title and the front cover are meant to be tongue-in-cheek, but also play to public perceptions of hair metal being populated by materialistic prima donnas—ergo, the title kind of backfires.

| 1985 | 1986 | 1987 | 1988 | 1989 |

BILLY CHILDS:

[Videos] were just an insanely powerful marketing tool, back then more so than today, because MTV had just launched, in what, 1980, 1981? And so in those years, MTV viewership was absolutely huge. So videos were the biggest paid-for infomercials you'd ever seen in your life. And the reason they cost so much money is because the production values are so high on them. Let's face it—they don't have to be as expensive as they are. When you're in the music business, especially as a musician, you start to notice early on as you're doing these things, there's a whole sub-network of people, and they are making all the money off the artist. Whether they be hairdressers or clothes designers or video directors, there are a million of them. So you start to see early on that these are the people that really make the money. Because you're only there for a few years. These guys are going to continue making videos and making clothes and doing people's hair. They're the reason why videos used to cost, oh, anywhere from $80,000 to $250,000. We did videos that cost almost $200,000 ourselves.

CARLOS CAVAZO (GUITARIST, QUIET RIOT):

We had the typical deal most bands had, which is fifty percent recoupable. Anything they spent on videos, the band pays half and the record company pays half. So yes, it did get out of hand. But again, it's competing, that whole competition thing. You're competing with other people's videos . . . $250,000, $275,000. "The Wild and the Young" video. And that was riding the height when everybody was trying to outspend each other. It was a good video, but it was probably overspending.

RUDY SARZO (BASSIST, WHITESNAKE):

The biggest expenses at that time was something that everybody, not just Whitesnake, was suffering with, and it was the videos. The videos got out of hand. We'd spend more money on the videos than we did on the actual recording. We did three videos on the *Slip of the Tongue*, and, oh my God, they were each about $350,000. And that's all nonrecoupable—the band paid for that. But then again, actually, in those days, the record company, the management, would have a meeting with MTV, and MTV, by the end of the '80s, they would basically tell you what they wanted included in the video. And if those certain things did not meet the criteria, they would just decide not to play it, which means you just wasted $300,000.

BEAU HILL:

Those were the [director] Marty Callner video days, where everybody wanted to get him to do their video, and he was a $100,000 price tag, was the last that I heard, just for him. And then you have all your other video costs. So yes, the videos were starting

1980   **1981**   **1982**   **1983**   **1984**

to get ridiculous. Where there are like $350,000, $500,000, $750,000 for a rock band video. And unless the contracts stipulated that the label was going to absorb part of that production cost, it went right back onto the band. So yeah, some of those guys probably didn't make as much as they would have liked, to absorb that cost.

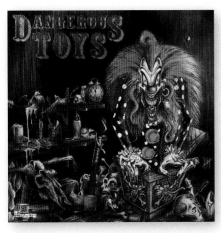

Early 1989: Dangerous Toys from Austin, Texas, issue their self-titled debut album. Produced by Max Norman and issued on Columbia, it goes gold.

February 1, 1989: Tesla issue their second album, *The Great Radio Controversy*, which eventually achieves double-platinum status.

March 14, 1989: Boston's Extreme issue their self-titled debut album, arriving late to the hair metal game.

I saw this happen a lot of times, with Ratt, Warrant, and Winger to a certain extent. When you have guys who are broke on Monday, and then a month from Monday they are all millionaires . . . obviously that's an exaggeration; I've condensed the timeframe, but it still exists. Ratt, when I met them, if they had fifty cents between them, I would be shocked. And then at the end of that particular album and tour cycle, they all had a net worth of seven figures. When you're a young kid, some people can really put that in proper perspective and some people can't. As well as the concept that, we are so lucky and that this gravy train is not going to last forever. That was my philosophy, was don't get cocky because just as quickly as this thing started, it can stop. I was battling that with these guys. Because when people start looking at their bank account and they start believing the press that is written about them, then they have someone like me coming in and sort of dousing the flame and going, "Okay guys, that's really great. Now let's get back to work." It was a wet blanket, I guess.

There was a lot of pressure being put on us to deliver a sophomore album, but it's a great album. "Love Song" is one of my favorite songs of all time that we've done. But it still felt a little unfinished.

The people who know Extreme know we weren't a hair band. Everybody at that time had long hair and bad high school shots [laughs]. Everybody has a bad high school photo, so looking back at it, you laugh when you think of what you wore and the hair that you had. But Extreme, to me, if anything, we took our cue from Queen. Not comparing in sound or voice, because he da man, but Extreme was more ambitious than a lot of the bands out there. We didn't quite fit into the hip Chili Pepper thing going on. We certainly weren't as fluffy as Poison, even Bon Jovi. I thought Bon Jovi was the best of the pop metal stuff. But I wasn't a big fan of theirs; I thought the music was a little too poppy. What Extreme had was that kind of metal funk going on. And that was a combination of mine and Nuno's writing. And I really think some of the stuff holds up well today.

The majority of me wants to say no. But in all fairness, I'm sure it had influenced us. What we realized is that there was definitely a scene going on in the mid- to late '80s. There was an aspect of the spirit of it that we connected with, but obviously, musically, we were kind of outside the box. We were always a bit of a bastard child of what was going on. We were doing a bit of funk stuff, and people are saying, "Well,

1980　　　**1981**　　　**1982**　　　**1983**　　　**1984**

where can you put that from a rock standpoint?" And even the acoustic stuff—there wasn't much acoustic stuff going on. It was all the big production power ballads. So we were always stuck in the middle of all that. And with every genre of music, at that point, there was a handful of great bands and the result was the stuff that comes afterwards, the watered-down versions of those bands.

April 1989: San Francisco's Sea Hags issue their Mike Clink–produced debut, on Chrysalis. They are immediately associated with Dangerous Toys as part of a punky, rootsy new form of hair metal.

April 10, 1989: The Cult issue *Sonic Temple*, widely considered enough of a hair band album for the band to run (with an uneasy lack of irony) in those circles.

GARY CHERONE:

That Queen comparison really makes sense, because you've got a sort of exhilarating, energetic vocalist and a like-minded guitarist at the same time. That's how it all started. Nuno and I met talking about *Queen II*, and we hit it off, and we had an explosion of songwriting in a short amount of time, and that was Extreme.

NUNO BETTENCOURT:

It was important to us to stay where we were, because of who we were and what we sounded like. There were definitely thoughts of, "Do we actually think it's possible to get a record deal in Boston?" But then again, we looked around us and saw that even Boston had a great scene. It wasn't L.A., but I think that was the good news. It was flourishing. There were a lot of clubs and bands in Boston that were being sort of L.A.-ish, doing that glam metal that was going on. And we connected more with New York than L.A. We would always pair up with bands like Kix and things like that, which we always thought were a bit more rock 'n' roll and blues-based. So L.A. never really occurred to us. We definitely saw that as, the aliens were on the other side.

IAN ASTBURY (VOCALIST, THE CULT):

Sonic Temple was more of a commercial interpretation of where we were at. It was like a combination between *Love* and *Electric*, kind of glossed over for the mass market in a lot ways. But making it, that certainly wasn't the intention behind it. Certainly for me it wasn't. I mean at that point I wanted to deconstruct it. I wanted it to sound like Cream's *Disraeli Gears*. But I think that [producer] Bob [Rock] and [guitarist] Billy [Duffy] had a different vision. And I have a great respect for Bob, so . . . in that sense it was as much an artistic statement as it was a career statement. . . . I think that *Sonic Temple* will be remembered more for the time than the actual content. Whereas I think *Electric—Love*, certainly—and the last Cult album, the self-titled, I think they're our most accomplished records, in terms of artistry.

1985   **1986**   **1987**   **1988**   **1989**

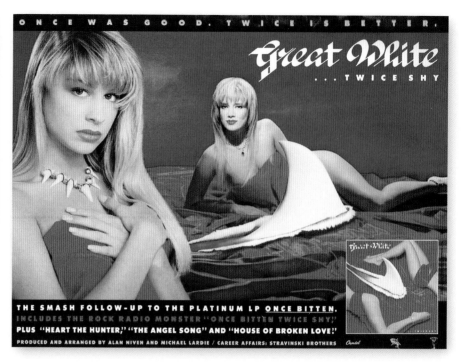

April 12, 1989: Great White issue . . . *Twice Shy*, which, like its predecessor, sells double-platinum. The band scores a hit with a clinical hair metal cover of Ian Hunter's "Once Bitten, Twice Shy," illustrating a connection between two glam realms.

JACK RUSSELL (VOCALIST, GREAT WHITE):

The cover songs? I mean, a song is a song is a song. And I'm a singer and I like to sing good songs. And just because "Once Bitten, Twice Shy" became a big hit, I never thought it was going to be because I never liked the song to begin with. I was blown away. I still can't believe that song was a hit. It's a fun song to play live, but it's one of the songs I never rehearsed. It was like, "Yeah, I know it," know what I mean? But no, a song is a song is a song. I mean, there are a lot of '50s artists and country artists that didn't write any of their own material. A lot of people like the songs and they like the music and we wrote a lot of our own stuff. A lot of our hits have been our own songs. As long as people show up for the shows and buy the albums and like the music and we're making some positive changes to people's lives. . .

JOE ELLIOTT (VOCALIST, DEF LEPPARD, ON THE PSYCHOLOGY OF RECORDING COVERS):

That's great—that's the first time I've been asked this question. Great. In fairness, I think the essential beginnings of the cover goes back to the '40s and '50s—people used to do them all the time. Very few performers even pretended to write songs. It was a completely new thing really, thirty-five years ago or so. In essence, the A&R men, at some stage in the involvement of music, decided that one way to help break a band—or at least the manager would say to the band, once they started to play gigs and they didn't have a record deal—one way to attract attention and see yourself in a positive way, is to do a cover version of a song the audience is most likely to know, and to do it as well as the one they know in their head. So what it does is, it gives the people in the audience the opportunity to compare. Because it's

1980   **1981**   **1982**   **1983**   **1984**

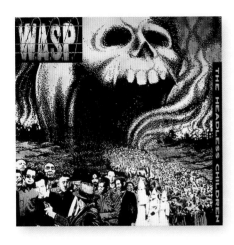

impossible to compare something to something you've never heard. If a band writes new music, maybe they can be impressed by the musicianship or the melody of the song. But if they don't know it . . . but if they do a cover of "Johnny B. Goode," which everybody did do in the '60s and '70s, people can compare. Unless of course it's Hendrix's version, where there's no comparison at all [laughs]. So I would say that in the embryonic stage of, "Hmm, covers, great idea," it was probably an A&R man trying to break bands.

CARMINE APPICE (ON BLUE MURDER):

Basically, John [Sykes] had this deal on Geffen and we were supposed to go to Vancouver and work with this new producer named Bob Rock, who was known for engineering a lot of big records but had never produced any, and this was like his first production deal. And believe it or not, we got Bob Rock for like $30,000. And we had this other guy named Mike Fraser who was same thing, big engineer, and here he was working for $2,500 a week. Making more than Bob, actually [laughs]. Tony Martin from Black Sabbath was supposed to be the singer, but, long story short, based on John's singing, they gave him the deal, because he was fresh out of Whitesnake and I was on that Pink Floyd record [*Momentary Lapse of Reason*], and we were side-by-side with each other on the charts [laughs] at that point in December '87.

April 15, 1989: W.A.S.P. issue *The Headless Children*, which finds Blackie Lawless distancing himself from juvenile hair metal and horror conceits and instead offering sociopolitical lyrics and dark cover art to match.

April 24, 1989: Kingdom Come issue the credible *In Your Face*, which shows the band as much more than Led Zeppelin wannabes.

April 25, 1989: Supergroup Blue Murder issue their self-titled debut, on Geffen. The band consists of John Sykes (ex-Whitesnake), drummer Carmine Appice (previously back in the game with hair metal band King Kobra), and bassist Tony Franklin. They are yet another band touted as the second coming of Led Zeppelin.

1985   **1986**   **1987**   **1988**   **1989**

May 11, 1989: Accept finally give in and go hair metal, releasing *Eat the Heat* with an American singer (David Reece) and glossy, mechanized production.

May 11, 1989: Badlands issue their classic self-titled debut. The band is a bit of a hair metal supergroup, featuring Ray Gillen (ex–Black Sabbath) and Jake E. Lee (ex–Ozzy Osbourne) with drummer Eric Singer and bassist Greg Chaisson. Pictured plainly on the front cover in sepia tones, the band's visual image matched the music within—no-nonsense, rootsy metal, essentially the antidote to hair metal—even if their sound bore a resemblance to the stadium rock of cream-of-the-crop Whitesnake from the early to mid-'80s.

STEFAN KAUFMANN (DRUMMER, ACCEPT):

Eat the Heat was a huge mistake. Some good songs on it, but the wrong production and a different singer. It had nothing to do with Accept anymore.

DEE SNIDER (VOCALIST, TWISTED SISTER):

I think the '70s and '80s set in stone that live is live and the studio is the studio, and your tempo for live is one thing and the tempo for the studio is another. The attention to everything had to be perfectly doubled, perfectly in pitch—perfect, perfect, you know, this Mutt Lange-ish. You heard stories about Mutt Lange recording one string per track for a chord on the guitar for Def Leppard. And I think that was thrown out the window, courtesy of the alternative bands, and rightfully so. So much, I feel, is lost, from my band Twisted Sister for example, and some of the other bands, of the real essence of a band, in an effort to be studio-perfect.

BEAU HILL:

Without any disrespect, I knew that things were happening in our industry, or in that particular genre, when bands like Dangerous Toys and Danger Danger and Bang Tango could basically go out and record anything and be assured at least of a gold record. And in my opinion, they certainly weren't meritous of that. So when it became that easy and all you had to do was wear tight clothes and have a singer that was kind of cute, that was it, that's the criteria, then I'm sitting around waiting and going, "Oh, something's going to change."

ALICE COOPER:

We took three days writing ["Poison"]. Now, usually I say a hit is written in five minutes. So maybe the basics of "Poison" was written in a half-hour. But when you're working with Desmond Child, he is a song doctor, he is a surgeon. He spent two days just on the background vocals. I mean, he really, really made that song work. The basics were written, yeah, in maybe an hour. But he really sat down at the piano and worked out every one of those background vocals, which is something I never would be able to do. Desmond was good, because Desmond came from a whole different place and, yeah, Desmond did push me. He wasn't satisfied with "That's a good song." He was a song doctor, and he would sit there and go, "Yeah, it's good. It's not great." And he would just work on that song until it was great. And that's why *Trash* sold three, four million copies, because there was somebody at the helm that really, really was working there but also making sure the album was great.

1980   **1981**   **1982**   **1983**   **1984**

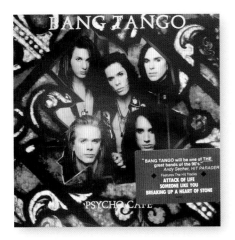

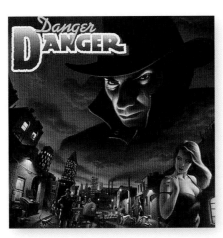

May 29, 1989: Bang Tango issue their Howard Benson–produced debut, *Psycho Café*, which proposes hair metal with a whiff of funk, like Extreme.

June 15, 1989: Nirvana issue their debut album, *Bleach* (recorded for $606.17).

June 20, 1989: Hair metal supergroup Mr. Big issue their self-titled debut. The vibe is of a band of players with more chops than average playing simple songs busily, somewhat in the spirit of David Lee Roth solo, from which bassist Billy Sheehan hails.

June 26, 1989: Diane Warren–penned ballad "When I See You Smile" vaults Bad English's self-titled debut to platinum status. The band is a supergroup, principals being John Waite from The Babys (vocals) and Neal Schon and Jonathan Cain, both from Journey (Cain also being ex-Babys).

June 27, 1989: New Yorkers Danger Danger issue a self-titled debut that goes gold.

July 20, 1989: The talented Steve Blaze and Lillian Axe issue their well-regarded second album, *Love + War*.

July 25, 1989: Alice Cooper issues *Trash*, the biggest hit among his hair metal albums. There are four videos from it. Rote and synthetic power ballad "Poison" is by far the biggest hit. The other singles/videos are "Bed of Nails," "House on Fire," and "Only My Heart Talkin'." Jon Bon Jovi and Steven Tyler guest star. Nine of ten songs are cowrites with producer Desmond Child.

1985   **1986**   **1987**   **1988**   **1989**

172

August 10, 1989: White Lion issue *Big Game*. The album is considered eclectic, with the band burned out by too much time on the road. It peaks at No. 19 on Billboard, quickly going gold but no further. The album's main hit is "Little Fighter," and it also includes a cover of Golden Earring's "Radar Love."

August 12–13, 1989: The Moscow Music Peace Festival features Cinderella, Gorky Park, Scorpions, Skid Row, Mötley Crüe, Ozzy Osbourne, and Bon Jovi. The concert is a plea for world peace and for fighting the drug war in Russia, but by all accounts, it was a horrendous, drug-fueled party for the bands involved. There were also huge ego clashes among Mötley, Ozzy, and Bon Jovi. It was believed that Bon Jovi was given preferential status (i.e., longer sets, more elaborate staging, and headliner status). The fest was set up by Doc McGhee for his Make A Difference Foundation, which he put together as a condition of his parole for his drug smuggling conviction. Ozzy and Sharon fought, too. And apparently there were crowd problems. It was the first rock concert in Lenin Stadium, which fit 100,000 but, for this debacle, had 120,000 jammed in. The event inspired Scorpions' political power ballad "Wind of Change," but the real story was the hypocrisy of hair metal bands.

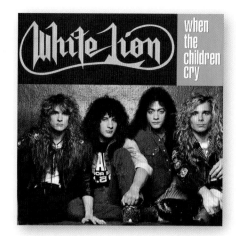

WHITE LION BIG GAME

The follow-up to their Double Platinum debut album, *PRIDE*

Includes the single, **"Little Fighter"** and the songs **"Goin' Home Tonight"** and **"Cry For Freedom."**

IT'S THE ONLY GAME IN TOWN

PRODUCED, RECORDED AND MIXED BY MICHAEL WAGENER FOR DOUBLE TROUBLE PRODUCTIONS
Management by
LOUD & PROUD

DON'T MISS WHITE LION ON TOUR WITH OZZY OSBOURNE FROM JUNE 15 THROUGH AUGUST!

On Atlantic Records, Cassettes and Compact Discs
© 1989 Atlantic Recording Corp. ◯® A Warner Communications Co.

1980   **1981**   **1982**   **1983**   **1984**

MOSCOW MUSIC
PEACE FESTIVAL
SKID ROW ▪ CINDERELLA
BON JOVI

1985   **1986**   **1987**   **1988**   **1989**

August 15, 1989: Aerosmith issue "Love in an Elevator" as a single from *Pump*. Its party vibe, lyric, and backing vocals are hair metal personified.

August 22, 1989: Chicago's Enuff Z'Nuff issue their self-titled debut. The album and band (known for their superior songwriting and Beatle-esque harmonies) represent hair metal maturing and exploring fresh avenues.

ERIC BRITTINGHAM (BASSIST, CINDERELLA, ON TRAVELING TO THE MOSCOW MUSIC PEACE FESTIVAL):

That was a blast, sitting on a plane, talking with Geezer Butler, having him tell stories. Ozzy was like a bit out of it [laughs]. He sat directly behind me, him and Sharon, and Sharon was like the nursemaid/mom to him. I just remember him getting annoyed with Sebastian Bach, because Sebastian was very hyper, running up and down the aisles, being loud, and Ozzy was like, "Please, will someone shut him the fuck up?" But it was funny, just sitting there, listening into his comments. I think one of the best ones was Jason Bonham. He was out for that thing, and he was telling stories about his dad and everything was about his dad, and he said something, and Ozzy said, "You know what? I'll tell you something about your dad. He was a drunk and a fucking junkie." And I was like, "Oh my God. Why did you bring that up, you little shit?" Oh, man. But he just came along, sat in or something.

It was pretty dreary. This is before the fall of the Iron Curtain. Everything was like gray and dismal, dreary. That's how I would sum it up today. And we were staying in, like, Stalin's Seven Stars, this famous building or whatever, and this place sucked. I mean the water was fucking brown, cockroaches everywhere. Thank God I brought my own toilet paper, because the toilet paper was the frickin' consistency of writing paper. I was thinking, "Man, I do not want to live here."

Yeah, Moscow Music Peace Festival—Bon Jovi, Mötley Crüe, Scorpions, Ozzy, Skid Row, going to Moscow, and just did this big antidrug, alcohol thing, and we did that record. It was a three-day event, with just the one show. Yeah, pretty pathetic. There was plenty of drugs and alcohol everywhere. Everybody was up and roaming the halls until 6 a.m., like, fucked out of their minds [laughs]. So it was, like, "Yeah, this is really good," you know? It's an antidrug thing and everyone is frickin' stoned.

MIKE FRASER (ENGINEER, ON WORKING WITH AEROSMITH):

I have to admit, the whole time we were doing "Love in an Elevator" I hated that song. I thought, "Oh, what are they doing this for?!" Now, in retrospect, it's like, "Oh, okay" [laughs]. It's one of their biggest songs.

CHIP Z'NUFF (BASSIST, ENUFF Z'NUFF):

We started the band in 1984 in Grandma and Grandpa McNulty's basement, here in Blue Island (Illinois). He was a friend of ours and his grandma and grandpa had this house, and they were kind enough to let us rehearse down there. So [vocalist] Donnie [Vie] and I recorded about twenty songs on a little four-track. I played drums, bass, and guitar, and he sang and played a little guitar. And we took the tapes and played them for people and they were blown away. People were saying "Cheap Trick meets Elvis Costello." We thought, great. So we

1980   **1981**   **1982**   **1983**   **1984**

put a band together, it's that simple. We did an album called *1985*. Howard Stern did the liner notes for it. That would have been the first album we put out, but fortunately we wrote some better material, which we put out when we got signed in 1989. So we signed with Atco. Derek Shulman, who was the president of Atco, signed us. We had Doc McGhee, who manages Kiss, Bon Jovi, everybody back then, was our manager. So we put the first album out, then *Strength*, then *Animals*. *Animals with Human Intelligence* cost us $400,000; *Strength* cost us $350,000. The first album cost us $180,000. They've all cost us hundreds of thousands of dollars to record. We've shown all the labels that you can make records for a tenth of what they're doing. And all they're doing is incurring huge debts with the artists that you can't even pay back. The record company's gotta sell a million records before you see a penny.

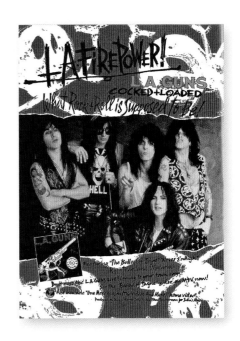

STEVE ALBINI
(GUITARIST AND VOCALIST, BIG BLACK, SOUND ENGINEER):

Heavy metal was laughed at. And the fucking fishnets and lipstick bullshit, that only happened in L.A. There may have been a few bands imitating that, in various places. I mean, I never saw a single band like that in Chicago. I think there was one kind of a cartoonish pop metal band called Enuff Z'Nuff, who were sort of like that in Chicago, but that stuff was a total fucking joke to us.

STEVE RILEY (DRUMMER, L.A. GUNS, ON *COCKED & LOADED*):

What makes up the sound is really a mixture of Tracii's guitar playing, and his guitar playing is some of the best around. It absolutely is, and it's not just because I play with him. Because I've been in a lot of bands on a lot of different labels. His guitar playing, if it's not underrated, it's just not quite realized. He's a super guitar player and he can write just about anything he wants. And the mixture in L.A. Guns starts with his bud that he brings in, and once the band takes hold of his writing session and [vocalist] Phil [Lewis] gets to put his touch on that, it's really Phil and Tracii's touch that makes up the L.A. Guns sound. I drive the beat home, but our sound is a mixture. We have a lot of influence from the '60s and the early '70s. And there's a lot of British influence in our sound. We love straight-ahead rock 'n' roll. We love Aerosmith, Rolling Stones, and other types of bands like Led Zeppelin and the Beatles, and we really do lean on all our styles. And our sound has always been quite versatile. I think that's why we stood out in the pack and had some credibility. We weren't afraid to mix it up on an album. We'll take it from one end to the other.

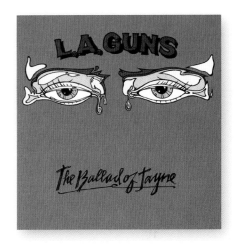

August 22, 1989: L.A. Guns' second album, *Cocked & Loaded*, hits the streets and goes gold on the strength of "The Ballad of Jayne" and "Rip and Tear." The record includes cameos from members of Cheap Trick. The band establish themselves as part of the "dirty hair metal" movement, along with Guns N' Roses, Skid Row, and Love/Hate.

August 29, 1989: Giant issue *Last of the Runaways*, on A&M; the "melodic rock" band is a vehicle for talented session guitarist and producer Dann Huff.

August 30, 1989: Molly Hatchet makes *Lightning Strikes Twice*, a total hair band album, forsaking their southern rock roots.

1985 **1986** **1987** **1988** **1989**

176

September 1, 1989: Mötley Crüe issue their *Dr. Feelgood* album, which arguably marks hair metal at its commercial zenith. The album is produced by Bob Rock and recorded in Vancouver, a route that had worked hair metal magic for both Aerosmith and Bon Jovi. *Dr. Feelgood* is eventually certified 6x platinum.

BOBBY INGRAM (GUITARIST, MOLLY HATCHET):

It was absolutely crazy, my experience with *Lightning Strikes Twice*. Are you ready? In the mid-'80s, we had management, agents, and record companies telling the band what the fuck to play, what the fuck to do, where to turn, where to shit, where to piss, how to do everything. It ripped the heart and soul out of the band. We were given songs that we have heard, fucking, maybe two or three times that wound up on the album. It made no sense to the group. We were being spoon-fed all this material, demoed to death, either to fuck with the band or make some people a lot of money, but not us. In the end it ripped the guts out of Molly Hatchet. They were great songs, don't get me wrong, but we didn't even get to meet the writers, just a little cassette tape. "Oh, let's work this up!" It wasn't the band's doing, trust me. It was all about making a lot of money, and taking it out of the pockets of the group. That is the truth.

TOMMY LEE (ON *DR. FEELGOOD*):

That was first time we'd worked with producer Bob Rock. We spent the time and money on it and that was a real signature time for us. Everybody was sober then as well and focused all their energy on writing a really great record, which is what we needed to do at that point in our career.

NIKKI SIXX:

You know, I said to Vince [Neil] one day—and he was aghast when I told him—"Do you realize that the band is fucking over?!" After *Girls, Girls, Girls*. And he said, "What are you talking about?! We're not over. A sold-out tour. . ." And I said, "You don't realize, we just made two fucking abortions of records. We made two records that might have equalled one. And we can't do it again. We have to fucking get serious now." And if we hadn't gotten serious, I think we would've been over at that point. You know, Vince is like heroin chic. Vince can be drunk and rock 'n' roll and looking at his watch because he's got four strippers waiting for him in the parking lot, and pull it off. What [*Theatre of Pain* and *Girls, Girls, Girls*] would have been if somebody would have said no to me, no to Tommy, no to Vince, and no to Mick, I don't know. We'll never know. But we know what *Dr. Feelgood* is. We know what happened.

VINCE NEIL (ON THE APPROACH TO *DR. FEELGOOD*):

We are completely sober. We made a pact together and said if we're going to do it and survive as a band we're going to be sober. Because it was always like there was one guy sober and the other guys not. Everybody was kind of like up here, down there, up here, down there. This was the first time we were all in the same spot. So when we recorded *Dr. Feelgood*, we'd moved out of L.A., up to Vancouver for like nine months, so there were no distractions, just recording. It was

POISON IVY

September 1989: Ex–Hanoi Rocks singer and hair metal fashion pioneer Michael Monroe's second solo album, *Not Fakin' It*, is issued on Polygram. At No. 161 on Billboard, it will be Moore's most successful solo album.

September 6, 1989: Faster Pussycat issue their second album, *Wake Me When it's Over*, which finds the band moving into a smarter, bluesier sound. The album sells gold on the strength of single and video "House of Pain."

September 12, 1989: Bonham, featuring Jason Bonham and now-deceased Canadian vocalist Daniel McMaster, issue *The Disregard of Timekeeping*, produced by Bob Ezrin. The band's sound is a hair metal–inflected yet high-quality take on Led Zeppelin.

good for us because we had Aerosmith right next door to us recording *Pump*, and we've been friends with them for a long time, and they were going through the same thing. It was a little tough because we had to live in Vancouver, and most of us basically just flew home on weekends, to L.A.

JOEY KRAMER (DRUMMER, AEROSMITH):

And that happens to be one of my favorite Aerosmith records. I love it. I was always happy with the playing on it and with the songs. For the time that we made the album, the production was top-flight. I still enjoy listening to it now, although it's a little on the wet side [laughs]. But that was a fun record to make and we worked really hard. It was basically the first record that we all made together when we were finally all sober. So that was kind of a landmark. And the playing and the songwriting on that was really us at our best.

TOM HAMILTON (BASSIST, AEROSMITH):

The *Pump* album really felt like the *Rocks* album. Those albums, I just remember feeling like they had an easy flow. They were both really challenging and really fun records to make, and the *Pump* album, we had already made a record up in Vancouver with Bruce Fairbairn [1987's *Permanent Vacation*] that we were really happy with, so we went and did [*Pump*], and that one was the equivalent of when we started with Jack Douglas with *Get Your Wings* and then did *Toys in the Attic* . . . it came out really good. Especially sonically; the production on it is just awesome. *Permanent Vacation* is, you know, a party album, a lot of different kind of stuff on it, but *Pump* sounds really brash. *Pump* is more of a hard rock album.

Bonham's Daniel McMaster.
© Rod Dysinger

1985   **1986**   **1987**   **1988**   **1989**

September 12, 1989: Aerosmith issue *Pump*, which includes another power ballad cowritten by Desmond Child called "What It Takes." Smarter ballad "Janie's Got a Gun" is the album's biggest hit. In total, though, the album is solid, nontrendy Aerosmith and goes 7x platinum. Aerosmith now is just Aerosmith, outside of trends, although perhaps this demonstrates that, despite it being the grunge era, there's still an appetite for traditional American hard rock.

September 12, 1989: Sweden's Shotgun Messiah issue a self-titled debut, on Relativity. Their sophomore album, *Second Coming*, is issued a couple weeks after Nirvana's *Nevermind*. By 1993, they will have gone industrial metal.

September 13, 1989: Canadian "metal queen" Lee Aaron issues her fifth and most successful album, *Bodyrock*. The album includes a cover of Montrose's "Rock Candy," although its big hit is "Whatcha Do to My Body."

October 1989: Iron Maiden guitarist Adrian Smith issues a hair band album, *Silver and Gold*, under the band name ASaP.

October 5, 1989: Überglamsters Pretty Boy Floyd issue their Howard Benson–produced debut, *Leather Boyz with Electric Toyz*, on MCA. The band is instantly accused, like Warrant and Winger, of hair metal leanings. Gone by 1991.

October 13, 1989: Ace Frehley issues a solo album called *Trouble Walkin'*, scoring a hit with his cover of ELO's "Do Ya" and also covering "Hide Your Heart" (written by Paul Stanley, Desmond Child, and Holly Knight), which will also show up on Kiss's *Hot in the Shade*.

October 17, 1989: Kiss issue *Hot in the Shade*, another substandard glam album that goes gold, nonetheless. Again, song doctors are all over the place: Vini Poncia, Desmond Child, Bob Halligan Jr., Holly Knight, and Michael Bolton. Gene Simmons admits taking his eye off the ball during this era and concentrating on movies and other business ventures.

1980   **1981**   **1982**   **1983**   **1984**

ADRIAN SMITH (GUITARIST, IRON MAIDEN):

I really liked where [Iron Maiden was] going with *Somewhere in Time* and *Seventh Son*. I thought they were a bit more mature and polished. That's where I was coming from and felt like going. I wanted to do something that is really polished. ASaP was kind of a shining, gleaming, produced record, which is what I wanted to do. I was quite pleased with it although, obviously, it was a radical musical departure, which threw a bit of a curveball.

DAVID COVERDALE:

The demos of the *Slip of the Tongue* album kick ass, the ones that I worked with [guitarist] Adrian [Vandeburg] on. And then, of course, it just got overdecorated. The way *Slip of the Tongue* was, it was Tommy Aldridge wanting to get all his licks in, Rudy Sarzo was trying to get all his licks in, Adrian Vanderburg was trying to get all his licks in, Steve Vai was . . . there was no foundation. Everyone was just being overtly flamboyant. And there's a picture I have at home just to remind me to never go there again, where I'm standing in the middle of this utter chaos. And you know, I can hear what it was like. The look on my face was like, "Where the hell am I supposed to sing in here?!" So, not the fondest memories. Also, I was coming into a period of great fatigue after working nonstop for three years on that remarkable successful rollercoaster that we experienced and I just lost perspective. And my private life was just the distraction from hell. And of course, normally, I would be able to seek solace within my professional life, but it was not to be this time! But like I say, I'm the Edith Piaf of rock, so I have no regrets. Everything that's ever happened to me has been necessary for learning this or learning that. "Judgment Day" is a corker, though, isn't it?"

KEITH OLSEN (PRODUCER):

Well, let's see, we sold twelve million copies of the one before, in fifteen months. Wow! [laughs]. Then we go in to start work on *Slip of the Tongue*, and [A&R man John] Kalodner says, "I want to do it in a similar way that we did the other one. That means, Keith, I want you and Clink—because Mike is a good buddy—and kind of do it together, kind of the way you did the last record with Mike Stone." And I said, "Okay, but you do realize it costs twice as much and it takes twice as long." And Kalodner says, "I don't care. We made more money than God on the last record!" The power ballad was the big thing that year, and so they went out and they toured that album, and everybody was saying, "Oh, such terribly disappointing sales." Well, okay, we only did four million copies. I'm serious! We did four million copies of that album in sixteen months, where the other one did twelve. Okay, so our business is really down. Well, no, they called it a stiff and the beginning of the end, because it only sold four million copies! [laughs] It was hideous, what the market did, and what the record company deemed as hits or misses, or successes or failures, and they called an album a failure because it only did four million copies. And only had one big hit on it.

1985   **1986**   **1987**   **1988**   **1989**

November 9, 1989: Fall of the Berlin Wall. Some claim this seismic event was hastened by the Moscow Peace Festival and the flood of western culture that it represented.

November 18, 1989: Whitesnake issue *Slip of the Tongue*, which goes 4x platinum in the US. It's much glammier than the band's preceding album, with even the rockers sounding "cheap." The big ballad is "The Deeper the Love."

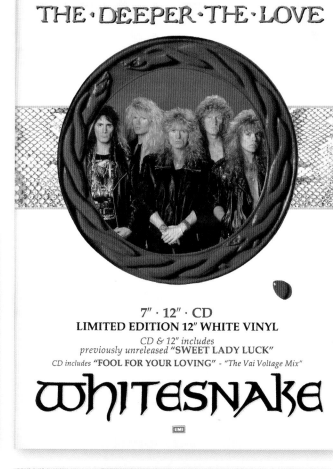

1980   **1981**   **1982**   **1983**   **1984**

BILLY CHILDS (ON BRITNY FOX'S FASHION CHOICES):

Well, we used to view it as, okay, this is the band. When the band is playing, this is the uniform we wear. If the band is doing a photo shoot, in support of that, sometimes we wear them, and occasionally not. But all that kind of went away after the first album, anyway. That idea was all Dean [Davidson]'s, our first singer. The whole look. And it was fairly unique at the time, and it was way over the top, and that's really what you had to do to get noticed in those days. So that happened, and we had earlier versions of that as well, that involved tying many things around ourselves. And, oh man, it would take an hour to get dressed and two hours to get undressed, because the shit would be wet. So we are playing these festivals outdoors, and it's 110 degrees, and we're wearing the suits all the time, man, the Britny suits, the uniform, whatever you want to call them, and it started to get pretty old. After the first album, it pretty much served its purpose, and then we started to move in a slightly different direction. And I, for one—and I think I can speak for everybody—was really happy to get out from underneath that. It's got to be incredible for someone like Kiss to have to wear that make-up for twenty-five years. Anyway, it made us look like a cool, sexy glam rock band. There's no hidden meaning behind that, man. But upscale. It was Dean's idea to go with that Amadeus kind of thing. And it just worked. It really worked for the band at that time period, and, as I say, it was unique. That was really a hard thing to achieve, especially during that particular time when everybody and their brother was spiking their hair up and wearing something fancy.

As prefabricated as the look itself was—and the look was very important in those days, Martin—people say, "Why did you guys look that way?" You had to understand, you are not going to get a record deal unless you did one better than the guy who just got one, you know what I mean? It was pretty much that kind of thing. Not only for us, but I would probably assume almost every band out there that had achieved our level of success, or greater or even close, their look was a prefabricated thing. You had to have that image in mind. But as prefabricated as our image was, our tunes were very much organic. We were pretty naïve, I guess, really. We never wrote in terms of, "Oh, this will make it big, this will be a big chorus, this will be a big hit. . . ." Not in the beginning anyway. We were just coming up with good riffs and somebody would sing something cool over it, and, hey, we had something that we liked. And when we liked it, we would play it, and the crowds seemed to like it. So that's how our tunes were written. It was never—I can say this with complete candidness—we just never really thought that way. We'd always been organic. Meanwhile, at the same time, we did come up with things, I mean, "Girlschool," for example, a very double-edged sword, that song. But we knew that would be big. We knew that video more or less wrote itself, and that would be very appealing, and would be very big. So we did come up with those things, but ironically they were more byproducts more than the content.

December 17, 1989: Britny Fox issue their second album, the Neil Kernon–produced *Boys in Heat* (Kernon also produced Dokken's *Back for the Attack*). It includes a cover of Nazareth's "Hair of the Dog." While Britny Fox's debut had gone gold and hit No. 39, this one misses certification and stalls at No. 79.

| 1985 | 1986 | 1987 | 1988 | 1989 |

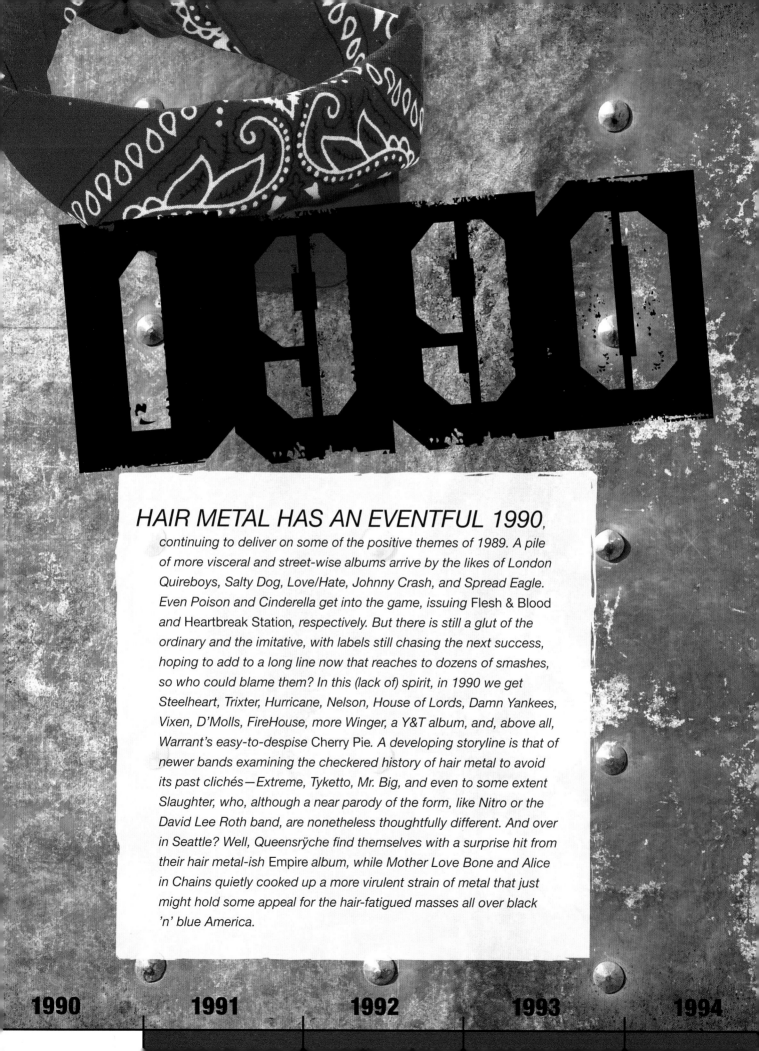

HAIR METAL HAS AN EVENTFUL 1990, continuing to deliver on some of the positive themes of 1989. A pile of more visceral and street-wise albums arrive by the likes of London Quireboys, Salty Dog, Love/Hate, Johnny Crash, and Spread Eagle. Even Poison and Cinderella get into the game, issuing Flesh & Blood and Heartbreak Station, respectively. But there is still a glut of the ordinary and the imitative, with labels still chasing the next success, hoping to add to a long line now that reaches to dozens of smashes, so who could blame them? In this (lack of) spirit, in 1990 we get Steelheart, Trixter, Hurricane, Nelson, House of Lords, Damn Yankees, Vixen, D'Molls, FireHouse, more Winger, a Y&T album, and, above all, Warrant's easy-to-despise Cherry Pie. A developing storyline is that of newer bands examining the checkered history of hair metal to avoid its past clichés—Extreme, Tyketto, Mr. Big, and even to some extent Slaughter, who, although a near parody of the form, like Nitro or the David Lee Roth band, are nonetheless thoughtfully different. And over in Seattle? Well, Queensrÿche find themselves with a surprise hit from their hair metal-ish Empire album, while Mother Love Bone and Alice in Chains quietly cooked up a more virulent strain of metal that just might hold some appeal for the hair-fatigued masses all over black 'n' blue America.

1990   1991   1992   1993   1994

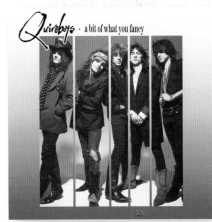

1990: Supporting the British reputation for a gritty, bluesy form of hair metal are Quireboys, with *A Bit of What You Fancy*. Barroom party rocker "7 O'Clock" is a minor hit, even in the US.

1990: Keel's Marc Ferrari forms Cold Sweat and issues a self-titled major label debut that explores a trending return to a heavier metal for some hair metal musicians.

1990: San Francisco's Cry Wolf see their Japan-only self-titled debut issued in the states as *Crunch*, through Grand Slamm/IRS.

1990: Dutch hair metal band Sleeze Beez issues their US major label debut, *Screwed Blued & Tattooed*, which sells well due to MTV hit "Stranger than Paradise."

January 1990: Y&T issues the impossibly glossy, void-of-personality, and corporate *Ten*, their last before a long hiatus and rethink.

DAVE MENIKETTI (VOCALIST AND GUITARIST, Y&T):

When we were doing *Ten*, I remember the head of the art department at Geffen was pushing this really lame idea of having these big giant Y&T letters and we would be hanging off of them and around them. It just reminded me of something that the Beatles or the Monkees would have done. We're just like, "Oh my God, what are these guys thinking?!"

1995   **1996**   **1997**   **1998**   **1999**

January 1990: Atlanta's Black Crowes present their debut, *Shake Your Money Maker*. The band, previously psychedelic paisley pop, find instant success straddling the dirty hair metal wave begun by Guns N' Roses and the "keep it real" blues metal wave as demonstrated by Cinderella. As well, the band's evocations of Humble Pie and the Faces aligns them with UK rockers The Quireboys and Thunder.

January 27, 1990: Las Vegas' Slaughter come late to the party with *Stick It to Ya*, which goes 2x platinum. "Fly to the Angels" is the record's egregious, melodramatic power ballad that gets it there, although the main single is party rocker "Up All Night." The band includes vocalist Mark Slaughter and bassist Dana Strum from Vinnie Vincent Invasion.

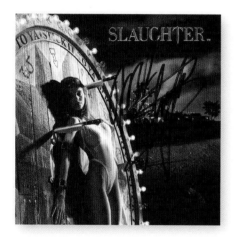

MARK SLAUGHTER:

I think the key point with Slaughter is that, first of all, it's got a very strong rhythm section, a very good bottom to it. My voice, over the top of it. And my voice is very high and it's got a very distinctive tone. You're either going to love it or you hate it— it is what it is. But by that, it has its own sound—no excuses. You know, we've done what we've done over the years and we're proud of it and we're the only band from our genre that wrote and produced and performed our own music, from the very beginning. As for production, it's very distinct. Our idea was the infusion of all the classic rock elements as well as the current thing that was going on at that time. It's funny, in fact, Slaughter never played a live show until we played with Kiss. We wrote the songs, we played in the studio, knocked it out there, but as far as an actual live show, the first show we ever played was in Lubbock, Texas, opening up for Kiss. And, actually, when we came off the stage, we had a gold record waiting in our dressing room from the record company. So it was very not typical, how it happened.

1990   **1991**   **1992**   **1993**   **1994**

TOM ZUTAUT (A&R MAN):

When I signed Salty Dog, the party was still rolling. I mean, Salty Dog, Roxy Blue, and Phantom Blue, being the female band, I felt that the party was still rolling. By the time their records came out, you know, that Nirvana record had come up. I had another band in the grunge metal area called The Nymphs, with Inger Lorre. And actually her record predated both Nirvana and Pearl Jam—probably her record was the first grunge record. But she made her record, and then her record got put on hold, because her producer ended up mixing *Use Your Illusion*. So her record was delayed a year and a half, due to Bill Price going off and doing the GN'R record. That's why she got pissed off and urinated on me in my office.

February 1990: Salty Dog issue their lone album, *Every Dog Has Its Day*, on Geffen. Lead singer Jimmi Bleacher and bassist Michael Hannon were both from Columbus, Ohio. The album sold well, but the band was dropped before they could issue a second. (Hannon now fronts American Dog.) The band's sound was a cross between the new, raw, bluesy hair metal and Led Zeppelin.

February 9, 1990: Johnny Crash joins the line of credible too-late-to-the-game hair bands. Their lone Columbia-issued album features the lead vocals of Vicki James Wright, formerly of NWOBHM outfit Tokyo Blade.

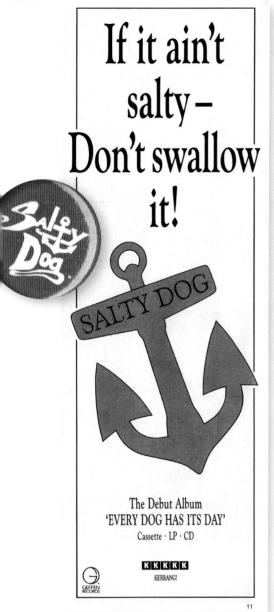

If it ain't salty – Don't swallow it!

SALTY DOG

The Debut Album
'EVERY DOG HAS ITS DAY'
Cassette · LP · CD

KKKK
KERRANG!

GEFFEN RECORDS

11

DAMN YANKEES — HOT DAMN!

TED NUGENT, JACK BLADES, TOMMY SHAW AND MICHAEL CARTELLONE ARE OUT TO PROVE THAT THERE'S ONE THING AMERICANS STILL DO BETTER THAN ANYONE ELSE.

DAMN YANKEES ONE NEW ALBUM THAT'S WORTH FIGHTING FOR.

FEATURING THE SONG "COMING OF AGE"

© 1990 WARNER BROS. RECORDS INC.

LOVE/HATE
BLACK OUT in the red room

| 1990 | 1991 | 1992 | 1993 | 1994 |

JIZZY PEARL (VOCALIST, LOVE/HATE):

Yes, the records sound really good now, and, yes, people really like them now, but why didn't people go crazy in 1990? I don't know. I mean, our second record, the label really didn't like it. They wanted us to come out with *Blackout II*. And we wanted to graduate a bit and get a bit more serious, and we kind of weren't allowed to get serious. We were still supposed to be fuckups and drunks and, you know, break windows, just be juvenile. I think, maybe if we would've made a more aggressive second record, it would have carried on. But that is the past. A lot of the time fans will come up to me and they'll have a bit of a chip on their shoulder, saying, "Man, why didn't you sell as much?" and "It's just a damn shame." And I say, "What? It would have been a damn shame if I didn't make any records at all." To me, it's all good. I got to tour the world and I got to play and I still play today. Poison comes into our dressing room, and I mean, they love the *Blackout in the Red Room* record, and I've never met these guys.

February 22, 1990: Ted Nugent, Tommy Shaw (Styx), Jack Blades (Night Ranger), and drummer Michael Cartellone of hair metal supergroup Damn Yankees issue their self-titled debut. The album goes double-platinum on the strength of power ballad "High Enough."

February 22, 1990: Love/Hate's *Blackout in the Red Room* is issued, on Columbia. It rises only to No. 154 and the band tour it, supporting Dio and then AC/DC. "Why Do You Think They Call it Dope?" is a minor MTV hit. This underrated band is arguably the finest of the dirty, sleazy hair metal subgenre led by GN'R.

April 4, 1990: Rare UK hair metal entry Thunder bring a rootsy, bluesy sound to their EMI/Geffen debut, *Backstreet Symphony*.

April 25, 1990: New York transplants hailing from Boston, Spread Eagle issue a self-titled debut, on MCA. The well-regarded act is a dirty metal bridge from Guns N' Roses and Skid Row to Love/Hate. Still, the noble effort comes too late.

May 2, 1990: Tough-guy rockers Little Caesar issue their gritty self-titled debut, which coughs up a hit in "Chain of Fools," driving the album to No. 139 on the charts. The band is A&R'd by John Kalodner and the record is produced by Bob Rock. Singer Ron Young later joins The Four Horsemen.

May 10, 1990: Trixter, from Paramus, New Jersey, issue their self-titled debut, on MCA. It goes gold and hits No. 28 on the charts, somewhat fueled by a boy band angle, given their tender ages. The album is recorded in Hollywood. They tour opening for Stryper.

May 10, 1990: Connecticut's Steelheart is another late arrival with their self-titled debut, on MCA.

May 15, 1990: Lita Ford issues her fourth studio album, *Stiletto*, but the band peaked with "Kiss Me Deadly" two years earlier.

June 12, 1990: Bad Company issue *Holy Water*, their last record to go platinum and the second to last of the Brian Howe era.

RIKKI ROCKETT (DRUMMER, POISON):

We're a good band and we have a lot of hit songs. Basically, when you see us, you get an hour and a half of hit songs and we deliver it with complete high energy and a show, and that's important. We're an important band for that reason. I mean, we may not be everybody's cup of tea, but nobody is everybody's cup of tea. I mean, look, I'm not a music critic. I enjoy the bands who are out with us. Cinderella, we actually toured with back in 1986, and both of us opened for Loudness. And of course we would get the snide critic-y reviews and they would get the great reviews, and look where they're at now, so take note, Martin! And you know what? This is what I don't understand. And let me just ask you this. If you were at the show and someone wrote a review about it and you wrote a bad one but somebody liked what they saw, they know what they saw, so what difference does it really make what you wrote?

1990   **1991**   **1992**   **1993**   **1994**

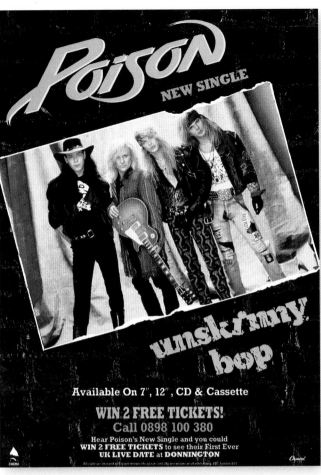

June 21, 1990: Poison's issue their third album, *Flesh & Blood*, which sells seven million copies worldwide. Recordings made on the tour will become the band's bloated double live album, *Swallow This Live*, which, given its release on November 12, 1991, six weeks after Nirvana's *Nevermind*, helps put a fork in the near-decade reign of hair metal.

June 26, 1990: One of the last breakout hit successes for hair metal is Nelson, whose debut, *After the Rain*, goes triple-platinum on the strength of No. 1 hit ballad "(Can't Live Without Your) Love and Affection." The band features the flowing blond locks of Matthew and Gunnar Nelson, twin sons of Ricky Nelson, and represents a considerable stretch of the hair metal rulebook toward pure pop.

June 27, 1990: Cheap Trick release another glam album, *Busted*, with overproduction similar to *Lap of Luxury*, a handful of song doctors, three videos, and a No. 12 chart placement. The record doesn't sell as well as *Lap of Luxury*, and a few months later Epic drops them.

June 28, 1990: D'Molls release their second (and last) album, *Warped*, also on Atlantic.

July 1990: Vixen's *Rev it Up*, their second and last (until reunion), rises only to No. 52 in the US. Neither Vixen album achieves gold status.

July 19, 1990: Mother Love Bone issue their *Apple* album—their lone release due to the heroin overdose death of lead singer Andrew Wood. *Apple* is the last Seattle grunge album to retain any vestige of a glam metal influence.

MARK ARM (VOCALIST, MUDHONEY, ON MOTHER LOVE BONE):

I know at the time [Mother Love bone and, later, Pearl Jam bassist] Jeff Ament was really into Zodiac Mindwarp, which had kind of a biker pose but also pretty funny lyrics. To me, glam was the stuff that was happening in the '70s with Sweet. I guess that term totally morphed in the '80s to mean any metal band that dressed in women's clothing. But there's a very different feeling between most of those bands and Sweet or the New York Dolls. Mother Love Bone, I don't think was as serious as Guns N' Roses, if you know what I mean. There's more levity in the record. Guns N' Roses, they have that Robert Williams painting of the machine raping the woman on the cover of the first record. There was that intensity, and also I think an unintentional goofiness. But there was nothing tongue-in-cheek about it, whereas I think Andy was very clever and very funny.

TERRY DATE (PRODUCER):

I remember somebody saying early on that Mother Love Bone wanted to be Montrose [laughs]. I always thought that was funny. And I remember very distinctly reading a review, and somebody calling Mother Love Bone a metal band, and that just surprised me. Although there wasn't a grunge scene at that time. I think the word "grunge" and the labeling came later. To me it was just an evolution of a local town's musical evolution. These guys seemed to be rejecting the hair metal, the butt rock that was going on [laughs]. And I, to be honest, wasn't that involved with the very early parts of that, because I was in the studio recording some of that butt rock [laughs].

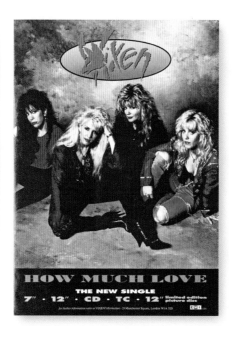

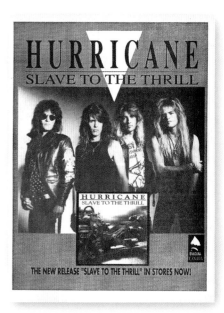

1990　　**1991**　　**1992**　　**1993**　　**1994**

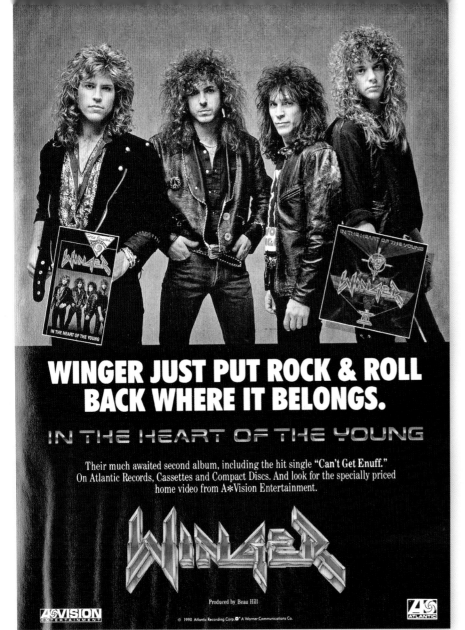

July 23, 1990: Hurricane issue their third album, *Slave to the Thrill*. The original cover art was a very sexist depiction of a woman on a machine. Shortly thereafter, the woman was removed, leaving only the machine. The band featured vocalist Kelly Hansen as well as guitarist Doug Aldrich, later of Whitesnake.

July 24, 1990: Pantera's major label debut, *Cowboys from Hell*, is by some measures the heaviest record ever as of 1990. It's certainly robustly antiglam, and its success in a major-label environment helps usher in a new era.

July 24, 1990: Winger issue their second album, *In The Heart of the Young*.

ROD MORGENSTEIN (DRUMMER, WINGER, ON REFORMING):

You know, Kip has mixed feelings. All the Winger bashing that we received, I feel for the most part that was uncalled for, because I know in my heart that the musicianship in Winger was at a very high caliber, especially for that kind of music. Kip's fear is that since the band is really his name on the line, he's really not that sure that he wants to relive all of that bashing again. And justifiably so. I mean, I'm staring at a photo from one of our early photo sessions that Kip just sent me, and it's hilarious. Our hair can't even fit on the page, it was so big. I think if people could just go beyond that . . . I mean, it's almost like looking back to the 1700s, when they wore all the wigs and stuff. Just try to get to the heart of the matter, they would see that there was a lot of substance to the band. It was not the garage band approach. It was very fastidious, and it would take months to complete a record.

1995   **1996**   **1997**   **1998**   **1999**

We all hated it. Everybody hated it. With the exception of, say, Metallica and Slayer, which were considered cool. And you know Priest, everybody grew up on JP. But '80s metal, such as it was, I don't consider '80s metal *metal*, other than the obvious exceptions. It was pop metal. And it really was not particularly metal in any sense of the word. Pop metal, meaning the sort of Def Leppard et al, Winger, and Warrant, all the L.A. hair metal bands—nobody considered it metal. It certainly wasn't . . . it was barely rock. That stuff was absolutely despised up here. There was a scene of that kind of music that existed in Seattle, as it existed in pretty much all suburbs throughout the United States at the time, but it didn't really get anywhere. I think the only bands that successfully came out of that '80s metal scene here in Seattle were Queensrÿche and the original version of Alice in Chains, kind of came out of that scene, and they were smart enough to evolve and change their sound. And Queensrÿche just happened to be very good at what they did, so they rose to the top of the pile, but they certainly didn't come out of any punk rock background or do the club scene or any of that "paid our dues" thing.

August 7, 1990: Extreme issues their second album, *Extreme II: Pornograffitti.* It is considered a thinking man's hair metal album, with thoughtful lyrics and tasteful guitar work, the type of album deemed at the time welcome and even necessary to keep the party going. However, the album goes double-platinum on the strength of an acoustic ballad ("More than Words"), much like Kiss did with "Beth" back in 1976, causing some grousing among fans of the band's otherwise hard rock direction.

Though not my favorite Extreme record, that was the record that put Extreme on the map. I think Nuno's guitar work on that record was the best. He wrote a hell of a lot of riffs. And if you want to edit it down to one statement, you can say that *Pornograffitti* is much more than "More than Words," because there's a lot of great stuff on that record and "More than Words" was the vehicle for people to hear it. I'm sure there were a few hundred housewives returning it after hearing "Get the Funk Out" and "Suzi (Wants Her All Day Sucker)" [laughs].

The first headline tour we did was playing to mostly empty clubs with Alice in Chains opening for us. I remember even Tom Morello from Rage Against the Machine, he said he was at those gigs. But then we went from the tour with Alice in Chains to, all of a sudden, bizarre sorts of combinations. We'd be touring with ZZ Top and then opening for David Lee Roth. Nobody knew what to do with us [laughs]. There wasn't any specific genre they could put us into, so they didn't know what the hell to do with us. But Alice in Chains, we loved them. I remember walking out to sound check and hearing them do "Man in the Box," thinking, "Man, this is really cool." There was definitely a difference in the feel. And the crowd . . . the cool thing I remember about that, before it became hip to be kind of grunge, I remember the crowds loving all of it, which is kind of great. It wasn't like this "Oh my god, that's an Alice in Chains fan; that's an Extreme fan." People were just packing clubs and coming in to listen to music. And I think when it

1990　　　　**1991**　　　　**1992**　　　　**1993**　　　　**1994**

becomes what it becomes and people figured out what it is, then they put a name to it, and there's a scene and it gets segregated. Then the clubs start happening—"I belong to this club; I belong to that church." That's when it started changing.

GEOFF TATE (VOCALIST, QUEENSRŸCHE):

Empire was a huge, massive commercial success for us. And I think there were some good songs on it, too, from an artistic standpoint. But we toured for eighteen months on that record. We got off that tour and we just didn't even want to play music anymore. We were just so burned out. And just being together all that time, and on the road, it really kind of fractured the band. So we took a year off. And I remember during that year we hardly spoke to each other. And then a good solid year went by, and somebody called me, I think it was [guitarist] Michael [Wilton], and he said, "We should probably make a record."

SCOTT ROCKENFIELD (DRUMMER, QUEENSRŸCHE):

[1988's *Operation:*] *Mindcrime* took almost a year to write and make that record. It was a pretty deep, fine-tuned concept. We completely turned left field and said, "Screw that, let's not make a concept record or theme, let's just write a bunch of songs." So we wrote twelve songs and put them on a thing called *Empire*, stuck it out. And the first single, "Empire," just went through the roof. So we toured for fourteen months, went around the world twice on that record. But it was nice, because it was the first opportunity we had to really headline in the full-on sense of being a global headliner.

C. J. SNARE (VOCALIST, FIREHOUSE):

When we brought [bassist] Perry [Richardson] back in again, we were still White Heat, and there were so many "white" bands out there—the Canadian White Heat, Whitesnake, White Lion, Great White—that the record company was like, "You know, let's not do the White thing," and that's how we came upon FireHouse.

BILL LEVERTY (GUITARIST, FIREHOUSE):

We're a melodic hard rock band with a positive message and diversity. It's something that young kids can enjoy listening to and older people can enjoy listening to, and the older people aren't embarrassed to play it for the young kids. We don't have a lot of controversial lyrics in our music for the most part. The worst thing we would end up talking about is mild in comparison with a lot of other bands. Other than that, we just have good vocals and good musicianship. The one thing that I think is unique is that everybody in the band is a quality singer. Our vocals are all strong and our lead singer is really good. If we had four of him, we would be really something, but we have three guys that back him up that sing real well, and I think that sets us apart. The

Queensrÿche's Michael Wilton.
© Rod Dysinger

August 20, 1990: Queensrÿche issue what is widely considered their hair metal album, *Empire*. It's a huge success, selling 3x platinum on the strength of singles "Silent Lucidity," "Jet City Woman," and "Empire."

August 21, 1990: FireHouse, from Charlotte, North Carolina, issue their self-titled debut. It goes 2x platinum on the backs of four singles, including huge power ballad "Love of a Lifetime."

August 21, 1990: Ratt issue *Detonator*, which goes gold (all of the band's four previous albums went platinum or multiplatinum). The band had broken with producer Beau Hill and brought in Desmond Child, who, of course, cowrote the whole record except for a 55-second guitar intro. Two years later, Ratt breaks up.

August 21, 1990: Ex–glam band Alice in Chains from Seattle issue their classic grunge debut, *Facelift*.

first album, we had a lot of time to write those songs. One thing we've always concentrated on was to make sure that when we put out an album we had an album's worth of quality material, not just one good song and the rest throwaways, which a lot of bands tend to do. But we had a huge success with that first album. When I look back at the promotion we had with that, the timing, it was just wonderful. MTV was playing that kind of music all the time, radio was playing it, the "rock 40" format was so hot back then. And we were on some great tours.

GREG PRATO (AUTHOR, *GRUNGE IS DEAD*):
Alice in Chains started off as more of a glam metal band. They were drawing direct influence from Poison, GN'R, and Kiss, and it seemed like when they first started, that's what they wanted to be also. And then, I think, they discovered Soundgarden, and that's when they changed the way they dressed and down-tuned and started to sound more Sabbath-y like Soundgarden, and they found the formula for what they are today, and what people love them for. But I know some of the grunge guys liked Def Leppard. Mike McCready, who is the guitarist for Pearl Jam, I know he cited Def Leppard as a pretty big influence, and also Stone Gossard—he dug *Pyromania*. But as far as Poison and those bands, I don't think many of the grunge bands liked that. I think some of them liked the first Guns N' Roses album, but that's the closest it got.

BILLY CHILDS (BASSIST, BRITNY FOX, ON THE CHANGING OF THE GUARD):
I guess the first physical signs of it I began to see was when we started doing record-release shoots. And we used to go to L.A. for all that, and I started to see a different breed of band that wasn't there before. I started seeing bands like Love/Hate and LSD. They didn't get really big but they were really interesting. And I started meeting these hybrid kind of grunge/glam guys. So it was obvious it was being taken seriously. And then I remember doing early radio, when [1991's] *Bite Down Hard* was just coming out, and I remember sitting with the band one day, and the [DJ] finished, okay—"And that was 'Louder' off of *Bite Down Hard*. And here's something new, by Alice in Chains: "Man in the Box"— and I'd never heard of that. And I really dug the '90s stuff. And I remember saying to the guys, "Wow, this is kind of like the latest thing that seems to be rolling here." And they go, "Oh man, this seems like a fad." I was going, "No, I don't think so." And unfortunately it turned out I was right. And I also remember, too, when we started out the *Bite Down Hard* tour, we're playing huge clubs, nice clubs, sold out all the time, and by the end of it we played a place in Florida called the Good Food Sports Pub, which actually had booths, and it was like, "Wow, it's pretty obvious that this is over."

1990   **1991**   **1992**   **1993**   **1994**

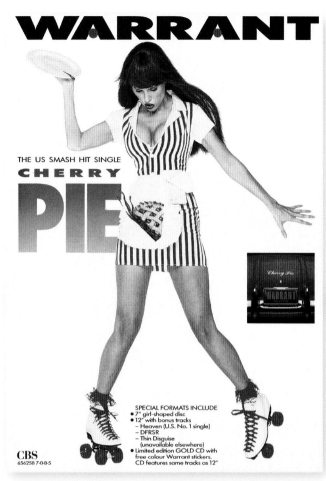

HOUSE OF LORDS go in for the kill with "SAHARA" the blazing new album featuring their searing version of Blind Faith's "CAN'T FIND MY WAY HOME" plus "SHOOT" and "KISS OF FIRE."

Produced by Andy Johns and House Of Lords
Executive Producer: Gene Simmons
Management: Ken Adamany Associates

On Simmons/RCA Records cassettes, compact discs and albums.

THE US SMASH HIT SINGLE
CHERRY PIE

SPECIAL FORMATS INCLUDE
● 7" girl-shaped disc
● 12" with bonus tracks
   – Heaven (U.S. No. 1 single)
   – DFRSR
   – Thin Disguise
     (unavailable elsewhere)
● Limited edition GOLD CD with
   free colour Warrant stickers.
   CD features same tracks as 12"

CBS
656258 7-0-8-5

JERRY DIXON (BASSIST, WARRANT):

Cherry Pie is the better record because we weren't so green in the studio. Musically, we played a lot better. But pretty much those first two records [*Dirty Rotten Filthy Stinking Rich* and *Cherry Pie*] are made out of the same piece of wood. We were in the same frame of mind; [vocalist Jani] Lane was writing the same kinds of songs. Those were two very similar records, which was good because that's what people wanted at that time. What I liked about Beau Hill is the preproduction side of it. He wants to make sure . . . he's not worried about the recording end of it. He's worried about what you're recording. What is the song about? Is it a hit? Is it not a hit? Rewrite this part. So it's the making of the record even before you go to tape. Lyrics . . . our lyrics tended to always be about girls. They tended always to be about sex. And you know, at sixteen, that's all we knew [laughs]. Or all we cared about. But as we developed and did [1992's] *Dog Eat Dog*, there was a bit heavier lyrical content, like on "April 2031," which is about the future. So we kind of grew up a bit; we went from talking about chicks to a little bit more serious subjects. You tend to write about where you're at in your life and what you know. So those first two records, all we knew was cherry pie was good and girls were good.

August 21, 1990: House of Lords issue their second album, *Sahara*, on Simmons/RCA.

September 11, 1990: Warrant issue their second album, *Cherry Pie*, the title track of which is derided as completely cliché hair metal in every way imaginable, from production to vocals, sexual lyrics, and juvenile video.

1995   **1996**   **1997**   **1998**   **1999**

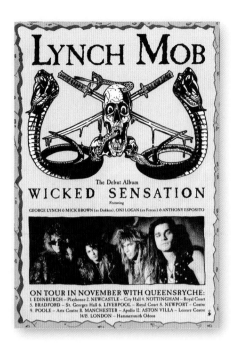

October 23, 1990: Lynch Mob, featuring Dokken guitarist and consummate hair band shredder George Lynch, issue their debut album, *Wicked Sensation*, on Elektra. Despite the waning popularity of the hair metal sound, the album achieves gold status.

BEAU HILL (PRODUCER):

Warrant, to me, was a vehicle for Jani. No disrespect to any of the guys in the band, Jani was really the driving force behind that band, from my perspective. And Jani was a very good writer, and, again, if you don't have any songs, then you can have all the long hair and silly clothes and good looks that you want, but then you're going to wind up being one of those second- or third-tier hair bands. And I think it was Jani's writing and his showmanship that really pushed Warrant to the top. And the other thing was, now that I think about it, the guys in the band really instinctively knew that Jani was an exceptionally talented guy. So I never got the sense that there was the internal strife like there was in Ratt. The guys knew that Jani was a good writer and there was a lot of cooperation. It wasn't done in a way that was ego-driven. It felt cooperative.

JERRY DIXON:

We upped our budget by about $100,000, longer lunch breaks, a little longer on everything. But a record label is like a bank, you know? You're preapproved for this. And if you want it, take it. But our philosophy was, we may never see this money again. True, you gotta pay it back and you've got to sell records to pay it back. If they're going to give it to you, take it, man. You know, you fudge the budget a little bit and all of a sudden everybody gets a little salary. It doesn't all go to the recording studio, so that's why people do that. You take it from those bastards when you can get it [laughs]. You want to give us an advance? Hell, yeah! We may never sell a damn record. But then, it did bite us in the ass because we did sell a lot of records. And then it turns out you have a shitty deal. So it's a double-edged sword. Together, between those first three, we sold six million records. *Cherry Pie* is almost three million, worldwide—Japan, Europe, everywhere. *Dog Eat Dog* went gold in the States, almost platinum. *Cherry Pie* was about two and a half million. *Dirty Rotten* was over two million.

STEVE ALBINI (ON HAIR METAL PRODUCTION):

The slick, pop, glam, hard rock records—most of them used techniques that were taken from jingles and pop music: many layers of guitar overdubs, many layers of vocal overdubs, drums being replaced either by drum machines or supplemented by samples. Everything was played to a click track. The guitar sounds and vocal sounds were quite processed using a lot of electronic effects. The records were taken out of the realm of documentary recording and put into the sort of Spielberg realm of production. It bore much more relationship to soundtrack music or jingle music than it did to the kind of punk aesthetic of making a quick, cheap, accurate recording of a band. And the grunge recordings were . . . more like punk records in the technical execution than they were like the glam records. I mean, the thing is, I don't know anybody from that era, of those bands, that aspired to sounding like that L.A. shit. Nobody wanted to sound like Guns N' Roses or Mötley Crüe. Nobody wanted to sound like that.

JERRY DIXON (ON HAIR METAL PRODUCTION):

Well, the reverb button [laughs]. I don't know what the hell that was. I think the oddest thing about that sound was the drum sound. It was like they would use triggers, which was a big deal. That way when the drummer hits the kick, you could trigger it in the studio to play like a sampled kick, and he would put ten of those on one kick drum, and put a reverb on that and make this *ccchhh*. And fifteen hundred guitar tracks. If you could sum it up, just overdoing everything. To the point where you can't understand it. Like, I will say though, our first record, one good thing about that era is that it really made your band a lot better than the newer bands, because there wasn't overdubs and there wasn't ProTools and copy and pasting. You had to play the whole song all the way through. If you made a mistake in the very end, it was, "Okay, start from the beginning." And the drummers especially; they had to take it from the beginning to the end. There was no fixing the tempo or moving a kick up, or sanitizing anything. And that was kind of neat. We worked on a two-inch machine, all that kind of dinosaur stuff. And it kind of made us a better band. And now people don't even have to sing and they sound like Mariah Carey. "Oh, we can fix that."

RUDOLF SCHENKER (GUITARIST, SCORPIONS):

When we came up with *Crazy World*, I think that was the peak of '80s rock . . . 1991, we had a big success, seven or eight million sold around the world. And then grunge came; even when we were on tour in America with the album *Crazy World*, grunge was already there. We said, "Hmmm, something has changed. We can't do the same thing again." When we started in the '70s, we tried to experiment and find our right style, and then in the '80s we found our style and we played our style until 1991, when the timing was perfect for that. And then when grunge came out, we feared that the times had changed drastically.

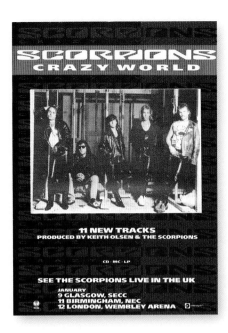

November 6 1990: The Scorpions issue *Crazy World*, which includes political power ballad "Wind of Change," a huge flashpoint song coming nearly a year to the day after the fall of the Berlin Wall. The band even produces a Russian-language version.

November 13, 1990: Tesla score a surprise hit with an acoustic live album called *Five Man Acoustical Jam*, powered by the smash status of the band's cover of "Signs," originally by Five Man Electrical Band.

JEFF KEITH (VOCALIST, TESLA):

We were out with Mötley Crüe when we did the acoustic album. They had prior commitments on a couple of nights off and we said, "Hey, instead of having two nights off on the road, let's go out and play some acoustic guitar and stuff," and the next thing you know we got a killer album from it. So they're all good memories; there aren't really any bad ones. I'm the kind of guy who tries to find positive out of everything.

**ERIC BRITTINGHAM
(ON NOT GETTING RICH FROM CINDERELLA):**

No, not like what you would think [laughs]. Because back then there was a lot of expense, too. You had to recoup on the videos and all that, and videos were like a half-million dollars each. So per record, you spend two million on the videos and you have to recoup that. And recouping is like, you know, a band gets a very small percentage of the retail price on a record. On our first record I think we were getting about seventy cents per unit, and out of that seventy cents, you've got to pay them back. And you're paying back like a couple million bucks. But it's like a promotional thing. Put it out, and in the mid-'80s, that was the big thing to do. You had videos that cost an arm and a leg. And then look at Van Halen's "Jump." That was made for like about eight grand, the whole thing, with a hand-held camera. Set up and frickin' did it. Then you had ours. I think the cheapest video we ever made was $300,000 or $400,000, and most of them topped half a million.

DEREK SHULMAN (A&R MAN, ON WHAT SUNK CINDERELLA):

The truth is, I would say the advent of MTV. And the very quick rocketing to fame from a track or two, and the heavily played video on MTV in the early days of MTV. In the early days, MTV would unfortunately bag a band, who perhaps would've had longer runs. I mean, it was a shortcut to success, to a certain degree, but it was also a millstone around your neck in certain respects, too. Bon Jovi was a band that was able to get out of that. Because Jon is so smart and forward-thinking, he was able to circumvent the stigma of MTV. Unfortunately, when people think of Cinderella, they think of the hair band videos and the whole aspect of what they looked like, where they discount the music. To be honest with you, it was certainly easy. The first album we put out went straight to the top of the charts, and in a lot of ways, the band was catching up with their fame, as opposed to having the groundswell that other bands should have today, because of a fan base. So it was very quick in coming.

1990   **1991**   **1992**   **1993**   **1994**

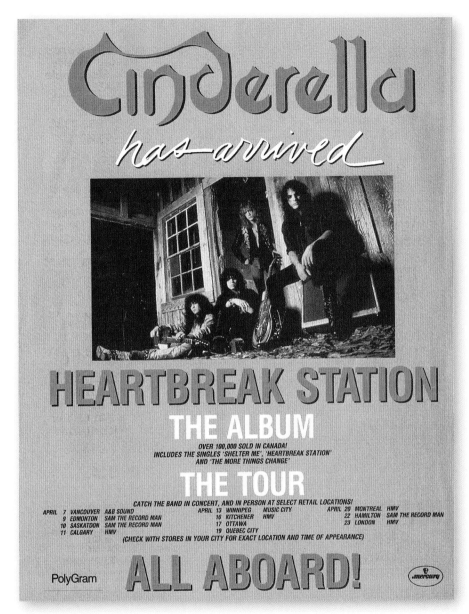

ERIC BRITTINGHAM:

We always did well touring, but by the end of the tour we'd either break even or take a loss. That's not keeping on the ball. And in hindsight, you're like, "Well, we could've done without this and this and this and put a lot more money in our pockets." At the end of the day, you look back, and it's like you lose a couple hundred thousand from touring and it's like, "Hmmm." But our biggest loss was on the *Heartbreak Station* tour, because the record company did a really big push on it, and the record was well-received from the critics, but it didn't sell like the first two records did. And we geared up and had our own staging built, reinvested a lot of money before we even toured.

November 20, 1990: Cinderella's *Heartbreak Station* is the band's most down-dressed and bluesiest album yet. It goes platinum and hits No. 19. "Shelter Me" is the album's biggest hit; the title track and "The More Things Change" are also singles.

1995   **1996**   **1997**   **1998**   **1999**

1990

AND SO HERE WE ARE, the apocryphal last hurrah for hair metal, even if some of the finest albums loosely attributable to the genre would see the light of day in 1992, after no one cared enough to take them seriously. Actually, there are a lot of interesting hair metal records issued in 1991—and some that are not particularly interesting, but just really high-quality participants to the tale, such as rollicking rounders from White Lion, Kingdom Come, BulletBoys, Mr. Big, Tesla, and, arguably, Britny Fox. A bit more off the map are debuts from Saigon Kick and The Four Horsemen: the first very forward-thinking, the latter charmingly reactionary. In the "we try harder" department, Skid Row shocks the industry with their toothsome Slave to the Grind, while Van Halen smartens up and toughens up for the uncharacteristically ambitious For Unlawful Carnal Knowledge.

Still, as our tale comes to an end, 1991 features a final battle royale. Ah yes, what to say about Guns N' Roses, who, after years of false starts, hit us up with two long studio albums at once—the Use Your Illusion bookends. They are either a very egregiously hair metal band or some sort of anti-hair band. And therein lies their mystique. Whatever you may think of them—and they certainly live on past 1991—they are the "chosen" band in our happy hair history, putting out (with much hoopla) their big pair at the exact same time Nirvana explodes like a supernova with Nevermind. And as our dear tale-tellers relate, all attention and resources and assets and goodwill . . . well, it's all gone in a flash. As the popular telling tells it popularly, artifice is replaced by authenticity, and hair metal is sent off to die an embarrassing death.

LOU GRAMM (VOCALIST, SHADOW KING):

I thought it was a pretty fine band, and I like the one album we did a lot. I think the songs were extremely strong, and the playing was very loose and a real joy to hear and to play with, in the few gigs that we did. But that whole album was undermined by the people at Atlantic Records, as I remember. There was some collusion with management from Foreigner and Atlantic, more or less, to put a stop to Shadow King's promotion. And after starting out very good, in the first four or five weeks, it just stopped dead in the water. And we knew that it could never do that, the way it went down. We all kind of felt that we had been tampered with.

RIKKI ROCKETT (DRUMMER, POISON):

Look, any band that had an image the way we did, whether you put a safety pin in your cheek or whether you spray-paint your hair to Mars, there's issues there. And if you crack open the lid a little deeper you'll find all those interesting things. The fact that we're from the '80s, this and that, all of that is the least interesting thing. There is so much more there. Poison sells a lifestyle, not just a song or a video.

VICKY HAMILTON (EX-MANAGER, POISON):

There were all these metal guys doing the glam thing. Next thing you know they're in flannel shirts and not combing their hair anymore. My favorite part of the whole thing was that the metal bands did not see it coming. At that point they were riding the wave of, "We are the rock gods of the world" and all of a sudden it was like they were mashed like a pancake. And it wasn't relevant anymore. I remember during that time period, I went to a Poison concert at the Blockbuster Pavilion . . . I'd managed Poison and I sold the contract to Howie Huberman and they signed a deal with Enigma Records during that time period for like $25,000. And then Tom Wally took over Capitol and they got the huge record deal and had the huge success, so they were saying, "Ha ha ha" to me or whatever . . . and we were talking to [bassist] Bobby Dall—I'd stayed pretty friendly with him. And it was like half-filled, the

1991: Hyper-glam Nitro issue their second and last album, *II: H.W.D.W.S.* ("hot, wet, dripping with sweat," natch). The band is most notorious for crazy-looking guitars and a particular band photo in which they prove themselves to be the band with the biggest hair ever. Like the modern-day Steel Panther but not quite, Nitro, to their credit, considered themselves a somewhat tongue-in-cheek parody of the form.

1991: The UK's Little Angels propose a clinical, syrupy-sweet—and ill-timed—hair metal concoction with their second full-length, *Young Gods*, their first to see distribution stateside.

1991: Tyketto issue their Geffen debut *Don't Come Easy*, adding to the evidence that, generally speaking, the new hair bands arriving late were of a much higher quality than the bands that had arrived in '87 and '88, and that they were at least cognizant that they had something of more substance to offer.

1991: Shadow King represent another attempt at a hair band supergroup, principals being Foreigner's Lou Gramm and Dio's Viv Campbell (soon to leave for Def Leppard). The band's lone, self-titled album is produced by hair metal icon Keith Olsen.

January 8, 1991: Def Leppard guitarist Steve Clark is found dead in his London home. Cause of death is explained in the coroner's report as an accidental mix of alcohol with painkillers and antidepressants.

January 15, 1991: David Lee Roth issues his third solo album, *A Little Ain't Enough*, featuring Jason Becker on guitar. The album scores gold within four months on the strength of medium rotation singles like "Tell the Truth," "Sensible Shoes," and the title track.

January 23, 1991: Poison's "Something to Believe In" single goes gold, one of four Poison singles to do so. It's one of hair metal's top dozen or so quintessential power ballads.

February 12, 1991: Florida's Saigon Kick issue their self-titled debut, one of a handful of records late in hair metal's lifecycle that propose a hybrid between melodic hard rock and alternative rock.

February 26, 1991: Great White issue their *Hooked* album. Triple indications that hair metal might be running out of steam: a) the band seeks recognition with yet another cover, and a second originally by Angel City; b) the front cover features a typical design by Hugh Syme, this one featuring a naked blond straddling a fishhook; and c) the album merely achieves gold, when both before it went double-platinum.

March 12, 1991: The much-hyped BulletBoys follow up their gold debut with the well-regarded *Freakshow*, which doesn't reach certification.

March 26, 1991: Mr. Big follow their self-titled debut with *Lean into It*, which, the band estimates, has sold about 1.2 million copies worldwide—not implausible given their uncommon and longtime fan base in Japan. The band scores a US hit with the enlightened and mature strains of "Green-Tinted Sixties Mind," as well as campfire acoustic ballad "To Be with You," a style of soft rock that has done well for a number of melodic rock acts by this point.

Blockbuster Pavilion. And Jennifer said something about, "Bobby, what are you going to do about all these empty seats?" And he said, "Oh, they're not a problem. We're going to get another semi for our next tour and we're going to put stand-ups in the empty seats." A semi full of stand-ups to put in the empty seats.

JERRY DIXON (BASSIST, WARRANT):

[1992's] *Dog Eat Dog* was good. It was out about six months and then comes Nirvana, Pearl Jam, Alice in Chains, who were on our label— they were like the new Warrant. They were getting the attention and it was all about that. It's a business. It's not snowing out and you're trying to sell snow hats, and it wasn't working. Switched gears and went with Alice in Chains. Shocking to us, all right [laughs]. We went out on tour on that record, and on past tours there were radio people—Sony and Colombia, they usually had a rep that would drive to each show, and they would pick you up, take you to radio, do that whole thing, and you would do interviews with them all day. And on that tour, there was nobody out there. And I was kind of scratching my head going, you know, "Where's Joe Blow from Michigan? He's always at the shows, and we've got nothing planned today . . . . what?" So that first tour going out to support that record, that's when we realized, "Oh shit. No more."

JACK RUSSELL (VOCALIST, GREAT WHITE):

The *Hooked* album was a mess because we all shoulda been in rehab at that point instead of making that record.

PAUL GILBERT (GUITARIST, MR. BIG):

We went to Europe and supported White Lion [laughs]. Career-wise, on stage, they sounded great. They were supporting an album that didn't do all that well, but I really liked a lot of the stuff on it. But career-wise, they were kind of going down, were arguing with each other, and they took it out on us [laughs]. We had no lights, no PA, we had to go on a half-hour before the tickets said the show started. But it toughened us up. And then we came back and went to the Japan, the States, Southeast Asia, and "To Be with You" went number one, and it exploded after that. That song, [vocalist] Eric [Martin] had this demo and he played it, almost shamefully presented it to me one day, like, "I wrote a song, you won't like it, it's not metal" [laughs]. So he played it, and I just sort of liked it but I couldn't get it out of my head. A month later, I said, "Would you give me a copy of that song? I just want to hear it." I didn't even think about doing it. I just liked the tune. So I listened to it again, and I used to make the rehearsal tapes for the whole band. And I put Eric's demo "To Be with You" at the end, and everyone called me up later that night, "What's that song at the end?! It's great!"

1990   **1991**   **1992**   **1993**   **1994**

March 27, 1991: Britny Fox issue their third album, *Bite Down Hard*, featuring a new vocalist named Tommy Paris, guest performances from Zakk Wylde and Rikki Rockett, a switch from CBS to EastWest, and a naked blonde on the sleeve. The album is produced by John Purdell and Duane Baron, the team behind Ozzy's *No More Tears*. The record fails to chart; it is the band's last album until 2003.

April 2, 1991: Thinking man's hair metal band White Lion issue their final album, *Mane Attraction*. Well-regarded by fans, the record stalls at No. 61 as industry attention turns to Seattle. It doesn't even go gold. There's the very real possibility that White Lion got stung worse than most because their name started with W, as "Winger, Warrant, White Lion, and Whitesnake" became a war cry for those who wished glam metal dead.

BILLY CHILDS (BASSIST, BRITNY FOX):

Earlier on, we didn't have a really good grasp of the whole melodic thing. That took a lot of time for us to develop. Initially we were just a heavy, straight-ahead band with a lot of screaming. By the time we got to our third album, you'll notice a completely different vibe. It's more homogenous. All those other things are still there, but just with a greater melodic influence. I guess that's how I see us musically. I guess pop culture basically. Hey, I thought we were pretty good at what we did. And there was a certain uniqueness we brought to it. I would say uniqueness within a very homogenous genre, if that makes any sense.

MIKE TRAMP (VOCALIST, WHITE LION):

When [guitarist] Vito [Bratta] and I decided to end the band, we ended on a semi-high note. We hadn't totally faded away, or were totally flopped. Basically, White Lion, toward the end, we weren't together for the same reasons as when we started. We could feel, we could sense and we could taste, that the record company had left the band, and that the new kid in town had already taken over. So I just said, you know, "Motherfuckers, fuck you, this is the way I'm going to go out."

JERRY DIXON:

It's just natural. The funny part is, shit, when Nirvana came out, I loved that stuff. I thought this is real music to me. It changed me. It's like, this is what music should be like. They didn't have the eighteen drums and fifteen hundred guitar tracks. It was just really rock. But with anything in life, when you are all the way at the top, there's only one way to go—right to the bottom. And we went a lot faster than we thought we would [laughs]. Honestly, the personalities bugged the shit outta me, because they had none. "Oh, we're badasses and we're wearing flannel," and it's like who cares? That didn't really rub well, but the music trumps that for me. It wasn't like I was going to go out and start looking like Pearl Jam. Because they had no look. That was their look [laughs]. Stare at the floor and play. Completely against all rules. You put on a show. But glam was just getting so ridiculous. And you know what happens to any good thing is that it just gets saturated. There's a Warrant and there's a Poison and then they sign twenty-five baby Warrants and keep putting them out, and then pretty soon those twenty-five baby-band Warrants have twenty-five baby bands of their own. And all of a sudden, it all sounds the same, looks the same, and is just dead. Stick your finger down your throat. It's just overkill. And you know what? Absolutely, I think we were right in line with the groups before us. We were in line with Ratt, and maybe we were a baby Ratt [laughs], you know? We were a baby Mötley Crüe. Because they were the first ones and then our wave came. Yeah, absolutely.

MIKE TRAMP:

There was just too much of the same thing. I came originally to the US in '82, from Denmark. And I had already been in the music business and in a professional band since I was sixteen and a half—straight out of school, didn't even finish high school, did six albums. But in '82, it's when everything is sort of starting. MTV was starting, the next year *Pyromania*, *Shout at the Devil* was coming out. So I started watching the '80s being built on a hard rock level. And then when you look at the '80s in '91, I wasn't an original one. I mean, I was still a protégé of David Lee Roth, which is what had fueled me, had energized me. That was my carrot, what Van Halen stood for. More because they had taken the stage back to being a stage where you perform and you don't just stand there. David Lee Roth referred a lot to the American bands from the '70s as just musicians, but they didn't look like a rock star band. And Van Halen obviously changed that. So by the time we came in, there had already been three copies of Roth. And even though we wrote our own hits, and I still believe that I did what I did, when you get to '91. . . Atlantic Records had signed White Lion and then they had signed five other White Lions. So instead of going, "I've got a band here that we really, really want to build on," no, let's sign another six bands that have a blond lead singer and three guys with dark hair, the Mötley Crüe image, the Van Halen image, et cetera, et cetera. And by the time you see the last '80s videos, it starts becoming a fucking joke. The song quality is down, the bands, they're just pulling things out of fucking nowhere. I know that when I look at White Lion's history, we really paid the dues, but I know it got copied so many times. But I see the concept. By the time you want to copy a band, that band has already been around long enough creating a unique thing. By the time the iPhone is being copied, the iPhone has already been around for a while—it's the same with the music business. "Fuck, we should do an album like that band," and that band has already been working on that kind of sound for three or four years and prior to that in the basement creating that original sound. And the same thing when someone wanted to be like White Lion, and White Lion wanted to be like Mötley Crüe and Van Halen. It's like, fuck, we've spent the decade with this already, and you can't keep copying this. Because it can't be copied any more. So people turn on MTV and start laughing about it. They say, "Fuck, this is a joke!"

May 1991: After six years trying, Phoenix's Tuff score a major label deal, issuing *What Comes Around Goes Around*, on Atlantic. Its cover belies the blatant hair metal enclosed.

May 6, 1991: EMI try their luck with a hair band supergroup called Contraband, issuing a self-titled album produced by Kevin Beamish. Band members are Michael Schenker, Tracii Guns, Bobby Blotzer (Ratt), Share Pederson (Vixen), and, on vocals, Robin Black from Shark Island. The single is a cover of Mott the Hoople's "All the Way from Memphis."

1995   **1996**   **1997**   **1998**   **1999**

Skid Row is back grinding out unadulterated rock.
The result is the no-holds-barred album SLAVE TO THE GRIND, and the first track "Monkey Business" will blow you away.
SLAVE TO THE GRIND will kick your ass.

Produced by Michael Wagener for Double Trouble Productions, Inc.   Management: Scott McGhee for McGhee Entertainment Inc.

May 14, 1991: Burbank, California's Tattoo Rodeo are yet another perfect example of a band arriving too late for the party, their *Rode Hard—Put Away Wet* being a manufactured, corporate blues metal album.

May 28, 1991: Bang Tango put forth their sophomore effort, *Dancin' on Coals*.

June 4, 1991: Dangerous Toys' second album, the Roy Thomas Baker–produced *Hellacious Acres*, is released. The rough-and-ready Texans play a bluesy, rudimentary, barroom rock 'n' roll version of hair metal, arguably one more authentic than Tattoo Rodeo's version.

June 11, 1991: Skid Row issue their second album, *Slave to the Grind*. Highly regarded, the band shows foresight in eschewing their hair metal past, going for a sound that is squarely of a heavier traditional metal sound, with some elements of hair metal but also evocations of heavier fare like Metal Church, if not outright thrash. It is widely considered the first heavy metal album to hit No. 1 on Billboard. Hits include "Monkey Business" and power ballad "Wasted Time."

DAVE "SNAKE" SABO (GUITARIST, SKID ROW):
We had always been influenced by heavier bands, and that maybe doesn't come across as such on the first record. We had more of a voice to get out of us on the second one. And also we had come into certain things business-wise that [were] a total wakeup call in terms of how ugly this business can be, how many parasites there are. And again, your anger can be vented through a number of different ways. And for us, it was through our music. Love, happiness, sadness, and whatnot, but at that particular time, anger was the predominant emotion prevalent in the band. There was anger and willingness and desire to create a record that would show that we were more substance than show, that we were more about the music than how pretty our frontman was or how good-looking our bass player was or whatever.

RACHEL BOLAN (BASSIST, SKID ROW):
As far as *Slave to the Grind* goes, that was a big departure that might have alienated a bunch of people that were used to the other sound of Skid Row. But I think it made people realize that these guys aren't just going for the pop metal sound.

LIZZIE GREY
(GUITARIST, LONDON, ON THE CHANGING CLIMATE):
It became so packed. I mean, when you had bands like Warrant, that kind of music, same as Poison, you kinda lost a lot of your metal crowd. The crowd that still thought that Ozzy Osbourne was God could not relate to the prettiness of these bands. Like I said, in the '70s, pretty was shocking, but in the late '80s, pretty was pretty. And the music

1990 **1991** **1992** **1993** **1994**

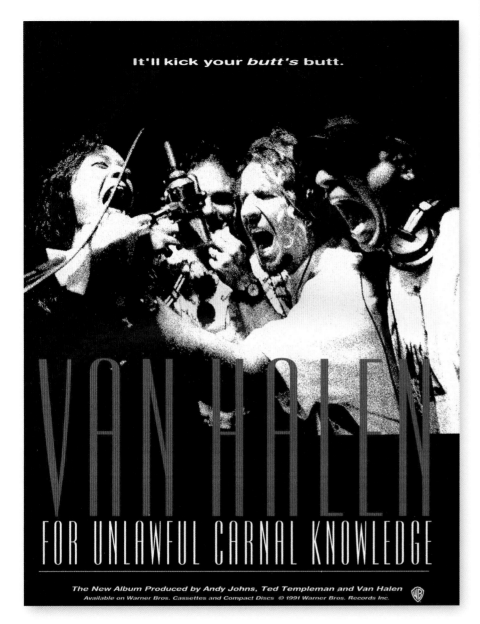

It'll kick your *butt's* butt.

VAN HALEN
FOR UNLAWFUL CARNAL KNOWLEDGE

The New Album Produced by Andy Johns, Ted Templeman and Van Halen
Available on Warner Bros. Cassettes and Compact Discs © 1991 Warner Bros. Records Inc.

June 17, 1991: Van Halen issue their tougher, longer, ninth album, *For Unlawful Carnal Knowledge*. Its lightest track, "Right Now," is a type of ballad, but more socially conscious and not a love song. The ambition, heaviness, and even sheer length of the album seem to signal that Van Halen sensed that the game was shifting and that phoning it in wasn't going to work anymore.

June 25, 1991: L.A. Guns issue their third album, *Hollywood Vampires*, and the decline in the band's fortunes seems to mirror that of every other hair metal act.

July 11, 1991: Kingdom Come bring their third album, *Hands of Time*, their last for major label Polydor.

was formula, all the songs started to become formulaic, and these guys would all hang around Hollywood, race to Hollywood to collect their platinum record deal, and I think something was lost. Their influences were not . . . they were influenced by Mötley Crüe! They were influenced by London. So they were like the next generation after us. I felt that there was something contrived about the approach of that stuff, even bands like Slaughter and Skid Row. It was so formulaic and lost its shock value; that was gone completely. Because young guys who are just having the time of their life wearing their mom's makeup and playing guitars. There's nothing wrong with that, but there was something missing that was alive and well in Mötley Crüe.

1995   **1996**   **1997**   **1998**   **1999**

July 1991: FireHouse release "Love of a Lifetime" as a single. The shameless power ballad kick-starts the band's run as a rare successful hair metal latecomer.

July 2, 1991: Alice Cooper presents the last of his big-budget corporate-rock kiddie-metal hair albums, *Hey Stoopid*. Song doctors are everywhere.

August 6, 1991: Canadian band Harem Scarem buck the trend and begin a long, successful semi–hair band career with a self-titled debut on Warner Bros.

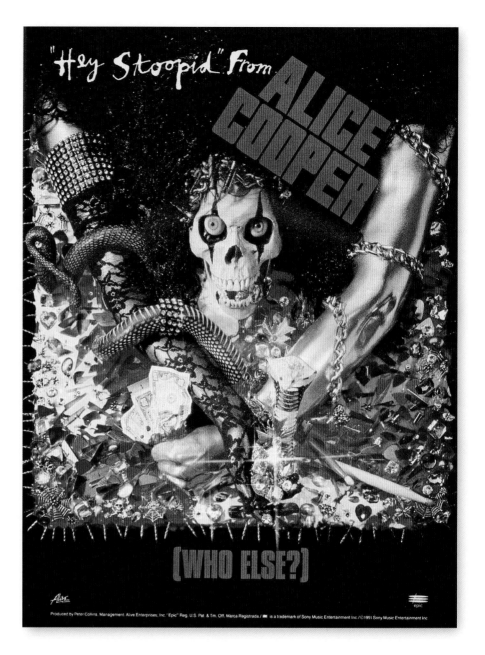

C. J. SNARE (VOCALIST, FIREHOUSE, ON "LOVE OF A LIFETIME"):

That was a big song for of us. I'll never forget, I had written that song on a Fender Rhodes piano and I remember bringing that song to Bon Jovi and he said, "Put that song away; it will ruin your career." I never found out what he meant by that. But as a young, green, easily influenced band, we hid that song. And we actually had a song called "Midnight Fantasy," which was the original ballad. And Epic said, "You know, this one just isn't strong enough; maybe we should bring in an outside writer to help you guys." And I said, "Well, I have a song," and I played it for him and he loved it and it became our first gold single and drove the sales of the first album up over platinum. And, God, it became this huge wedding song and we never thought that's what would happen. So it actually did the opposite. It gave us a career.

1990   **1991**   **1992**   **1993**   **1994**

August 27, 1991: Bad English follow their platinum debut with their second and last, *Backlash*, which doesn't achieve RIAA certification.

August 27, 1991: Pearl Jam issue *Ten*, which, at the time of writing, is 13x platinum. That's a lot of record sales not going to hair metal bands.

August 6, 1991: The Four Horsemen issue their Rick Rubin–produced debut, *Nobody Said It Was Easy*, which yields the hit title track as well as "Rockin' Is Ma' Business." The album was recorded in '89 but was delayed as vocalist Frank Starr languished in jail. Post-release, the band's career is further stalled by Starr being sent away for another year on new charges. A second album in '94 is followed by Starr getting into a motorcycle accident, falling into a coma for four years, and then dying in 1999. Stylistically, the band was part of the bluesy hair metal offshoot popularized by Badlands, Dangerous Toys, Sea Hags, and, to some extent, GN'R.

ROB DELEO (BASSIST, STONE TEMPLE PILOTS, ON HAIR METAL):

I mean, we were living it on Sunset Boulevard. I used to see those people come in immediately after they got signed and treat me like shit because I worked at a guitar shop and they just got signed. Those bands you're talking about, those glam or hair bands, were my blueprint to show me how to and how not to treat people. It wasn't just the music. It was the whole attitude that went along with it. I don't think our band has ever, again, you know, [been about] "Let's rape and fucking pillage and conquer, dude." That's not what we grew up on.

1995   **1996**   **1997**   **1998**   **1999**

August 30, 1991: Tesla issue their well-regarded and classic *Psychotic Supper* album, which in two years goes platinum. "Call It What You Want," "Edison's Medicine," "What You Give," and "Song & Emotion," all become medium airplay radio hits.

September 3, 1991: Atlantic issues a Ratt hits pack called *Ratt & Roll 81–91*, which goes gold.

September 17, 1991: Guns N' Roses issue, simultaneously, *Use Your Illusion I* and *II*. Each goes 12x platinum. *Use Your Illusion I* sells 24 million copies worldwide.

JERRY DIXON:

The commercial decline didn't really happen to us until like our third record. That's when Nirvana and Pearl Jam came out and just handed everybody their ass [laughs]. We call those the black years. But we got a couple of records out of it. We got to our third record in that time span of about four years, where that music was on top, and then one day, boom, there it went.

JEFF KEITH (VOCALIST, TESLA):

Psychotic Supper was great for me, personally, because we did crazy things and got to be more ourselves. Songs like "What You Give," which wasn't a big hit for us or anything, that's probably my all-time favorite Tesla song. "Edison's Medicine"—oh, man, tunes like that. I'd say *Psychotic Supper* would have to be my favorite, because it was true and honest. We didn't always take that easy route. We were the kind of band who said, "By God, we're taking the hard route for the sake of it." We always got lumped in with the hair bands, and, hey, we did use a little Aquanet in the first year or two. But we said, "Man, that's not what's important. What's important is that we're relating with the people and we're on the same level with them and we're enjoying the music and they're enjoying the music that we're writing for them. And when we get together for a concert, we're enjoying ourselves, having a good time." And that's what it was all about. It wasn't an image thing.

I think if [guitarist] Tommy [Skeoch] would have stayed in the band, we would have pulled out of this grunge movement thing. We would have survived. I know we always got clumped in with the hair bands, the '80s thing, and personally I've got no problem with that, because we were part of that era. But at the same time, that's not totally what we were about. I think that helped with our longevity. We'll pick up on that. We've got a lot of loyal fans out there still. But yeah, we did a headlining tour for *Psychotic Supper*. Things went fantastic, great. We were playing all these big arenas, selling them out, and everything was all peachy keen.

SLASH:

When we got into *Use Your Illusion*, which were two really, really hard . . . or one, really, really hard [laughs] bunch of songs that were really hard to write. That was more of an accomplishment, because the band was so dislocated at the time. And the playing on that record, just from a lead guitar player point of view, is ten times better all over the place, but it's all completely improv, almost everything on there. So it all sounds very fluid, but it's not as direct and to the point as, say, "Welcome to the Jungle," you know what I mean [laughs]? The solos were a definite arrangement type of thing. So I'm a fan of it, just because I thought it was a very fluid record guitar-playing wise.

DUFF MCKAGAN:

I remember when those records came out, the night it came out, the record company took Slash and I out to this dinner. You know the Tower Records on Sunset in West Hollywood? They open it up at midnight if a record like that is coming out. And the fucking line, half a mile down Sunset. And they took us to this place behind Tower Records and put us in this office where you could see down and watch the people coming in, through this one-way glass. And just watching this thing, these people going nuts for your record, you know? Waiting in line. . .

GREG PRATO:

There were a lot of similarities between Guns N' Roses and Nirvana, where at the time even Kurt was making it seem like they were two totally different factions. But they were both on Geffen Records and they were both against what was going on at the time in rock. They both were obviously involved with heroin [laughs], although not all of Nirvana

was into that, but Kurt obviously was. And also most of the Guns N' Roses members had problems with drugs. And there were certain rock bands that both had a mutual admiration for like Led Zeppelin, Aerosmith, Kiss. Obviously there were things they didn't have in common, like Guns N' Roses would hang out with porno stars and go to strip clubs, whereas Nirvana was more guys that you would just bump into on the street or at the local record store. Even Duff, when I interviewed him for [*Grunge Is Dead*], he totally agreed that they had more in common than not common.

DUFF MCKAGAN (ON THE BAND'S CHEMISTRY AT THIS POINT):

At that point, I mean, it's going to change. The amount of money we started to make. And more than that, yes men everywhere. People were just sycophants, just people kissing people's ass. And you can start believing your own hype after a while, and it's kind of a tragic thing to watch. Not just with our band. I've seen it all over the place and now I recognize what it is. And it's not real healthy. Sure, it's good for your confidence, up to a certain point. But after that it's just not real healthy. And that kind of stuff started happening with all of us but much more so with Axl.

1995   **1996**   **1997**   **1998**   **1999**

TOM ZUTAUT (A&R MAN, ON THE DECLINE OF GLAM):

Well, glam was really cool, but then all of a sudden every guy in a metal band was dressing like a girl and they were getting more feminine. So early glam was more rough and tumble, like a New York Dolls. And later glam was way more feminine, like, you couldn't tell the difference between guys and girls. Were the guys in the band the groupies? You had to you look at their shirts to see if they had tits or not. And I think it got way commercial, way overexposed on MTV and radio, and the almost instant response was sort of like . . . you know, and even Guns N' Roses on *Use Your Illusion* was way more commercial and slick than they were on their first record. A new generation of kids came along and it was like, "This is way too slick for us," and shoe-gazers like Nirvana and Pearl Jam came out, where it was almost like anti-hedonism of the '80s. It was like a new generation of kids and they wanted their own thing, and all of a sudden the anti–rock star shoe-gazers became super-important. This is all before digital downloads, but one thing about those grunge bands is that there's a minor dissonance in their songwriting and the chords they're playing, so they never really had the mainstream songs that hook lots of people. So you ended up where a lot of bands like Nirvana and Pearl Jam were not selling out stadiums the way the metal bands were, because they limited the amount of people that would fall in love with them because of the dissonance and the rebellion in the chords that they were playing. In other words, Mötley Crüe created rebellion, but it was really mainstream and parents were afraid of them and whatever. But the rebellion that was created by Nirvana and Pearl Jam, there was a dissonance in the chording of their music that gave it like a slightly sour tone where they couldn't really draw a mass audience to it. They could only draw their generation of kids who were into the shoe-gazers.

ZAKK WYLDE (ON HAIR METAL'S LAST HUGE SINGLE):

All I know is that the solo I did for "No More Tears," all the guitar work on that track is just one guitar. I remember I wanted to double the guitars. The guys were playing John Madden football at the time. And that solo I did was just one take and I said, "Oh man, I could probably get a better one; let's do another one." And they're all like, "Dude, it's fucking fine and anyway, we're fuckin' . . . we've got the playoffs going on right now." So they were playing video games and saying, "Dude, it's fucking fine, just fuckin' leave it." And I was always like, man, I wish I would have doubled it, but that's the way it was. The Madden was fuckin' more important than the record [laughs]. . . . We had a fucking great time making that record. Even if you ask Ozzy, because a lot of his recollections about albums, it's not even whether they sold the most or whatever, it's whether he had a good time making the record. But every album I've ever done, I mean, you're supposed to enjoy yourself and have a fucking good time. I've never done a record where I went, "Oh man, that was a lot of work." Man, get a job doing fucking construction. You'll see what work is all about.

OZZY OSBOURNE (ON HOW HE WORKS):

It's all a collaboration really. It's not all me at all. I mean, if anything, all I do is have the luxury of sticking vocal lines over some amazing guitar work. Or vice versa, if I get a vocal line. One of the more memorable albums was *No More Tears*. Randy Castillo, Zakk Wylde, and the rest of us sat down and we said . . . I never sat down and wrote airplay records. I just wrote albums, and if they got played on the radio, fine. But we all decided to sit down and say, "Okay, without going cornball, we've got to write each song with a treatment that it will at least have the possibility of being played on the radio." It won't be too whacked-out. I'm fed up with singing about "bloodbath in fuckin' paradise" and Satanic shit. I still wanted something dark, but in a different area, you know? So that's the way it came about. It was a lot of work, but it was a lot of fun, and it's the first time I'd ever done professional demos, which is a good thing and a bad thing, because I ended up bouncing a lot of the stuff off of the demos and onto the masters. For instance, the harmony section on the end of "Mama, I'm Coming Home," I bounced it.

MICHAEL HANNON (BASSIST, SALTY DOG):

I was at the Rainbow Bar and Grill [in West Hollywood] with some chick, just hanging out. There was Ozzy, and they were having a birthday party for one of his road crew guys, whose name was Ralph. I remember that, because he saved my ass. Salty Dog was still together and we were pretty hot at the time, and I was telling Ozzy how we recorded the album [*Every Dog Has Its Day*] at Rockfield Studios, which is where Black Sabbath recorded. And he was like, "That's great, Michael." You know how he gets. "Would you like to come back to the house? New songs we've got. It would be nice." So I was shitting my pants. Of course I'm going to go to fucking Ozzy's house and listen to some new Ozzy shit. This was *No More Tears* stuff. I said, "How am I going to get there?" And he's like, "Just follow the limo!" So there we are, he waves us on, and we follow him up to Coldwater Canyon, to his house. So we went in, everybody is hanging around drinking and stuff, and I do a big fucking line of coke with Ozzy. And this is the time where Sharon is just instructing him. Ozzy is just doing what Sharon says. It seems like he's pretty much out of it. We do this big line of coke, cool, and I'm walking around looking at shit and people are talking and they're playing the *No More Tears* stuff, and I'm looking at the World War II videos on the wall, and Ozzy is like, "Oh, it's so great that you're interested in other things." So we're standing there talking World War II, I quite like that stuff, I like the European Theater, I've read a lot of books on it, and he goes to me, "I want to tell you something. I don't do drugs and

1995　　　**1996**　　　**1997**　　　**1998**　　　**1999**

214

September 17, 1991: Ozzy Osbourne releases *No More Tears.* A big hit, it is nonetheless something of a second hair metal album for Ozzy, after skipping the conceit with 1988's *No Rest for the Wicked.*

neither should you." And I said, "Oz, we just did fucking lines a fucking foot long two minutes ago!" And he says, "No, what I'm saying is that I don't do drugs and neither should you." It was amazing, you know? It just made me realize that most interviews in most magazines are a bunch of bullshit. That is all you were reading at the time was him saying that. And I was hearing the song, "I Don't Want to Change the World," and that was my favorite so far that I had heard, and I said, "This is the one I really like." And he goes all sad, "Well, Lemmy wrote that one." And I was like, ugh. He was like a little kid. And then the other one I liked was "Desire," and I said, "Well, this one is really, really good too." And he's like, "Lemmy wrote that too." But, yeah, so I was looking at the videos, and he played this video of Hitler, and he goes, "That's really rare. It was never on any videos or anything, because it's really old stuff." And he pushes this button and this big screen came out of the ceiling and it was an incredible picture and this dumb fucking whore comes up and she's going, "Hitler was a bad man! You shouldn't be worshipping a bad man!" And Ozzy is like, "We're not worshipping. It's like, no shit he's a bad man, it's just interesting. This is old rare vintage video. You can't find it anywhere." And she's like, "I don't care, he's a bad man and you're a bad man for watching him." And Ozzy is really emotionally fucking cracked. And he looks like he's ready to break down. I could see that he was fading away. So I said, "You stupid fucking whore. Shut your fucking mouth and get away from us." So this really sends Ozzy into a tailspin. He sits down with his face down in his lap, his hands up in his face, just withdrawing. And everybody is like, "Uh-oh, party's over." So I remembered that this was a birthday party and there is this guy with a birthday, and I go, "Well, happy birthday Ralph!" And Ozzy just jumps up and goes, "Yes, happy birthday Ralph!" And it was like nothing happened.

1990   **1991**   **1992**   **1993**   **1994**

JONATHAN PONEMAN (COFOUNDER, SUB POP RECORDS):

There was a rejection of artifice, and I think that's the thing. People rejected not so much the music, though the music and the songs were banal and kind of idiotic, but banal and idiotic has its place, too, and I embrace it. The way it was marketed and the kind of mindless hedonism, it was lacking a certain dignity. Not to say that the bands up here [in Seattle] were about dignity overall, but there was a lack of pretention. . . . A lot of the Sub Pop bands would talk very much about how they were influenced by Kiss. There's not a rejection of a sense of humor or a pretense, but it was just the idea of embracing the archetype and then disposing of the ensuing generations after the archetype. Because Kiss always had . . . there was always a sense of, albeit varied, but a higher-minded satire going on. In some ways they were distant cousins of the Ramones, who were obviously the great inspiration for all the bands coming out of . . . well, practically any band that called itself punk rock traces itself back to the Ramones. But there's the same kind of conceptual coherence. Some people note that Kiss, the way they went about marketing themselves and going about their business, could have been seen as being incredibly cynical. But they also took some tool, some tips from the way the Beatles were marketed, for example, and applied them to the way they got their music and their image across. People were never conscious of their image in the way that the glam metal bands were, but I think not having that sort of awareness is not to say that you are unaware. There can be a calculated lack of awareness as well, but it's a calculation, if that makes sense. A question of where one puts one's priorities.

CARLOS CAVAZO (GUITARIST, QUIET RIOT):

I don't think we hated grunge music. I loved the music, but I think what we hated was the music industry changing and not accepting what we were doing anymore. And accepting them only. It would have been cool if they accepted that and us. But there were a lot of '90s bands who didn't even listen to '80s bands anymore. Which was kind of depressing. It almost felt like everything you did was a waste. Either you're a musician or you're not, and I still play no matter what. I'm a guitar player. It's what I do. Even though we don't sell as many records, I still gotta play. And the label, they'll just drop you, like all of a sudden not even call you anymore, not work with you. That's basically the way they operate. One day, you don't hear from them and everything is different. Or you go there and there's somebody else working there, and they don't know what to do with you.

DEREK SHULMAN (A&R MAN):

First of all, most bands literally have a lifespan, and if you look across the board, it's almost like organic.

September 24, 1991: Nirvana issue *Nevermind*, their second album, which becomes an instant hit, effectively, or in the lore of the times and, sure, in the book you are reading, "killing hair metal." Given the success of this album as well as Pearl Jam's *Ten* and hit records from Soundgarden and Alice in Chains, the industry abandons hair metal and goes grunge and then hard alternative. At this writing, *Nevermind* is 10x platinum. Big, but not as big as *Pyromania* or *Appetite for Destruction*.

1995   **1996**   **1997**   **1998**   **1999**

But obviously the advent, well, the advent of two things: number one, MTV being less important and also becoming much more broad-based in what they played musically, the urban hip-hop era, and then Michael Jackson getting on MTV. MTV was a very important factor in all of this—it and at the same time of course, the advent of grunge, the Nirvanas and Soundgardens, who discounted the look and raised the music. So the pendulum starts to swing, and when the swing starts, it affects the whole social structure. And MTV was affected and wanted to embrace hip-hop and rap music a lot more, and at the same time, the bands who'd been around for ten years or more, kind of were diffusing their efforts. So it was a natural evolution. You couldn't overcome that hum, and a lot of those bands could not. They went into oblivion or reformed, or reunited and were au courant just for the generation who grew up with them.

BEAU HILL (PRODUCER):

As we tend to do in the entertainment business in general, we kill the goose that lays the golden egg and just continue to push the envelope and push the envelope, and the backstory of that is, we just continue to try and get more and more money, and to do more and more and more stuff. I never saw it as glam, per se. And I tell people, I'm responsible for making the songs on the radio, yes, but I'm not responsible for the silly clothes and haircuts [laughs]. That's where I drew the line. But everything still got painted with the same brush.

BEAU HILL:

As soon as Nirvana came out with "Smells like Teen Spirit," every label in the entire universe was ready to cut bait on every band that was on the roster. If you didn't come from Seattle, you were on the chopping block. Nobody was spared the bloodshed, and that was it. It's very typical for the labels. They want instant gratification and no risk, and the whole concept of artist development, you know, had been on the way out for at least ten years, so by the time grunge came along, and it became popular to gaze at your shoes while playing, and indeed, you didn't have to be very good. Which is why, in the post-'80s era, you don't hear any blistering guitar solos, you don't hear anybody that's really pushing themselves vocally, just because it became acceptable. It was just the violent overreaction the other way. You know, some guys that would choreograph their shows and have big productions onstage and Vari-lites and pyro and all that stuff, it became popular to be the exact opposite. So everybody showed up in a dirty T-shirt, torn jeans, with crappy equipment that they could barely play. And everybody was like, "Oh, that was so honest and so cool!" [laughs]

1990　　　**1991**　　　**1992**　　　**1993**　　　**1994**

KEVIN ESTRADA (PHOTOGRAPHER):

I think glam metal rose and died because of MTV. With MTV, obviously it became very much a whole visual and stylistic thing for bands more than the music. Sure, Def Leppard had *Pyromania*, which was an amazing album, but Joe Elliott and his look really helped propel those bands with those videos. I think that's what really skyrocketed bands like Def Leppard and Bon Jovi. Then it got to a point where you didn't really have to have the great songs—you can just have mediocre songs. Then you had a good shot at being on MTV. The Wingers, the Slaughters, the Warrants . . . stuff like that started to scoot by. It wasn't really about substance, it was about their look. Maybe they did have a little hook here and there, but it became a real visual thing. And middle-America was all of a sudden discovering what was going on in Hollywood. They were rushing out to buy stretch pants and leather jackets and tease their hair and look like they were living in Hollywood even though they were living in Nebraska. The world opened up to what metal was at, at that point. Even though I don't really consider hair metal to be true metal—it was more pop. It was a completely commercialized world of metal, and that's how MTV, I feel, also killed metal—because they commercialized it so much and broadcasted it to the world, until everybody pretty much OD'd on it. It just became a joke and then was over as quick as it came.

NIC ADLER (OWNER, THE ROXY):

I was reading an article the other day that said from the first snare hit of Dave Grohl from Nirvana, that the scene on the Sunset had died. Cycling is a good word. I always looked at it as a graduating class, almost. With three, four, five years you spend, and then you get another scene that pops up. But it was a rough thing. We were all about glam and hairspray, being whatever you wanted, not being a tough guy, but being sexual and all those things, and then when the grunge scene came in, and it was a flannel shirt and greasy hair, it was like instantly, glam was out, the makeup was out, all those things the Strip really had its heyday in, in one single stroke, with "Smells Like Teen Spirit," it had been taken away. And then we had to look at ourselves, and a different scene started to come in. But for the Strip, that was the moment. Because we were always, up to that point, the ones that were pushing up the next scene and the next music, and then that was the first time I think we really noticed another community, Seattle, take hold of what we felt was our own. But the majority of what we were still booking was the glam rock, at that time. The Roxy had always been the place that had the popular music, whether it was hip-hop or rock or glam or whatever. So Nirvana played—you know, we had those shows at The Roxy—but it wasn't a scene. The bands weren't from there, they didn't play there weekly, there wasn't four or five grunge bands that made their way into that scene.

You know, living and playing in the same place creates something, and that's what we had for ten or fifteen years on the strip. So when you had a group of musicians, four, five, six, seven bands that were coming out, and they had never even been to the Sunset Strip, they didn't live there, they didn't know the Rainbow, they weren't going to watch some other bands—that was happening in Seattle. So we were just another tour stop in Los Angeles when they were coming through.

BOBBY DALL (BASSIST, POISON, ON HIS BAND'S STAYING POWER):

I think there's many reasons, but I think it goes back to, you know, in any genre there's going to be a bunch of bands that come out of it. I don't care what genre. The music business is cyclical. And when you get through the cycles, there's always going to be a handful that rise to the top. The cream rises to the top, so to speak. I know that sounds cocky or whatever, but in any cycle you're going to have that. And Poison stayed true to our roots. We worked our asses off and I know we were in the midst of the '80s, glam rock or whatever you want to call it, that explosion. We sold over 25, 26, 27 million records, we worked our asses off for ten straight years. We toured nonstop and built up a fan base. And in our genre that is unequaled and

1995   **1996**   **1997**   **1998**   **1999**

unparalleled in many ways by most bands. And there are still bands from our genre that still do it. Bon Jovi can still do it, Mötley Crüe can still do it, so could Guns N' Roses if they were to do it. If they want to or not is another question. Us four were really the biggest out of the epidemic of those type of bands, and I also like to take credit for not witnessing our demise because we didn't exist at the time. Really it was just timing more importantly than any great brains of our own. In other words, in '93, '94, when we disbanded—which we never really did with this band; we just stopped working and just retired basically—was when the whole grunge movement took off. And a lot of bands from our genre worked themselves down and diminished themselves. We didn't stop working because of grunge. We had just ran over ten years nonstop and it was time for a break. The band just could no longer work as a unit at that point. So we chose to stop working.

BILLY CHILDS:

We attempted to change a little bit, but I really don't think there's really any point of turning an apple into an orange. Britny Fox was too polarizing of a glam band to really try and change into anything else. We thought it was in our best interest to put out the best tunes we could, and hope that people could hear that we never really were basically an '80s band. We were just a rock band. That's all we ever were. And I don't really say that in a derogatory way, because I think that being a rock band is quite a noble thing, actually. There's no bullshit—you're a rock band. AC/DC's a rock band. Guns N' Roses, when they first came out, they were very much a hair band. People seem to forget that. But they immediately saw what was going on, and I mean, they got dirty real quick. You mention a band like Love/Hate. It's funny, because those guys seemed to catch . . . it wasn't just us that got caught up in all this.

And also too, Martin, I don't think grunge killed hair metal. Hair metal committed suicide. I think there were too many bad bands, too many guys who couldn't play, too many guys who couldn't sing, and it just got really bad. But, ironically, I look at a band like Love/Hate. Now had they come along . . . because if *Bite Down Hard* comes out two years earlier, I think we're looking at an album with four or five singles on it. That's how good I think that album is. I may not be right, but Love/Hate, I look at them, if they would've come along two years after they did, they probably would've been huge. Timing is everything. We were a little bit, at that point in time, on our way out, and I guess some would say more than others, and at that point they were on their way in, but the changing of the guard didn't help them either. They were just a little too soon.

I'll tell you something else interesting, real quick. And this will kind of summarize a lot of things for you about these bands. I don't think a lot of people realize this or notice this, but do you remember when Cinderella was spending a lot of money on *Heartbreak Station*? They recorded in like different studios all over the country, and I remember going to them, "What are you guys doing?! You're not thinking anymore." You know what I mean? And I saw people do this a lot. And I figured out what it was from my own experience, because you really can't see this. When you've been successful on that level and you're selling lots of albums, doing big tours and all that, even though you see it happening right in front of your eyes, and it's a very human thing that happens that says, well, it's happening to everybody else, but it's not going to happen to me. We're the guys who are just different enough to squeak through. And I think a lot of people thought that. Erroneously.

1990   **1991**   **1992**   **1993**   **1994**

postscript

**BILL LEVERTY (GUITARIST, FIREHOUSE,
ON THE ENDURING APPEAL OF HAIR METAL):**

[T]hat hard rock guitar, drums, and bass is a sound that will always be pleasing and popular with kids as well as adults. There's proof out there right now that people will always like their hard rock guitar. It's definitely coming back. I think a lot of these program directors are kicking themselves in the ass because they realize that these listeners that they have used to buy pimple medicine back when this was really in the mainstream. Well, now these people have gotten older and they're buying diamonds and cars and computers and that's exactly what their advertisers are. So they realize they have missed a decade of music by slamming the door shut on it. So they are opening the door again and what we need to do is get some songs on the radio again and hopefully we'll see the whole industry make a dramatic shift.

1995   1996   1997   1998   1999

credits

INTERVIEWS WITH THE AUTHOR

Nic Adler (The Roxy), Steve Albini (producer), Rick Allen (Def Leppard), Carmine Appice (Blue Murder), Mark Arm (Mudhoney), Ian Astbury (The Cult), Bill Aucoin (Kiss), David Bates (A&R), Nuno Bettencourt (Extreme), Rachel Bolan (Skid Row), Bobby Blotzer (Ratt), Eric Brittingham (Cinderella), Mick Brown (Dokken), Vivian Campbell (Dio), Carlos Cavazo (Quiet Riot), Gary Cherone (Extreme), Billy Childs (Britny Fox), Phil Collen (Def Leppard), Alice Cooper, David Coverdale (Whitesnake), Bobby Dall (Poison), Terry Date (producer), Dave Davies (Kinks), Dean DeLeo (Stone Temple Pilots), Rob DeLeo (Stone Temple Pilots), Brad Delp (Boston), Jerry Dixon (Warrant), Don Dokken (Dokken), Jack Douglas (producer), Kevin DuBrow (Quiet Riot), Joe Elliott (Def Leppard), Jack Endino (producer), Kevin Estrada (photographer), Kim Fowley (Runaways manager), Mike Fraser (engineer), Ace Frehley (Kiss), Jay Jay French (Twisted Sister), John Gallagher (Raven), Kelly Garni (Quiet Riot), Paul Gilbert (Mr. Big), Larry Gilstrom (Kick Axe), Lizzie Grey (London), Tracii Guns (L.A. Guns), Sammy Hagar (Van Halen), Tom Hamilton (Aerosmith), Vicky Hamilton (A&R, Geffen), Frank Hannon (Tesla), Michael Hannon (American Dog), Tony Harnell (TNT), Beau Hill (producer), Dave Hlubek (Molly Hatchet), Bobby Ingram (Molly Hatchet)

Matthias Jabs (Scorpions), John Paul Jones (Led Zeppelin), Stefan Kaufmann (Accept), Ron Keel (Keel), Jeff Keith (Tesla), Mark Kendall (Great White), Joey Kramer (Aerosmith), Blackie Lawless (W.A.S.P.), Tommy Lee (Mötley Crüe), Bill Leverty (FireHouse), Mike Levine (Triumph), Phil Lewis (L.A. Guns), Ben Liemer (Circus magazine), Troy Lucketta (Tesla), George Lynch (Dokken), Jim McCarty (Yardbirds), Andy McCoy (Hanoi Rocks), Duff McKagan (Guns N' Roses), Mark Mendoza (Twisted Sister), Dave Meniketti (Y&T), Rod Morgenstein (Winger), Michael Monroe (Hanoi Rocks), Ronnie Montrose (Montrose), Neil Murray (Whitesnake), Vince Neil (Mötley Crüe), Rick Nielsen (Cheap Trick), Ted Nugent (Ted Nugent), Keith Olsen (producer), Ozzy Osbourne, Stephen Pearcy (Ratt), Jizzy Pearl (Love/Hate), Joe Perry (Aerosmith), Doug Pinnick (King's X), Jonathan Poneman (Sub Pop), Greg Prato (author), Spencer Proffer (Quiet Riot manager), Richie Ranno (Starz), Robb Reiner (Anvil), Steve Riley (L.A. Guns), Rikki Rockett (Poison), Jack Russell (Great White), Dave "Snake" Sabo (Skid Row), Rudy Sarzo (Quiet Riot, Whitesnake), Tom Scholz (Boston), Billy Sheehan (David Lee Roth), Derek Shulman (A&R, Polygram), Nikki Sixx (Mötley Crüe), Mak Slaughter (Slaughter), Adrian Smith (Iron Maiden), C. J. Snare (FireHouse), Dee Snider (Twisted Sister), Jaime St. James (Black 'n Blue), Syl Sylvain (New York Dolls), Geoff Tate (Queensrÿche), Marq Torien (BulletBoys), Mike Tramp (White Lion), Joe Lynn Turner (Rainbow), Zakk Wylde (Ozzy Osbourne), Chip Z'Nuff (Enuff Z'Nuff), and Tom Zutaut (Geffen).

about the author

Martin Popoff has been described as "the world's most famous heavy metal journalist." At approximately 7,900 (with over 7,000 appearing in his books), he has unofficially written more record reviews than anybody in the history of music writing across all genres. Additionally, Martin has penned 44 books on hard rock, heavy metal, classic rock, and record collecting. He was editor in chief of the now-retired *Brave Words & Bloody Knuckles*, Canada's foremost metal publication for 14 years, and has also contributed to *Revolver, Guitar World, Goldmine, Record Collector*, www.bravewords.com, www.lollipop.com, and www.hardradio.com, with many record label band bios and liner notes to his credit as well. Additionally, Martin worked for two years as researcher on the award-winning documentary *Rush: Beyond the Lighted Stage* and on *Metal Evolution*, an 11-episode documentary series for VH1 Classic, and is the writer of the original metal genre chart used in *Metal: A Headbanger's Journey* and throughout the *Metal Evolution* episodes. Martin currently resides in Toronto and can be reached via martinp@inforamp.net or www.martinpopoff.com.

complete bibliography

Smokin' Valves: A Headbanger's Guide (2014)

2 Minutes to Midnight: An Iron Maiden Day-by-Day (2013)

Metallica: The Illustrated History (2013)

Rush: The Illustrated History (2013)

Scorpions: Top of the Bill (2013)

Epic Ted Nugent (2012)

Fade to Black: Hard Rock Cover Art of the Vinyl Age (2012)

It's Getting Dangerous: Thin Lizzy 81–12 (2012)

We Will Be Strong: Thin Lizzy 76–81 (2012)

Black Sabbath FAQ (2011)

Fighting My Way Back: Thin Lizzy 69–76 (2011)

The Collector's Guide to Heavy Metal: Volume 4: The '00s (2011; coauthored with David Perri)

The Deep Purple Royal Family: Chain of Events through '79 (2011)

The Deep Purple Royal Family: Chain of Events '80–'11 (2011)

Goldmine *Standard Catalog of American Records 1948–1991, 7th Ed.* (2010)

A Castle Full of Rascals: Deep Purple '83–'09 (2009)

Goldmine *Record Album Price Guide, 6th Ed.* (2009)

Goldmine *45 RPM Price Guide, 7th Ed.* (2009)

Worlds Away: Voivod and the Art of Michel Langevin (2009)

Ye Olde Metal: 1978 (2009)

All Access: The Art of the Backstage Pass (2008)

Gettin' Tighter: Deep Purple '68–'76 (2008)

Ye Olde Metal: 1976 (2008)

Ye Olde Metal: 1977 (2008)

Judas Priest: Heavy Metal Painkillers (2007)

The Collector's Guide to Heavy Metal: Volume 3: The Nineties (2007)

Ye Olde Metal: 1968 to 1972 (2007)

Ye Olde Metal: 1973 to 1975 (2007)

Black Sabbath: Doom Let Loose (2006)

Dio: Light Beyond the Black (2006)

Run for Cover: The Art of Derek Riggs (2006)

Rainbow: English Castle Magic (2005)

The Collector's Guide to Heavy Metal: Volume 2: The Eighties (2005)

The New Wave of British Heavy Metal Singles (2005)

UFO: Shoot Out the Lights (2005)

Blue Öyster Cult: Secrets Revealed! (2004)

Contents under Pressure: 30 Years of Rush at Home & Away (2004)

The Top 500 Heavy Metal Albums of All Time (2004)

The Collector's Guide to Heavy Metal: Volume 1: The Seventies (2003)

The Top 500 Heavy Metal Songs of All Time (2003)

Southern Rock Review (2001)

Heavy Metal: 20th Century Rock and Roll (2000)

Goldmine *Price Guide to Heavy Metal Records* (2000)

The Collector's Guide to Heavy Metal (1997)

Riff Kills Man! 25 Years of Recorded Hard Rock & Heavy Metal (1993)

See www.martinpopoff.com for complete details and ordering information.

index

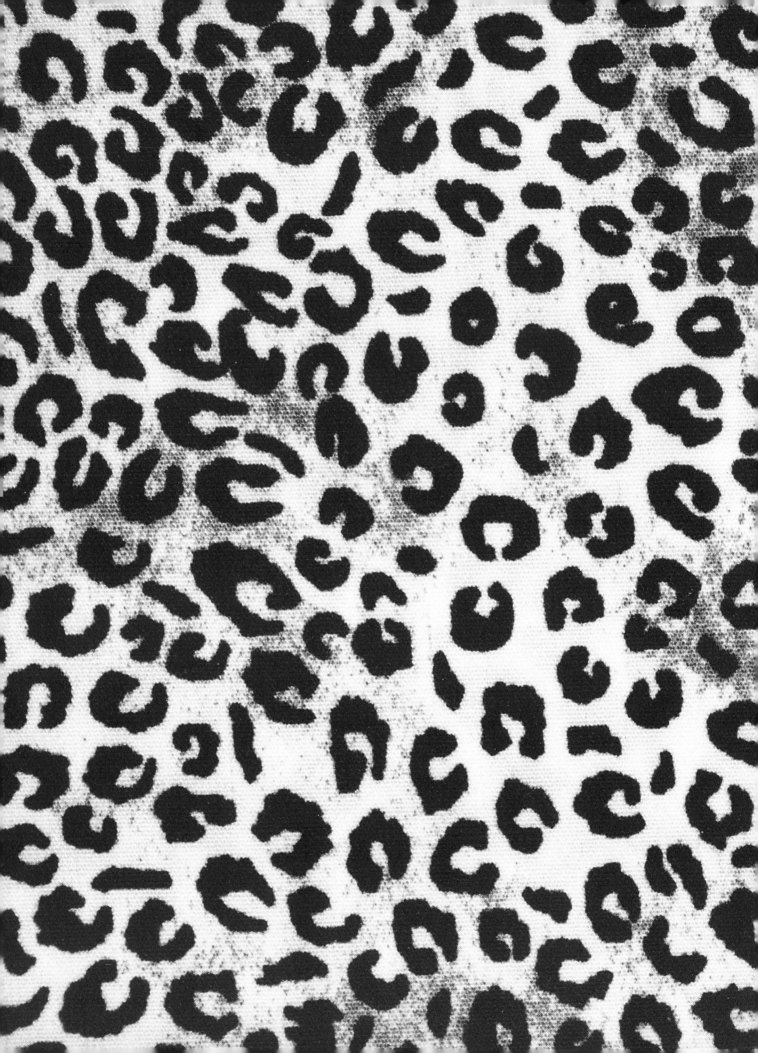